Crime and Punishment in Russia

THE BLOOMSBURY HISTORY OF MODERN RUSSIA SERIES

This ambitious and unique series offers readers the latest views on aspects of the modern history of what has been and remains one of the most powerful and important countries in the world. In a series of books aimed at students, leading academics and experts from across the world portray, in a thematic manner, a broad variety of aspects of the Russian experience, over extended periods of time, from the reign of Peter the Great in the early eighteenth century to the Putin era at the beginning of the twenty-first.

Published:

Peasants in Russia from Serfdom to Stalin: Accommodation, Survival, Resistance, Boris B. Gorshkov

Forthcoming:

The History of the Russian Worker: Life and Change from Peter the Great to Vladimir Putin, Alice Pate (2018)
Law and the Russian State: Russia's Legal Evolution from Peter the Great to Vladimir Putin, William Pomeranz (2018)
Marx and Russia: A History of Marxist Thought in Russia, James D. White (2018)
A Modern History of Russian Childhood: From Imperialism to the End of the Soviet Era, Elizabeth White (2018)

Crime and Punishment in Russia

A Comparative History from Peter the Great to Vladimir Putin

Jonathan Daly

Bloomsbury Academic
An imprint of Bloomsbury Publishing Plc

B L O O M S B U R Y
LONDON · OXFORD · NEW YORK · NEW DELHI · SYDNEY

Bloomsbury Academic

An imprint of Bloomsbury Publishing Plc

50 Bedford Square	1385 Broadway
London	New York
WC1B 3DP	NY 10018
UK	USA

www.bloomsbury.com

BLOOMSBURY and the Diana logo are trademarks of Bloomsbury Publishing Plc

First published 2018

British Library Cataloguing-in-Publication Data
A catalogue record for this book is available from the British Library.

ISBN:	HB:	978-1-4742-2436-9
	PB:	978-1-4742-2435-2
	ePDF:	978-1-4742-2437-6
	eBook:	978-1-4742-2438-3

Library of Congress Cataloging-in-Publication Data
Names: Daly, Jonathan W., author.
Title: Crime and punishment in Russia : from Peter the Great to Vladimir Putin / Jonathan Daly.
Description: New York : Bloomsbury Academic, [2018] | Includes bibliographical references and
index. Identifiers: LCCN 2017049011 (print) | LCCN 2017054825 (ebook) |
ISBN 9781474224376 (PDF eBook) | ISBN 9781474224383 (EPUB eBook) |
ISBN 9781474224369 (hardback : alk. paper) | ISBN 9781474224352 (pbk. : alk. paper) |
ISBN 9781474224376 (pdf) | ISBN 9781474224383 (ebook)
Subjects: LCSH: Crime–Russia–History. | Crime–Russia
(Federation)–History. | Punishment–Russia–History. | Punishment–Russia
(Federation)–History. | Criminal justice, Administration of–Russia–History. |
Criminal justice, Administration of–Russia (Federation)–History.
Classification: LCC HV7012 (ebook) | LCC HV7012 .D253 2018 (print) | DDC 364.947–dc23
LC record available at https://lccn.loc.gov/2017049011

Series: The Bloomsbury History of Modern Russia Series

Cover image © ullstein bild/Getty Images

Typeset by Integra Software Services Pvt. Ltd.
Printed and bound in Great Britain

To find out more about our authors and books visit www.bloomsbury.com.
Here you will find extracts, author interviews, details of forthcoming events and
the option to sign up for our newsletters.

For Upholders of Justice Everywhere

CONTENTS

LIST OF ILLUSTRATIONS

Figures

Six organizational charts have been provided throughout the text to illustrate the judicial hierarchy and configuration following periodic reorganization. Each chart simplifies in order to enhance understanding. For example, several independent or auxiliary courts have been omitted, such as ecclesiastical courts before 1917, Gulag courts after 1917, and transportation courts in the Soviet era. Although, before 1861, noble landowners ruled their estates like so many autocrats, meting out justice as they thought fit, they are also omitted from the relevant charts. So are both the peasant commune (*mir*), which managed petty crime until 1861, and provincial administrators, who exercised judicial authority under various names and guises de jure until the judicial reform of 1864 and de facto until 1917. Military courts were included in the chart for the early Soviet years, when they played a leading role, but excluded from the other charts for other periods, when their function was less central. In other words, the charts present the Russian judicial system not in all its complexity, but only in its main elements.

Maps

PREFACE

Russia developed as one of the most successful states in human history. Its territory expanded from some 430,000 km² in 1470 to more than 22 million km² at the end of the nineteenth century—a fifty-one-fold increase.[1] In the field of criminal justice, Russian journalists and rulers achieved major advances throughout the country's history. The *Ulozhenie* 1649 was one of the most detailed and elaborate law codes devised in the early modern world. In the mid-1700s, Empress Elizabeth curtailed and all but abolished the use of capital punishment a decade before Cesare Beccaria published his reformist treatise *On Crimes and Punishments* (1764)[2]—and over a century before a worldwide abolitionist movement gained momentum.[3] With the 1864 judicial reform, Russia became the first non-Western country to establish an independent judiciary functioning largely according to Western best practices. According to a leading specialist, the 1903 Criminal Code, while never entering force in its entirety, "represented the most advanced statement of criminal jurisprudence in the world."[4] And early Bolshevik criminal justice for regular (as opposed to "political") offenders aimed at a level of humaneness rare in the world in the early 1920s.[5] In the post-Soviet era, Russia's leaders have continued to devote enormous efforts to developing law in Russia, often seeking to implement international best practices. According to a leading scholar writing in 2009, Russia had at least nineteen separate law codes in force.[6]

Yet throughout these same years, Russia often deservedly acquired the reputation of a despotic power, where the rule of law was weakly rooted, the criminal justice system harsh and routinely unfair, administrative and judicial officials corrupt and partial, and the police distrusted and even feared by nearly everyone. Today, Vladimir Putin's Russia is a byword for arbitrary governmental power where political dissidents and critics of the regime not infrequently die under mysterious circumstances. How did Russia's historical evolution contribute to the emergence of this frightening polity? How can one explain historically both the striking harshness and humanity of Russia's criminal justice system over the past three centuries? In general, does one find clues in specific historical developments in the evolution of criminal justice in Russia to understanding the domestic and geopolitical successes of the Stalin or Putin regimes? Such were the questions animating my thoughts as I set out to write this book.

***

Many thanks to colleagues who shared published and unpublished work with me, including Kathryn Hendley, Rhiannon Dowling, Sergei Maksudov (Aleksandr Babyonyshev), Anton Weiss-Wendt, Jeffrey Hardy, Mikhail Nakonechny, and Tatiana Borisova. For incisive comments and bibliographical references, I am grateful to Evgenii Akeliev, Janet Hartley, William E. Butler, Richard Wortman, Aaron Retish, Matt Rendle, David Shearer, James Heinzen, Lauren A. McCarthy, Tatiana Borisova, Jörg Baberowski, Mikhail Nakonechny, Kathryn Hendley, Marc Elie, William Pomerantz, Laura Hostetler, Leon Fink, and Joaquin Chavez. Sergei Antonov, Richard Robbins, John LeDonne, Peter Solomon, Theodore Taranovski, and Sofia Villafuerte read and offered invaluable comments and criticism on the chapters in various stages of completion. For their efforts, I am deeply thankful. Michael Melancon's confidence in my ability to carry out this project is the only reason I made bold to try. Finally, the editorial and production team at Bloomsbury—in particular, Beatriz Lopez and Rhodri Mogford—were a pleasure to work with and collectively made this book far better than it might have been. It goes without saying that any remaining errors are my sole responsibility.

A Faculty Scholarship Support Program grant from the University of Illinois at Chicago generously supported my research.

* * *

Russian is a Slavic language that uses the Cyrillic alphabet. To convert text (transliterate) from Cyrillic into languages with a Latin script like English obliges one to follow certain conventions. I adhere to them with some exceptions. Thus, I write not "Trotskii," as the Library of Congress system of transliteration demands, but "Trotsky," following everyday norms of spelling.

While researching this book, I consulted hundreds of scholarly books and articles. Given the nature of this book series, it was possible to mention only a fraction of these works throughout the text. As a rule, references have been provided only for quotations, statistics, and especially important historical points.

CHRONOLOGY OF EVENTS

1696		Sole rule of Peter; Preobrazhenskii Chancellery as secret police; penal laborers assigned to building fortresses
1697–1698		Peter's first visit to Europe; revolt of musketeers crushed
1701		Investigation Chancellery abolished
1708	△	Establishment of *gubernii* (provinces)
1711	△	Governing Senate established
1715		Inspector-general instituted to supervise Senate; Military Criminal Code adopted
1718		Administrative colleges instituted; Tsarevich Alexis dead; five-tiered court system set up; Chancellery for Secret Inquisitorial Affairs created
1719		Internal passport system created; smaller provinces (*provintsii*) instituted
1720		General regulation on procedural norms
1722		Office of procurator general created
1723		Decree on judicial procedure reinstituting accusatorial trial for lesser offenses
1730		Succession struggle; "Conditions" rejected
1754		Capital punishment abolished provisionally
1757		Exiled women exempted from nostril slitting and branding
1760		Landowners granted right to exile serfs to Siberia
1762		Manifesto on rights of Nobility; Chancellery for Secret Inquisitorial Affairs abolished
1762		Secret orders for torture to be used sparingly

	1765	Landowners empowered to assign selected serfs with Admiralty College for hard labor; restricted knouting of persons 17 or older
	1767	Great Instruction; Legislative Commission meets (till 1774)
	1773–1774	Revolt of Pugachev
	1775	Provincial and judicial reform
	1781	Work house (*rabochii dom*) instituted
	1782	Forced-labor prison (*smiritel'nyi dom*) for crimes against property; Police Ordinance
	1784	Senate review required for sentences to harsh punishments
	1785	Charters to Nobility and Towns
	1796	Judicial reorganization
	1797	Recentralization of bureaucracy
	1801	Curtailment of judicial torture; partial restoration of prior judicial organization; commission to draft new law code
	1802	Ministries replace colleges
	1805	Committee created to combat political sedition
	1807–1811	Reforms of Speransky
	1815	Alexander grants liberal Constitution to Congress Poland
	1817	English prison reformer Walter Venning permitted to inspect Russian prisons
	1819	Prison supervisory board instituted
	1822	Secret organizations prohibited
	1825	Decembrist Uprising
	1826	Third Section of His Imperial Majesty's Own Chancellery created
	1827	Continental-style gendarmerie instituted
	1830	Russian law codified and published in 48 large volumes
	1832	Digest of Laws

1835   Imperial School of Jurisprudence opens

1839   Township courts for state peasants

1845   Penal Code; knout abolished

1849   Petrashevtsy arrested; Dostoevsky sentenced to
        forced labor in Siberia

1861   Emancipation of serfs

1864   Judicial reform (four statutes: on judicial
        institutions, criminal procedure, civil procedure,
        and rules for justices of the peace)

1866   Dmitrii Karakozov attempts to assassinate tsar;
        security bureau set up in St. Petersburg

1867   Societies of political, nihilistic, or atheistic
        tendencies outlawed

1871   Nechaev trial; gendarmes made primary
        investigators of state-crime cases

1874   Trial of Mother Superior Mitrofaniia

1877   Jacks of Hearts Club trial; "Trial of 50"; "Trial of
        193" (till January 1878)

1878   Zasulich wounds St. Petersburg city governor
        Trepov; law banning jury trials for attacks on
        officials; secret order empowering gendarmes
        or police officials to verify "political reliability"
        (*politicheskaia blagonadezhnost'*)

1879   People's Will Party established; governors general
        empowered to transfer to military courts persons
        deemed potentially harmful to public order

1880   Bomb blast in Winter Palace; Third Section
        replaced by Department of Police; security bureau
        created in Moscow

1881   Assassination of Alexander II (March 1); Security
        Law

1882   Rules regulating living conditions of
        administrative exiles

1884   Rules adopted to increase proportion of educated
        people in jury pools

1889	Justices of peace abolished save in major cities; office of land captain created
1897	Law on release of juvenile offenders to custody of parents or guardians
1901	Corporal punishment abolished for hard-labor convicts; administrative exile by urban communities abolished and by rural communes restricted
1903	Criminal Code partially adopted
1905	Bloody Sunday; General Strike; October Manifesto; December armed uprising
1906	Fundamental Laws; First Duma; military field courts; punitive expeditions; Duma votes to abolish capital punishment
1907	Second Duma; new electoral law
1909	Law on parole
1910	First juvenile court opened. St. Petersburg
1912	Judicial authority of land captains revoked; elective office of justice of peace restored; higher rural court created
1917	
March	Nicholas abdicates; crowds ransack police stations, courts, prisons; Provisional Government, Soviet established; police institutions abolished; amnesty of political prisoners; administrative exile abolished
September	Military Revolutionary Committee created
October	Bolshevik coup
November	first decree on courts
December	Cheka instituted, Panina trial
1918	
January	Constituent Assembly meets and is immediately dissolved
February	Second decree on courts
May	War on peasant bourgeoisie declared; Supreme Revolutionary Tribunal instituted

June	Cheka "troika" and revolutionary tribunals empowered to impose execution; Shchastnyi trial
July	Murder of Tsar Nicholas II and his family; third decree on courts
September	Red Terror declared
November	Statute on People's Courts of RSFSR
December	universal labor obligation established
1919	
April	Statute on revolutionary tribunals
May	Decree on concentration camps
October	Revolutionary tribunal established under auspices of Cheka for grave crimes
December	Guiding Principles of Criminal Law of RSFSR
1920	
March	Chekas authorized to incarcerate violators of labor discipline
May	Chekas empowered to function as military revolutionary tribunals
October	Office of people's investigators instituted
1921	Decree on deporting undesirables
1922	
February	Cheka replaced by GPU
May	Criminal Code and Criminal Procedure Code; statute on *Advokatura*; statute on Procuracy supervision
Summer	Show trials against Socialist-Revolutionaries and Russian Orthodox church leaders
August–November	160 to 400 leading intellectuals banished abroad
November	Revolutionary tribunals abolished, unified system of courts created
1923	OGPU replaces GPU; RSFSR Code of Criminal Procedure
1924	Fundamental Principles of Criminal Law of USSR adopted

1926	Criminal Code of RSFSR; Statute on Military Tribunals and Military Procuracy; OGPU given orders to help collect grain
1927	OGPU forbids mention of grain problems; anti-counterrevolution campaign in countryside
1928	Shakhty trial
1929	Collectivization begins; assault on church begins; death penalty for "kulak" terror
1930	"Dekulakization"
1932	Law on theft of socialist property; internal passports reinstituted
1934	Special committee for administrative punishments established; law on treason; political police reorganized as NKVD; Kirov assassinated; expedited criminal procedure adopted for state crimes
1935	Civil police sentencing boards (*militseiskie troiki*) instituted (till 1937)
1936	Stalin Constitution; abortion recriminalized; first Moscow show trial
1937	NKVD Operational Order No 00447 issued; Great Terror begins
1938	Terror ends; criminalization of labor shirking
1941	German invasion of USSR
1946	Officials directed to work harder to root out bribery
1948–1949	Campaign against acquittals
1948	Collective farm assemblies allowed to impose administrative exile on shirkers
1953	Stalin dies; Gulag amnesty decree; Beria executed
1954	Aggravated intentional murder made capital offense; parole reinstituted
1955	Reduced punishments for petty theft of state and public property
1956	Abortion legalized; work shirking decriminalized; administrative exile boards abolished; Khrushchev's "Secret Speech"

1959	Khrushchev speech on mental illness of dissidents
1960	Criminal Code of RSFSR; Code of Criminal Procedure of RSFSR
1961	Anti-parasite law adopted in RSFSR; law on grave economic crimes
1964	Joseph Brodsky trial
1965	Decree "Measures to Improve Procuracy's Investigative Machinery and Maintenance of Public Order" issued
1966	Laws on fighting crime in general and hooliganism in particular; Andrei Sinyavsky and Yulii Daniel trial for anti-Soviet activity
1978	KGB status raised
1979	Resolution adopted on crime-fighting
1983	Revisions to Russian Criminal Code, emphasis on crimes against public and personal property
1986	Chernobyl disaster; Gorbachev's anticorruption campaign
1988	Defense advocates permitted during preliminary stage of criminal proceedings; term of office of judges up from five to ten years; judges required to complete higher legal education and qualifying examination; trial of Churbanov, Brezhnev's son-in-law, for bribery and extortion
1989	Both suspects and accused gain right to counsel "at moment of detention, arrest, or indictment"; remaining political crime statutes repealed; rehabilitation for people repressed under Stalin
1990	Legal assistance ensured for indigent suspects; permanent committee on combating crime created
1991	Constitutional Court of Russian Federation (July); attempted hardline coup (August); USSR ceases to exist (December)
1992	Law on Procuracy of Russian Federation; Law on Status of Judges, including lifetime appointment
1993	Federal Law on State Secrecy; new Criminal Code; homosexual acts among consenting adults

K

B

G

decriminalized (June); government forces storm parliament building (October); Constitution of Russian Federation (December) establishes right to jury trial and presumption of innocence

1994	Amnesty for political and economic crimes
1996	Russia joins Council of Europe; judges' salary increased; death penalty suspended
1997	New Criminal Code enters force
1998	Court bailiffs introduced; judicial departments created to supervise courts; justices of the peace reintroduced
2001	New Code of Criminal Procedure: burden of proof on prosecution
2002	Single Advocates' Chamber instituted; advocates required to provide legal services to disadvantaged; juvenile offenders must be informed of right to counsel; law "On Combating Extremist Activity"
2002–2006	Funding for the courts dramatically increased
2003	Jury trials allowed for political cases; form of plea-bargaining introduced; law against human trafficking
2004	Terrorist attack in Beslan, North Ossetia; trial against Mikhail B. Khodorkovsky
2008	Jury trials disallowed for state crimes like treason and terrorism
2009	Sergei Magnitsky dies in jail
2010	Ban on pretrial detention for persons suspected of business-related crimes; Khodorkovsky convicted a second time
2011	Package of reforms tending toward more leniency in criminal justice; police reforms
2012	Protections for judges adopted; Pussy Riot performance in Cathedral of Christ the Savior; restrictions on NGOs adopted
2013	Kidnapping and sexual offenses put under the jurisdiction of district courts; ban on homosexual propaganda to minors

2014	Crimean Peninsula annexed by Russian Federation; "rehabilitation of Nazism" made a crime
2017	Decriminalization of domestic battery for first-time offenders; Aleksei Navalny found guilty of fraud

developing countries are supposed to follow →

Introduction

This book recounts the evolution of criminal justice in Russia over the past 300 years. It surveys developments in crime, punishment, the law, criminal investigation, judicial institutions, and kindred topics from the reign of Peter the Great to the rule of Vladimir Putin. Throughout these centuries, successive governments reformed or attempted to reform the practice and institutions of criminal justice, to strengthen law and legality, to impose administrative regularity and predictability, or to radically recast the very idea and practice of criminal justice.

Already beginning in the early modern era, Russia's leaders began to look to Europe for guidance in developing and strengthening the state, including its legal and judicial institutions. Under Peter the Great, following Europe became an obsession. In this sense, Russia constituted the world's first developing country. And follow they did. Within a century, Russia was among the powers triumphant over Napoleon's Grande Armée, and 100 years after that, it was one of the great powers of the world. A half-century later still, Russia was one of the world's two-ever superpowers. Obviously, Russia successfully adopted and adapted recipes of power devised in the West. But could it assimilate such subtler achievements as the rule of law, the curbing of arbitrary authority, due process, and the guarantee of individual rights?

Russian criminal law before Peter the Great

Criminal law developed in Rus' (the East Slavic lands before the emergence of Russia) and Europe in a similar manner, though with a time lag. Inquisitorial procedure dominated for many centuries and only gradually and quite late gave way to adversarial procedure with two parties making their case before an impartial judge. Judicial ordeals and swearing oaths served to find guilt or innocence in the absence of trained police forces and criminal investigators. Official law slowly replaced customary law or traditional norms. Detailed legal codes were compiled. In some areas, the lag was especially great. Legal experts in Russia began to grapple with questions of judicial philosophy many centuries later than their Central and Western European counterparts. For example, the widely circulated and oft-republished Germanic *Sachsenspiegel* (early 1200s) affirmed that "God is Law itself; therefore, justice is dear to him."[1] Such a conception of the law as an emanation of the divine and therefore higher and more authoritative than monarchs could not have been formulated in an official Imperial Russian or Soviet law book, though some scholars (under European influence) began to articulate such ideas in the late 1700s. Innovation and reform occurred in Russia but nearly always from the top down and only rarely, unlike in Europe, from political and intellectual movements promoted by powerful nongovernment elites.

In the centuries before Peter the Great, there was no system of courts, no permanent judges, no possibility of appeal, no legal profession, and no legal theorizing. Officials of the prince, who also managed administrative and military affairs, presided over judicial proceedings, applied the rules, and collected fees.[2] A series of law codes defined crime and governed its punishment. The codes (*Sudebniki*) of 1497 and 1550 placed the state and its agents at the center of the process. Procedurally, the emphasis was not on the free testimony of witnesses and a reliance on divine intervention but instead focused on confessions extracted by torture and evidence set out in written documentation. As in early modern Europe, the penalties (mostly corporal punishment and the death penalty) were harsh because their purpose was to frighten potential criminals and to assert the power and majesty of the ruler. No distinction was made between premeditated and unpremeditated criminal acts, and no account was taken of happenstance, carelessness, self-defense, and other extenuating circumstances.[3]

In ordinary times, the Russian monarchs applied the law as stated in the code and statutes, but they were not constrained institutionally, legally, or by tradition. Political power remained arbitrary. The best proof of this was the *Oprichnina*, created as a state within a state by Tsar Ivan IV, "The Terrible," in 1565–1572. During these years, Ivan's agents, or *oprichniki*, went on a rampage, expropriating noble estates, plundering towns and villages, and killing thousands of people. Scholars are divided over whether they were driven mostly by Ivan's paranoia or by a calculated plan to destroy potential social and political opposition to his absolutist rule. In a sense, the true motivation little matters: in either case, Ivan could disregard tradition, the law, custom, and common sense as he saw fit. No monarch of Europe had such power or authority. The despotism—manifest or latent— of the tsars was, moreover, paralleled by despotic governance of secular and ecclesiastical elites up and down the social hierarchy. Precisely in the sixteenth century, the vast majority of peasants in Russia became enserfed.

In the sphere of criminal justice, serfs fell completely under the sway of their landlords, unless they committed grave crimes.

Following a massive rebellion in Moscow in 1648, a committee drafted a new law code. The *Ulozhenie* (1649) drew heavily on earlier Rus' and Muscovite law codes, as well as Byzantine and Lithuanian law. Laying the foundations for both criminal justice and governance for nearly two centuries,[4] it spelled out in 967 articles organized into 25 chapters many details of civil and criminal law and social organization.[5] Pride of place—the first five chapters—went to protecting the representatives and institutions of, first, the church and, next, the tsar and state. Any words or deeds that might harm or bring disrespect to these pillars of the social order were to be punished more mercilessly than any other illicit acts. Blasphemy and insult to God and the church came first—persons who "cast abuse" on God, Mary, the cross, or the saints were to be burned to death in a cage—followed by assault on the person of the tsar and treason. The reach of the law in matters of state crime was wide indeed. Anyone, even relatives, was required, on pain of death, to report to the authorities any "conspiracy and gathering or any other evil design against the tsarist majesty." Capital punishment was to be imposed for all political crimes, including the failure to denounce such crimes to the authorities, as well as the forgery of official documents, counterfeiting of money, some types of manslaughter, some forms of robbery or stealing, rape, and arson—some sixty crimes. Most other crimes (140 in all), such as first and second offenses of stealing, were punishable by flogging with a knout (an exceptionally cruel form of whip), often followed by bodily mutilation and exile, which also served as stand-alone punishments. Imprisonment was rare in Muscovy as it was in early modern Europe, for prisons were expensive to build and maintain.

The code spelled out rules of judicial procedure. By requiring the careful keeping of judicial records, the code established written documentation as the supreme form of evidence in a court of law. In fact, for the most part, oral testimony and argument before the judge were replaced by a written case file presented to him. Torture was specified as the main method for assessing guilt and was often applied even to suspected accessories, potential witnesses, and plaintiffs. Such judge-centered—as opposed to "witness-centered"—procedure is known as "inquisitorial" (*sysknoi*) and was typical in early modern Europe as well. A key feature of inquisitorial procedure was presumption of guilt; a second was the lack of defense counsel at any stage of the investigation or trial. The code affirmed the principle of legal consistency: "All justice shall be meted out to all people from highest to lowest according to the law."[6] This was not, however, an expression of the principle of equality before the law, since the code also specified differentiated treatment of persons depending on their status within the strictly delineated social hierarchy. Insulting a nobleman, for example, was a far graver offense than insulting his serf. Corruption, bribe-taking, and favoritism by officials acting in a judicial capacity were to be punished severely, though such punishments were statistically only seldom applied. Central control was simply too weak, and local officials too often left to their own devices.[7]

The *Ulozhenie* was one of the most comprehensive law codes of the age. It "certainly dwarfs any French achievements in the form of Royal ordinances," according to William E. Butler.[8] At the same time, however, the code failed to distinguish between or to separate judicial and executive or administrative authority. Justice was dispensed by administrative officials, typically with military training and experience, though their clerks were often practical legal experts.[9] Similarly, many of the dozens of central administrative agencies (*prikazy*) decided criminal cases, though a few specialized in fulfilling judicial functions, like the Investigation Office (*Sysknoi prikaz*). Highly important cases, including those calling for the death penalty, were sent to Moscow to the *prikaz* to which the specific governor was subordinated. The tsar's council (*Boyarskaia duma*) and the tsar himself adjudicated most such cases.

In the second half of the 1600s, exile with flogging, bodily mutilation, and branding was often substituted for death sentences. Exile as a judicial punishment was now also resorted to more frequently, with Siberia the most common destination.[10] According to one estimate, 7,400 people were serving terms of exile in Siberia in 1662.[11] Seven years later, a statute made possible the exile by administrative process of suspected criminals whose guilt could not be definitely proven.[12] Such was the beginning of what would gradually become the chief method of punishing malefactors in Russia, at least before a large-scale prison-building campaign commenced in the late 1800s. Russia had a vast and often underpopulated territory, which exile served to colonize. It was, moreover, a relatively inexpensive criminal sanction. Perhaps most distinctively, administrative officials continued to send large numbers of people into exile as late as the mid-twentieth century, thus meting out punishments completely outside the formal bounds of the judicial system.

A second area where informal rules exerted a decisive impact was customary law, which stemmed from ancient Russian moral norms and traditions. As criminal justice grew more orderly, systematic, official, and institutionalized, customary law remained in use for the peasantry, who constituted most of the population, right down to the time of the Revolution of 1917 and even beyond.

Under customary law, crimes were viewed primarily as personal offenses, as violations of the moral, not the legal order.[13] Calculations of who suffered from an act determined culpability in the peasant mind. Wood-poaching from the state or landlords with vast tracts of land could not easily be conceived of as crimes. Clearly comprehensible harm was required for a crime to be thought to have occurred. If a villager stole, say, lumber from a neighbor, but returned it after having been caught, it was as if no crime had occurred, the more so if the offender plied his fellow-villagers with vodka. If the offense occurred against an outsider, less harm was done. Stealing from

[handwritten margin note: how were class relations maintd? Surely not just ideological conditioning? Force is necessary]

a poor person was seen as a crime; from a rich person was not. Committing an offense while drunk or in anger or with good intentions—such as killing a person while trying to exorcise a demon—mitigated culpability. Generally, the intent of the offender determined the level of guilt. Distinctions between civil and criminal cases were not made. Sentences were understood as effecting retribution or vengeance. Guilt could be collective, and a crime with multiple participants would typically result in like punishments, no matter the distinctions of participation. The ancient custom of collective responsibility (*krugovaia poruka*), which bound individuals and households to the broader community, was widespread in Eastern and Central Europe and to a lesser extent in Western Europe in earlier times.[14] It reinforced the norms of customary law and persisted in Russia into the Soviet era.

Whereas official law was objective and rational, customary law was subjective, governed by feeling, and aimed at restoring concord. General principles were not articulated, and every case was treated as entirely unique. Customary law permitted mob justice (*samosud*), sometimes involving savage forms of murder, against horse thieves, for example, because they stole property on which livelihoods depended. Many acts forbidden by official law, by contrast, were permitted under customary law, such as insulting officials, felling trees in state forests, stealing to eat, and incest. Then again, some behaviors, which were not illegal, such as lechery or drunkenness, might be punished under customary law, per circumstances.

Within the context of inquisitorial tendencies above and customary norms below, Peter the Great carried out his radical transformation of Russian government in general and criminal justice in particular. As official law and legal institutions were built up under successive rulers, authoritarian officialdom and autarchic traditional ways of the common people persistently characterized the relations of state and society and both facilitated and hampered efforts at reform.

How this book is organized

Chapter 1 surveys the Russian criminal justice system in the 1700s. Peter the Great opened the century with a series of administrative, economic, cultural, military, legal, and judicial reforms instituted in conscious imitation of European models. In the judicial sphere, he created a central judicial agency, the College of Justice; a central executive organ, the Senate, which became the highest court of appeal; a system of judicial oversight, the Procuracy; and a short-lived uniform hierarchy of courts. At mid-century, Peter's daughter Elizabeth suspended capital punishment. She also extended to rural communities and landlords the power to dispose of "undesirables" by means of administrative exile. In the last third of the century, Catherine the Great devolved more judicial authority to the provincial and local levels, restricted the use of judicial torture, banned the application to minors of harsh forms of corporal punishment, and invested landowning and urban elites with civil rights for the first time in Russian history. Throughout, administrative officials continued to wield great power over the judicial system, and no independence of the courts was achieved. The French Revolution, which broke out in 1789 and led to the trial and execution of the king in 1793, triggered a political crackdown in Russia.

Judicial developments in the first half of the nineteenth century are the subject of Chapter 2. After a brief attempt by Paul I to recentralize the judicial system, his son Alexander I endeavored to undertake its liberalization. Although judicial torture was officially abolished, along with some of the more heinous forms of penal bodily mutilation, no major changes ensued. During the reign of Alexander's younger brother, Nicholas, Russian law was codified for the first time since 1649. Criminal law was somewhat softened. The knout was abolished, but harsh punishments for political dissidence were retained. Legal training expanded. By mid-century, the criminal justice system had grown more efficient and fair, but remained arbitrary.

Following an ignominious defeat in the Crimean War, Alexander II undertook major judicial reform, a central topic of Chapter 3. He instituted a uniform hierarchy of courts, jury trials for serious crimes, an independent Bar, and adversarial procedure. These were important steps on the path toward the rule of law. A campaign of political terrorism, however, prompted the government to remove "political crime" from the purview of the ordinary judicial system and to invest administrative officials with broad punitive authority. Efforts to scale back the judicial reforms during the following reign, of Alexander III, were only partially successful. The Revolution of 1905–1907, which saw terrible violence by both revolutionaries and government officials, resulted in Nicholas II granting basic civil rights. Political repression gradually waned in the years before the First World War. Popular discontent swelled during the conflict, however, and brought down the Imperial regime in early 1917. The resultant Provisional Government dismantled nearly the entire repressive apparatus and freed thousands of political prisoners.

The Bolsheviks came to power in late 1917 with an even more radical vision of reform, as recounted in Chapter 4. The early Soviet regime, led by Vladimir Lenin, obliterated the reformed judicial system, unified judicial and executive power, and repudiated the very idea of the rule of law. Henceforth, judges were to be guided by "revolutionary consciousness" based on class solidarity and ideological knowledge. In the early Bolshevik years, legal experts still took inspiration from progressive Western reformers, emphasizing, for example, the impact of environmental factors in triggering criminality. Social liberalization also ensued, including the decriminalization of abortion and homosexual acts between consenting adults. At the same time, however, political control grew more repressive. Thus, the Soviet criminal justice system was even more dualistic than before 1917. While political opponents faced harsh repression and few legal guarantees, ordinary criminals, especially those of the lower classes, could expect significant due process and even relatively lenient treatment. Private trading, made a grave criminal offense during the Civil War (1918–1920), was legalized in 1921. One might have imagined the Soviet system evolving toward judicial liberalization.

As Chapter 5 makes it plain, however, Stalin, who came to power in the late 1920s, engineered a radical break toward almost complete lawlessness. His mass collectivization of agriculture in the early 1930s harnessed both the political police and the criminal justice system to the political demands of the state and its helmsman. Millions of people were uprooted, shot, transported in boxcars to distant localities, persecuted, and prosecuted for the most ordinary behaviors. From this point until the collapse of communism in 1991, the political police became the key bulwark of the regime. The high point of arbitrary state power came with the Great Terror in 1937 and 1938, when hundreds of thousands of people were executed without a trial. In the late 1930s, failure to show up for work and kindred offenses were often punished with sentences to penal servitude. At any given time, 3 or 4 million inmates were crowded into labor camps and settlements. The conditions of incarceration were especially grim during the Second World War. After the war, political repression wound down, but the regular criminal justice system remained unforgiving.

Stalin's death in 1953 marked the end of state terror in Russia. Criminal justice grew more rational, predictable, and lenient, as shown in Chapter 6. Millions of inmates were liberated from the camps and settlements, and many were rehabilitated. Soon a crime wave broke out, however, prompting the government to shift gears back toward severity. Popular participation in law enforcement and criminal justice was strongly encouraged, though under tight government supervision. Even so, the justice system remained far more predictable and fair than under Stalin. Political deviation was still severely punished; psychiatric incarceration without cause was a common method of fighting against freethinking. Yet dissidents were not executed. A regular criminal, by contrast, could hope for at least a modicum of due process, so long as no influential person took an interest in his or her case. In the later Soviet years, the shadow economy and official corruption flourished. Gorbachev sought to reform the criminal justice system, but communism collapsed before great progress could be made, once the population discovered, thanks to his glasnost—or openness policy—the colossal social, economic, and political ills, which the elite had been hiding for decades.

Chapter 7 chronicles the significant change in criminal justice that became possible only after the collapse of the Soviet Union in 1991. Boris Yeltsin launched a series of reforms intended to expand judicial independence, reinstitute the right to a jury trial for serious crimes, assert the presumption of innocence of defendants, and move the system toward adversarial judicial procedure. Yet the decade also witnessed a surging crime waved. Vladimir Putin, who came to power in 2000 and again in 2012, as well as Dmitry

Medvedev who served as president in 2008–2012, endeavored to further strengthen the judiciary. Still, accusatorial bias, the dependence on superiors of judges, administrative interference, and official corruption persisted. The criminal justice system was now less arbitrary, politicized, and stringent for both regular and "political" criminals than under communism. The likelihood of a fair trial, however, was slimmer than during the post-reform era of Imperial Russia.

1

Eighteenth-Century Russia

For over two centuries, Russia's rulers had looked West for ideas, institutions, and practices to adopt as they built up state power. Peter the Great in particular was an avid Westernizer. Much of his cultural and institutional transformation of Russia was inspired by European models. He and his successors throughout the eighteenth century worked hard to develop a Europe-oriented criminal justice system. Inculcating respect for the law was one of their highest priorities. So was creating a uniform hierarchy of courts. But was it possible for the rule of law to develop in a society in which the power of officials and social elites was all but unconstrained by constitutional or administrative rules?

The era of Peter the Great

Peter Alekseevich I came to the throne in 1682 conjointly with his half-brother Ivan V and became sole ruler in early 1696. From early 1697, he traveled widely in Europe and diligently studied its institutions and government. He returned to Russia in August 1698 to crush a musketeer rebellion. Dissatisfied with the original investigation and sentences imposed on the rebels, he ordered a new trial, resulting in the execution of 1,182 mutineers and the flogging and exile of 601 others.[1]

Peter came home determined to impose not just political conformity but a cultural transformation. He personally shaved off the beards of his leading advisors and decreed the adoption of Western-style dress, to replace what Europeans viewed as Turkish-style garb. He founded a new capital city, St. Petersburg, closer to Europe and modeled it on European cities (see Map 1.1). Education and high culture were expanded and transformed. Peter sponsored mapmaking, geographical surveys, scientific expeditions to Siberia and the Far East, and the development of scientific advancement of all kinds. The military was

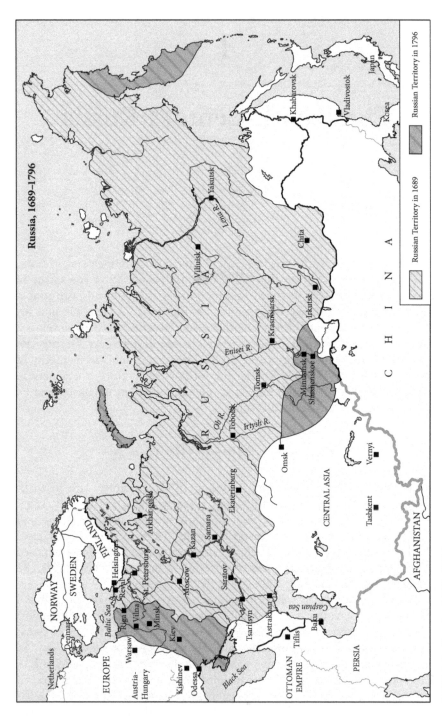

MAP 1.1 *Russia, 1462–1796.*

built up and modernized. It was a transformation probably more successful and more rapid than any ever undertaken (the Meiji Restoration being the only rival in world history).

Such changes came at a price. Russia's elites, who generation after generation grew closer to European ways, became as strangers to most Russians. The elites also inevitably saw themselves as more advanced, as justified in their greater power and wealth. They tended to view ordinary people in a paternalistic way. Peter, moreover, encouraged Europeanization selectively. Technology, high culture, technical education, administrative methods, and science were all welcome. Political philosophy, imposing limits on rulers, constitutional law, representative government, and the rights of individuals or groups were not. Consequently, the ruler continued to be viewed as all-powerful and above the law. Moreover, just as the ruler stood above the law and was not limited in any way by the law, so also his entire administration, including the system of criminal justice, depended more on the will of magistrates than on the letter of the law.

To finance reform and continuous warfare, Peter raised the peasants' taxes, imposed a lifetime draft, authorized industrialists to use enserfed labor in factories and mines, employed tens of thousands of convict laborers on major building projects, and developed an internal passport system. Such pressures drove millions of peasants to flee to the borderlands and in 1707–1708 to join a massive rebellion seeking to restore "the good old ways." Thousands of captured rebels were tortured or executed. Thousands more fled further south. Far from improving the lot of most peasants, the rebellion brought ruler and elites closer and intensified their exploitation of the lower orders.

When Peter came to power, criminal cases were not brought to specialized courts, but to chancelleries (*prikazy*) with administrative authority over a particular function—or life-or-death power over a population group (such as serfs and noble servitors). Some chancelleries specialized in judicial matters more than others. The Investigation Chancellery (*Sysknoi prikaz*), for example, prosecuted murder and armed robbery. In Moscow, the Office of the Land (*Zemskii prikaz*) prosecuted felonies. Judgments were often reached as a function of the authority and influence of officials, not of procedural norms. (Peter shut down the Investigation Chancellery in 1701 and transferred its authority to various other jurisdictions, including that of provincial governors.) The final arbiter of the entire criminal justice system was Peter himself, though he only occasionally took part.

Political cases could also be handled by a wide variety of chancelleries in Muscovite Russia, though ad hoc chancelleries were sometimes set up to deal with specific political threats. Nearly all political cases were triggered by a denunciation, the number of which increased dramatically in the second half of the 1600s. Such cases were labeled "the Sovereign's Word and Deed." Essentially any manner of intended or even unintended harm or criticism of the ruler, his family, or his rule was treated as a potentially serious crime.

Can they deny?

The denouncer was required to substantiate the accusation and, failing that, suffered punishment. Thus, in political cases there had to be a guilty party. The tsar served as final judge in most such cases. Mere suspicion of guilt was sufficient for imposing capital punishment. The traditional understanding of the ruler as sacred remained strong in Russia. Crimes against faith and the church were also deemed heinous, and their number, as defined in statutes, expanded enormously during the reign of Peter.[2] In 1696, Peter created a high court for investigating and trying cases of state crime within the already-existing Preobrazhenskii Chancellery and expanded its scope in 1702. This body also handled a wide variety of nonpolitical cases.

In 1708, Peter decentralized government administration into eight big regions, called *gubernii*, each headed by a governor and centered on Moscow, St. Petersburg, and six borderlands.[3] In 1711, he instituted a Governing Senate to supervise the machinery of government, to serve as a first-instance court for political crimes and cases of corruption of high-ranking officials, and to rule conditionally in his absence. Simultaneously, he created a network of officials, called *fiskaly*, to seek out and denounce malfeasance or corruption within the government. As an incentive, they were promised one half of any resulting fine and could not be prosecuted for false accusations. In 1722, Peter instituted the office of procurator general to watch over the administration throughout the country, to ensure that the Senate fulfilled all its duties, and to supervise the *fiskaly*. It was a common practice in Russian history for rulers, who often distrusted the bureaucracy and most officials, to deploy ad hoc representatives to watch over the entire executive apparatus. This was a prime example of the strong personal, informal factor in Russian governance. It was also an instance of the Russian preference for the rule of authoritative persons rather than of law.

In 1718, Peter replaced the dozens of chancelleries (though not the Preobrazhenskii Chancellery) with a set of ten (later thirteen) colleges, or collegial administrative agencies, following the Swedish model.[4] There was still considerable overlap. Although the College of Justice was the most focused on judicial affairs, it also handled a wide variety of administrative tasks, while all other colleges administered justice, both civil and criminal, for specific categories of people. The College of Manufactures, for example, tried cases involving factory owners. No instruction was ever issued defining the authority, jurisdiction, and procedural rules of the College of Justice. Here was another example of a resistance to codify rules and procedures and a tendency to leave them up to the discretion of administrative officials.

The College of Justice created a five-tiered judicial hierarchy: two primary courts, at the district and provincial level; a higher regional court at the provincial level; appeals brought to the College of Justice; and final appeals to the Senate (see Figure 1.1). Appealing Senate decisions to the tsar himself was to be a capital offense. (The Preobrazhenskii Chancellery remained independent.) Yet cases did not always follow the established hierarchy, they

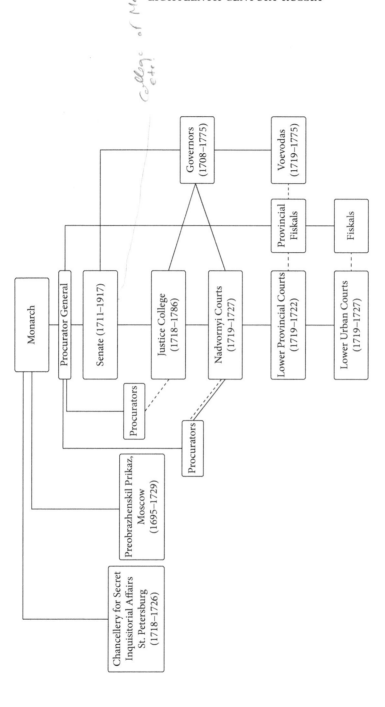

College of Manufactures etc.

FIGURE 1.1 *Judicial organization from the early 1700s to 1727. The central figure in the entire criminal justice system was the monarch, from whom all authority flowed. Justice was meted out by administrative officials typically with little legal expertise. Separate courts and treatment were reserved for each official social estate. Military courts tried many civilians.*

were often opened at any level, appeals were still made directly to Peter, and the Senate rarely heard appeals cases. In a word, the system was not systematic.

The court reform was intended to separate administrative from judicial authority, yet most judges remained military officers and administrative officials. This was not surprising, since Peter distrusted lawyers and judges. "Lawyers' useless lengthy speeches," he opined, "serve merely to complicate the judges' task and make for greater delay."[5] Nor were judges supposed to engage in legal interpretation. Clearly, Peter wanted to maintain personal administrative control over the criminal justice system. He was willing to delegate authority within the system, but primarily to administrative officials. These officials enjoyed broad power to adjudicate, but only within the framework of the law as issued in St. Petersburg. (In 1722, the lowest courts were reincorporated into the governors' offices.)

For Peter, creating the right atmosphere and impressing relevant symbolism on his institutions was always important. In 1722, for example, Peter decreed that all courtrooms in the Russian Empire must display a trihedral prism, called *zertsalo*, on the judge's bench. The three faces were required to exhibit the texts of three relevant edicts: concerning the preservation of civil rights, offenses and courts, and state statutes and their importance. Atop the prism stood a double-headed eagle, the Russian state symbol. When the judge left the courtroom, either the prism or the double-headed eagle also had to be removed.[6] This decree was meant to raise the prestige and authority of senior judicial personnel. Yet they enjoyed no independence from the tsar and his administration, unlike in all Western European countries where the judicial power of government had been separated from the executive power during the Middle Ages.

In 1719, to devolve more authority to the local level, the large regional administrations, or *gubernii*, were divided into forty-five much smaller provinces (*provintsii*), each headed by a governor (*voevoda*), most of whom were former military officers. (The *provintsii* were further subdivided into districts, or *uezdy*.) Overburdened with administrative functions, governors often found it difficult to focus adequate attention on judicial matters. Judges under their purview received inadequate pay, which naturally fostered bribe-taking. Official corruption, further exacerbated by a tendency for personal relations to trump formal rules, was a perennial problem in early modern Russia—despite extremely harsh punishments, including the flogging, bodily mutilation, and execution of dozens of senior officials caught in the act during Peter's last years.

Although the law code of 1649 remained in force, Peter supplemented it with the Military Criminal Code of 1715. This legislation was of utmost importance to criminal justice. It applied to regular criminal justice if the defendant was in the military or retired from the military and in cases where existing legislation did not specify a suitable punishment. It spelled out rules of interrogation in criminal cases and more carefully distinguished between murder and manslaughter than previous legislation. Henceforth, accusatory procedure was to be replaced by inquisitorial, with the apparent purpose of limiting the discretion of judges. The code also instituted some new harsh punishments, including execution by firing squad, running the gauntlet (for officers only), hanging by the ribs, and *shel'movanie* or deprivation of all status markers, like "civil death" in England. The code increased the number of capital offenses to 108 (English criminal law, by comparison, listed some 200 as late as 1819), including death by shooting for 47 offenses, by beheading for 11, by hanging for 25, by the wheel for 6, by quartering for 8, and by burning for 4.[7] Such harsher punishments were adopted in imitation of practices in Europe, where capital punishment was more broadly and frequently applied. How often such punishments were imposed in Russia is impossible to determine, because neither crime nor punishment statistics were systematically collected during this era. In other words, the functioning of criminal justice in Russia as conducted in courtrooms is impossible to know except anecdotally.

In both military and civilian trials, defense attorneys were not permitted. Confession was considered the most reliable form of proof, and therefore torture was regularly used to obtain one, as in the early modern European countries. Noblemen, the aged, children, and pregnant women were exempted from torture, except in cases involving murder and actions deemed harmful to the state, the ruler, or the church. Despite this apparent equivalency, in both theory and practice murder was considered far less grave crime than attacking—even nonfatally—the highest religious and secular authorities. This particular disparity remained a key feature of Russian criminal justice for most of the past 300 years.

In 1723, Peter issued a decree on judicial procedure that reinstituted the accusatorial form of trial for lesser offenses, where a plaintiff and a defendant argued their case before a judge, though inquisitorial procedure persisted for serious crimes.[8] The decree also prescribed hefty fines for violating procedural rules. Some punishments were softened, for example, beheading instead of force-feeding molten metal for counterfeiting. Others were made harsher: embezzlement of state revenue became a capital offense, in keeping with Peter's goal of augmenting the authority and prestige of the state, ostensibly at the expense of the person of the ruler. Since he did not create an independent judiciary or work to institutionalize the law as standing above himself and his officials, however, the net effect was to enhance the power of the state and its bureaucracy without lessening the awesome status of the monarch.

Indeed, the gravest crimes remained attacks on the ruler, treason, and rebellion. Next came murder and other violent crimes, which entailed the death penalty. Then followed vagrancy and fraud, to be punished with exile, hard labor, or corporal punishment. Defendants were presumed guilty, kept in detention during investigation, and pressed at great length for a confession. Even when insufficient evidence was available to convict a suspect, he or she might be left "under suspicion," a status that could count heavily against the person in possible subsequent criminal investigation. Court documents frequently referred to people as "guilty" before they had even been brought to trial. All lesser crimes required a plaintiff to bring charges to administrative officials and to press his or her case with witnesses and evidence. Making an accusation against a person in a position of power and authority was, in such a starkly hierarchical society, no easy task. Indeed, respect for persons and positions was far greater than for law and procedure within the Russian judicial system and indeed Russian society more generally.

During Peter's reign, the death penalty was resorted to less frequently than previously, and people of higher status suffered corporal punishment less often, except for state crimes. Corporal punishment and hard labor were preferred to the death penalty, because of the state's need for labor. Nostril slitting, which had existed in Muscovite law, became under Peter a routine bodily marking for penal exiles. Settlement before a judge became common for ordinary crimes, up to unintentional homicide, but even in such cases, corporal punishment was typically applied. The knout, a heavy flogging device that tore the skin, was the instrument of choice.

Peter's dramatic program of reform and transformation spawned vehement opposition in nearly every corner of society. Even his own son, Alexis, apparently conspired against him. To investigate the suspected conspirators, in 1718 Peter instituted an office dedicated to investigating political and state crimes. Called the Chancellery for Secret Inquisitorial Affairs (*Kantseliariia tainykh rozysknykh del*), it was created without mention in any published law, and its functioning remains veiled in shadows.[9] This was, of course, an instance of irregular justice outside the normal bounds of the law and thus likely to reinforce the tendency to arbitrary governance and punishment.

Over the course of several months, dozens of suspects were tortured and flogged or executed in various gruesome ways, including impalement. Among the victims was Alexis himself, who died under mysterious circumstances, apparently following torture overseen by his own father. Clearly, Peter considered threats to his rule to be among the most dangerous offenses conceivable. The head of one alleged conspirator, Avraam Lopukhin, was left on public display for five long years.[10] It seems that the history of Russian criminal law reached a high point of punitive severity during the reign of Peter the Great (at least until the Bolsheviks came to power 200 years later).[11]

As in all early modern European polities, where criminal investigation was rudimentary and professional police forces nonexistent, rulers used such spectacles of judicial horror to make an example of the few who were caught in order to deter others. It was a crude but probably relatively effective means of inculcating respect for higher authority and the state. Since Peter was uprooting many traditions and reorienting Russia on a new path, he probably felt he needed to promote such respect even more than other monarchs.

The chief focus of the reforms of Peter the Great was strengthening the state and enhancing political absolutism. Like his predecessors, he avoided dividing sovereignty. Elites and officials were never allowed to amass power, develop regional power bases, form semiautonomous intermediary bodies, or coalesce into historically rooted and politically influential social estates. Unlike their French counterparts, Russia's rulers did not sell administrative offices and did not preserve regional administrative and judicial institutions, but created a unified and centralized bureaucratic system. Marc Raeff argued throughout his work that the absence of "intermediary bodies" in Russia meant that modernization along European lines inevitably resulted in a greater concentration of power and repressive institutions in the hands of the ruler, since no constituted and powerful institutions or influential social groups could act as a political check to counterbalance the overwhelming authority of the monarch.[12]

For all Peter's efforts and intentions to devolve power and build up institutions, Russia remained an autocracy. The emperor's power dramatically exceeded that of all officials and institutions. He also stood entirely above the law. Whatever he decided was the law. In the words of a preeminent Petrine scholar, "there were no limitations on the sovereign's power. Nobles were more than ever vulnerable to death or disgrace at the sovereign's whim. They were full-time servants of the State, appointed at random while still in their teens to a branch of the service."[13] In a similar manner, justice was rendered not by institutions and according to legal procedure, but by men, almost always officials of the executive branch of government, deciding according to circumstance, applying as best they could the statutes set out in the codes of 1649 and 1715. Ultimately, one can argue that Russia's rulers were more concerned with compiling decrees than promoting a legal consciousness, a disposition that remained relatively constant both before and after 1917.[14]

After Peter

The reigns of Peter's immediate successors—Catherine I (r. 1725–1727), Peter II (r. 1727–1730), and Anna Ioannovna (r. 1730–1740)—were relatively uneventful from the point of view of criminal justice. Obligatory service of elites and bondage of the masses continued. Established criminal law and procedure remained unchanged. The Chancellery for Secret Inquisitorial Affairs was abolished in 1726 but reinstituted in 1730–1731, with branches in St. Petersburg and Moscow.[15] The entire judicial system was returned to full administrative control in 1727 (see Figure 1.2). From this point, all judicial authority was given to the *voevody*, the governors, and the colleges. The College of Justice served as the main appeal institution for all chancelleries and governors. It also served as the first-instance court for crimes committed by officials and for serious criminal cases. Death sentences were imposed more sparingly. Penal exile was used more extensively. Penal laborers were increasingly assigned to Siberia's growing metallurgical sector as well as other industries.[16] No major popular rebellions occurred. Politically, and indeed throughout the entire remainder of the century, Russia's rulers were put in power amid struggles among guard officers, who also served as political advisors and officials in the successive reigns.

From the point of view of constitutional law, however, 1730 was a major turning point. In that year, Anna Ioannovna was placed on the throne by a cabal of high nobles gathered in the Supreme Privy Council. They sought to establish a system of limited government by imposing upon her a list of Conditions. Henceforth, no member of the nobility could be deprived of life, honor, or property without a proper trial. Fearing arbitrary rule by oligarchy, however, most noblemen urged Anna to reject the Conditions. With a flourish, she ripped the document in twain. Russia's transition toward a constitutional monarchy had to wait over a century and a half, until 1906.

The power of landowners over their serfs did not decline in this era; if anything it increased.[17] Custom forbade them to kill their serfs, but no law prohibited it. If a person killed the serf of another, the only recourse under the law was a civil suit. Otherwise, such crimes were handled "in-house" by landowners themselves. (One should not say "serfowners," because legally speaking the serfs' status was never made fully clear and they were never unambiguously categorized as property.) Yet few landowners murdered their serfs. Most were relatively careful about punishing them, to inculcate obedience but also preserve their worth as beasts of burden. Enlightened landowners adopted elaborate rulebooks for the application of criminal and civil punishment in respect of their serfs. As for serfs, they could not bring charges against their lords except in cases of high crime, such as treason and attempted regicide.

A momentous development in the criminal law occurred in the next reign, that of Peter the Great's daughter Elizabeth Petrovna (r. 1740–1762). Upon coming to the throne with the backing of guard officers, she spoke against capital punishment and issued a series of decrees requiring the Senate to review all death sentences. In 1753, the Senate requested her confirmation of 279 death sentences and 151 sentences to hard labor and reported on 3,579 further criminal cases that had not yet been decided.[18] It was in this context that her famous decree of March 29, 1753, was issued. It prescribed leading death row inmates to the place of execution and reprieving them at the last minute—a practice made infamous by such treatment of Dostoyevsky the following century. A decree of September 20, 1754, abolished capital punishment provisionally, until the adoption of a new law code. (Meanwhile, twenty capital offenses, including the theft of objects worth more than twenty rubles, remained on the books.)[19]

For the rest of Elizabeth's reign, relatively few death sentences were issued, and all of these were overturned by the Senate or the empress. For the next seventy years, only about a dozen people were executed on court orders

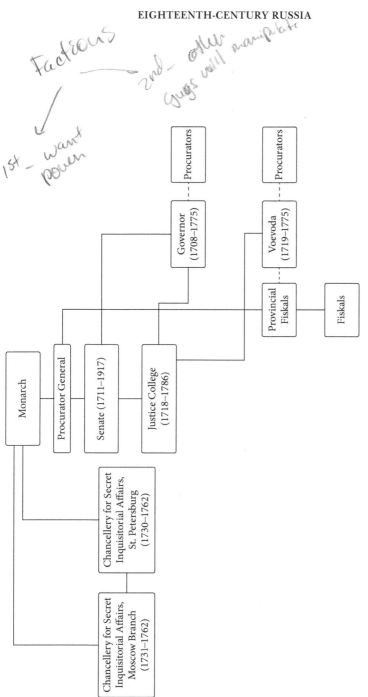

FIGURE 1.2 *Judicial organization from 1727 until the reforms of Catherine II in 1775. After the independent system of courts was abolished, their functions were transferred to the chancelleries of each governor or voevoda, who had continued in many ways to interfere in the judicial process.*

in the Russian Empire (though a few times that number were summarily executed during rebellions, civil strife, and bandit raids). Indeed, for several decades capital punishment was considered an exceptional measure in Russia. In England and Wales, by contrast, the *yearly* number of executions as late as the first decades of the nineteenth century was just under 100, before falling to roughly ten in the late 1830s.[20]

Even so, Elizabeth's reform was not necessarily as humanitarian as it might seem. The usual replacement punishments—flogging with the knout, bodily mutilation, and exile to Siberia or to hard labor in Siberian mines or building fortresses in the borderlands—were brutal, destructive of one's life chances, and sometimes resulted in death. In fact, all such punishments entailed civil death, or *shel'movanie*: the convict's property was placed in trusteeship for his children or was confiscated by the state if he had none, and his wife received the portion due to her as a widow. Any privileged status of the convict was obliterated. Yet even a conditional abolition of capital punishment a decade before the publication of Rousseau's *Contrat social* (1762) and Beccaria's *Dei delitti e delle pene* (1764) was a notable advancement in the realm of criminal law.

The powers of social control were dramatically enhanced toward the end of Elizabeth's reign, by a decree of December 1760. Henceforth, serf masters (both secular and ecclesiastical), as well as village and urban communities, were empowered to recommend to state authorities the exile of recalcitrant and other undesirable persons to settlement in Siberia for indefinite time periods. For each adult male, these landowners or communities would receive credit for a military recruit. It was clear from the wording of the decree that its purpose was not to strengthen the power of landowners over their serfs, though of course that was a prime result, but to promote migration to Siberia.[21] Three more decrees (1761–1762) confirmed and extended this power. One estimate holds that 35,000 males, along with perhaps an equal number of family members, were exiled to Siberia under the new provisions in 1761–1781.[22] The combined effect of these laws was to enable the main rural authorities—the landed nobility and peasant communities—to dispose of anyone who failed to conform to expectations. Thus began the systematic use of Siberia (though also, albeit less frequently, other remote regions) as a vast prison and exile as a means to people the empire's sparsely inhabited borderlands.

The chief accomplishment of the six-month reign of Elizabeth's son, Peter III, was emancipating Russian noblemen from service and explicitly exempting them from the confiscation of their estates for failing to serve the Imperial government. Although a large proportion of noblemen continued to enter service, particularly the military, a significant—and gradually increasing—number elected to settle in the provinces on their landed estates, contributing to the maintenance of order in the countryside. As previously, such landowners continued to exercise judicial authority over the serfs populating their estates. Those who resided on their estates passed judgment personally; absentee landlords devolved that authority to bailiffs. Peter III also abolished the Chancellery for Secret Inquisitorial Affairs and pardoned peasant participants in revolts on monastic estates and persons exiled for political reasons during Elizabeth's time of rule.

The era of Catherine the Great

In June 1762, Peter was deposed (and in July murdered) by guard officers in cahoots with his wife Catherine. She reconfirmed several of her deposed husband's reform measures, including the liberation of the gentry from state service. She also reconstituted the political police, now called the Secret Expedition.

In the same years when noble property rights grew more secure, peasant landholding remained conditional on service to the lords. Thus, the burden of state service fell disproportionately heavier upon the peasantry. In fact, soon after Catherine took the throne some 200,000 peasants—one quarter assigned to mines and factories in the Urals and the rest laborers on church lands who had expected to receive ownership of the land they tilled—were in open revolt. Her officials applied harsh repression but also regulated the work conditions of assigned peasants. Even so, until the abolition of serfdom in 1861, nearly all workers in the entire Urals metallurgical industry—except the most senior management—were ascribed serfs.[23] The next few years witnessed repeated unrest among serfs, apparently bitter that Peter and Catherine freed the nobles from service but did next to nothing to improve their own lot.

An important step in the evolution of criminal justice in Russia came with the Great Instruction, divided into 526 articles, which Catherine prepared for an impending Legislative Commission of 1767.[24] Its main purposes were governmental reform and the codification of Russian law. In preparing her Instruction, Catherine was strongly influenced by Montesquieu with his argument against torture and Beccaria, whose *Of Crimes and Punishments* she had carefully read in the 1766 French translation.[25]

Beccaria was the first thinker to argue that criminal punishment was not some arbitrary right of rulers but a mechanism for deterring crime and as such served goals of utility and humanity. He also argued from the concept of the social contract that the death penalty could never be legitimate since it could not have been a precondition for agreeing to form social and political bonds. Not above copying wholesale from European writers, Catherine concluded that law should aim at deterring crime, that it was better to prevent than to punish after the fact, that the nature and intensity of the punishment should correspond to the nature and gravity of the crime, and that the law should define crimes according to their seriousness. Punishment should also be swift and certain and should aim at deterring criminality rather than terrorizing the population. Capital punishment, she opined, should be resorted to seldom. Blasphemy and related acts should be conceived as offenses against decency rather than religious, much less, state crimes. Torture and bodily mutilation should be avoided. She also followed Beccaria in arguing against interpretation of the law by judges. On the contrary, the monarch should be the sole legislator. Such a view certainly fit well with Russia's autocratic tradition. Yet, the Instruction radically diverged from positive Russian law. And its conceptualization of the law in terms of the individual made no sense in the context of a culture lacking individual rights and abounding in collective responsibilities. Even so, the Instruction was well known throughout Europe and helped promote a positive assessment of Catherine's reign.

Representatives of Russia's social categories, or estates (but not serfs on private landed estates who made up 53 percent of the total population), were invited to submit petitions (*nakazy*) to the Legislative Commission. The majority of such petitions complained about the functioning of the justice system, especially its cumbersome nature, slow settling of cases, and perceived unfairness. Petitions from representatives of all social estates, from noblemen to peasants, urged draconian punishments for bandits and other criminals. They all also clamored for legal protection of their person, property, and interests.[26] Such complainers did not hope for the establishment of a strong independent judiciary, but rather the investment in local nobleman of the power to decide cases according to their conscience. This was in keeping again with the tendency in Russia to prefer a government of men rather than laws and to trust personal authority more than formal procedures.

The Legislative Commission ceased its work in 1774 without having proposed major legislative change or codified the law. Practically speaking, codification was difficult in Russia because tens of thousands of decrees—scattered throughout the administrative apparatus—had been issued by Russia's rulers since the *Ulozhenie* of 1649. In many cases, even legal experts and government officials had no idea exactly which laws should be applied when. Naturally, such problems were greatest at the provincial and local levels. It seems furthermore quite likely that Catherine understood explicitly or implicitly that establishing a true rule of law, as she had proposed in the Instruction, would limit her own autocratic power, a step she might have favored in theory but certainly not in practice.

Nevertheless, Catherine's reading of key works of Enlightenment thinkers strongly influenced her criminal justice policy. As early as December 1762, she had issued secret orders that torture was to be used very sparingly in order not to let the innocent suffer.[27] In February 1763, for example, she urged limiting recourse to torture and prohibiting its use in any case when a confession had already been given. A decree in 1765 limited the application of the knout to persons 17 years of those aged or older. Those aged 15–17 could be whipped with rods, those aged 10–15 with birch twigs, and those 10 and under should be released to their parents or landowner.[28] Catherine's Instruction itself, moreover, was not without subsequent impact. Judges and other officials intending leniency typically undergirded their decisions by citing the Instruction. Even the Senate not infrequently invoked the Instruction when formulating its judgments. Such practice continued into the reigns of Catherine's successors. Like Elizabeth, she preserved capital punishment on the books but rarely implemented it in practice.

The main reason for discontinuing the work of the Legislative Commission was a massive Cossack and peasant rebellion that broke out in the southeast and east in 1773. The leader, Yemelyan Pugachev, was captured, brought to trial in Moscow in 1774, and sentenced to quartering followed by beheading. Enlightened despot that she was, Catherine ordered that he be beheaded first. Yet she also approved a proposal that rebels, who collectively had killed thousands of government officials, be "put to death, after preparation according to Christian rites, first by cutting off their hands and feet, and then their heads, and placing the bodies on blocks beside thoroughfares." One official reckoned that 324 rebels were thus executed, 339 lost an ear before flogging with the knout, and 7,000 more suffered other forms of whipping.[29] Among the most important consequences of the rebellion was to draw the ruler closer to the landowning elites who relied absolutely on the military power of the state to maintain their privileged control over their serfs. This reinforced the nexus of autocratic power of both the empress and the landowners, each in their sphere of influence.

The uprising, the last great peasant rebellion in Russian history, further convinced Catherine that the organization of government in rural areas was completely inadequate. All rural governance, including the passing of justice, was carried out either by landowners or by peasant communes. This arrangement spared the treasury but left the government without its own agents in the countryside. In 1763, Russia had around 16,500 officials at all levels of government—roughly the same number as Prussia, a country with five times fewer people and a vastly smaller territory[30]—and only 5,000 mostly low-level officials scattered in rural areas.[31] In other words, nearly the whole of the Russian population escaped government oversight.

In 1775, therefore, Catherine completely reorganized local administration. First, she divided the country into forty-one (by 1796, fifty) roughly equally sized provinces (*gubernii*), which were subdivided into relatively uniform districts (*uezdy*), whose number increased from 169 in 1775 to 493 in 1796.[32] She appointed a governor to reside in the capital city of each province. They were to oversee new police, taxation, and general administrative officials, instead of these responsibilities being concentrated in the hands of the governors. Most important from the point of view of criminal justice, Catherine instituted a hierarchy of local, district, and appellate courts.

At the local (*uezd*) level, separate courts were established for nobles and their serfs (*zemskie sudy*), townspeople (*magistraty*), and state peasants (*raspravy*). (See Figure 1.3.) There was no requirement that elected judges of the latter two courts be members of those social estates; landowners or retired officials could also serve. The governor had to approve those elected.

Each court was divided into two departments, civil and criminal. As before, private serfs remained outside the system and completely under the power of landowners. Many landowners relied on customary peasant justice, though how much they wished to interfere and impose their own will depended entirely on the landowners themselves. The wealthy Sheremetevs granted fairly broad latitude to communal justice, but little is known about how the law functioned at this level on the thousands of estates throughout the Russian Empire. When a legal dispute involved members of two social categories, their respective courts settled the matter in tandem.

Above the district level, but below the provincial, stood three intermediate courts, also organized along estate lines. First was the upper land court (*verkhny zemsky sud*). It was also made up of two departments, civil and criminal. The chairman of each was appointed by the empress; each chairman was seconded by five elected assessors. In criminal cases, this court could not issue binding judgments but only provisory ones. The chairmen of the intermediate courts for urban dwellers and state peasants were appointed by the Senate; the assessors were elected.

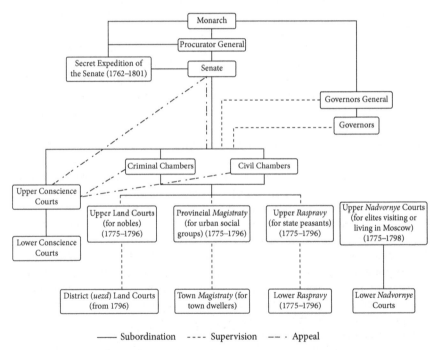

FIGURE 1.3 *Judicial organization following Catherine the Great's provincial reform of 1775. Estate-based justice continued. Specialized courts were created, though most judges remained retired noble army officers deciding cases based on written reports compiled by clerks. Administrative officials continued to exert influence throughout the system, including the authority to review court decisions.*

One more set of regular courts with territorial competence, called *nadvornye* courts, was created to handle cases concerning nobles and *raznochintsy* (persons outside the main social estates) from other jurisdictions who were conducting business in the two capital cities, Moscow and St. Petersburg. These courts also had separate civil and criminal departments and were established at both the district and the provincial levels. The personnel of these courts at both levels were appointed by the empress at the upper ranks and by the Senate at the lower ranks rather than elected.

Serious criminal cases—those liable to sentences of death, loss of honor, or flogging—could commence at the lower levels but were decided by the provincial criminal chambers (*palaty*). None of the members of these chambers was elected, though they seem to have defended the interests of the landowning nobility more than those of other social estates. All ten members of each judicial chamber were, by definition, hereditary nobles and typically landowners of the province where they served. Their decisions had to be confirmed by the governor, and, failing that, were sent automatically for review to offices of the Senate in either Moscow or St. Petersburg. (Cases involving nobles went directly to the Senate.) Convicts nearly always benefited from a review of their cases by the Senate, which much more than provincial officials tended toward leniency. The provincial chambers were the only institutions outside the central bureaucracy that were devoted exclusively to judicial affairs. All of the lower courts still handled a variety of nonjudicial matters.

The 1775 reform also created a completely separate court at the provincial level called the conscience court, or court of equity (*sovestnyi sud*). Judgments were passed in each such court by a judge along with two elected representatives from the nobility and from either the townspeople or state peasants, depending on the nature of the case being considered. The court's mandate was to "safeguard personal security," guided by an "aversion to the oppression of mankind."[33] These courts were to try cases involving the mentally ill, minors, and alleged sorcery, which according to the author of the statute inevitably involved "stupidity, deception, and ignorance." A person held in prison for more than three days without being charged with a crime could appeal to the court. People accused of lesser crimes could be released on bail by decision of the court. An upper conscience court heard appeals. The fundamental idea of the institution was that people not fully responsible for their actions should be removed from the regular criminal justice system. It seems that Catherine had been strongly influenced by her reading about the English justice system with its equity courts and the tradition of habeas corpus. The work of these courts in Russia seems to have varied from place to place, but they apparently introduced significant judicial discretion into cases with a variety of extenuating circumstances. These courts apparently heard serious crime cases even when there was no question of insanity and they passed judgment more rapidly than the regular courts. It seems therefore that many defendants sought to have their cases tried by these judges as a conscious way to improve their odds of receiving a favorable outcome. (The courts were abolished by the judicial reform of 1864.)

Regular judges and their assistants at the local level were elected by members of their social estate (nobility, townspeople, or state peasantry). They were also paid a decent salary and given ranks within the civil service. The same went for the intermediate judicial level, though senior positions in those courts were by appointment. At the provincial level, all judges were appointed by the empress and all were members of the nobility. At no level was any specific legal training required, and therefore in many, if not most cases, judges and their assistants were presumably ignorant of the law. It was the clerks, who often remained in their positions for many years and thus acquired intricate knowledge of the system, who were the legal experts. The wealthier and more powerful noblemen had no interest in serving as judges but expected their interests to triumph in the courts. They were also accustomed to commanding and had little habit of resolving differences through compromise. Nevertheless, hundreds of retired noblemen were available to take on the responsibility of administering justice at the local level, something that would not have been the case before their emancipation from compulsory state service.

The reformed judicial system started operations somewhat haphazardly. The new courts opened in St. Petersburg in 1780, but in Moscow only in 1782. The central judicial institutions (including the College of Justice) closed their doors a year or two later. The number of courts at the local level immediately doubled, while the personnel staffing them increased from a few hundred to a few thousand, about half of them elected noblemen. The change represented a clear devolution of authority to the local and provincial levels and for the most part to local landed elites. A clear and systematic separation of civil from criminal cases naturally fostered greater specialization and efficiency (obviating the need in many instances to travel to Moscow or St. Petersburg).

Although the *Ulozhenie* of 1649 and the Military Code of 1715 remained the basis of all criminal procedure and sentencing, Catherine introduced a few revisions and innovations. Some crimes were no longer severely punished, such as immoral behavior or growing a beard. Sentencing grew more lenient. Several decrees of 1775 reformed penal policy. A statute of limitations was instituted for the first time in Russia. Whipping was redefined as a severe and not a corrective punishment and therefore required confirmation by the local governor. The distinction was also made between heavy whipping by a specialized official and light whipping of a clothed offender by ordinary police officials. Decrees also limited the number of lashes to which convicts were subject as part of their hard-labor sentences, abolished the use of the knout against women, replaced the traditional slitting of the nostrils with branding, and ordered that prisoners who became injured or sick during the march into Siberia be hospitalized. In practice, however, executioners, guards, and administrators often ignored these rules.[34] Finally, a new form of forced-labor prison, *smiritel'nyi dom*, was instituted to incarcerate persons convicted of such offenses against society as sexual abuse and parasitism. In 1781, yet another forced-labor prison, *rabochii dom*, was established for persons found guilty of committing crimes against property, such as theft and fraud.

While Catherine's reforms did not explicitly include procedural changes, the conscience courts opened the door to recognizing mitigating circumstances. The provision that, in all except state-crime cases, suspects could appeal to a conscience court for release after three days of detention, pending trial, was tantamount to an assertion of habeas corpus, though it seems this provision was not consistently enforced, especially for lesser crimes and outside the provincial capitals. It was also not insignificant that the law narrowed the jurisdiction of the lower courts to exclude not only the most serious crimes but also those for which whipping of any kind was the penalty. A decree of April 1781, which redefined the crime of larceny, downgrading to the status of misdemeanor even three instances of stealing goods worth less than 20 rubles, also had significant procedural implications.

As noted above, a decree of 1753 required Senate confirmation for all death sentences, which in practice were few in number. Sentences involving death, dishonor, or whipping were sent automatically to the relevant provincial criminal chamber, which reviewed the case, confirmed or reduced the sentence, and then sent it on to the governor for final confirmation. Governors were administrative officials typically with a military background. Requiring them to provide confirmation of judicial sentences thus left the executive branch of government in firm control of the judiciary for most criminal cases. A decree of 1784 expanded the requirement of senatorial review to most serious criminal cases, and a decree of 1796 permitted judicial appeals to the Senate. Nevertheless, gubernatorial control over the judicial system at the provincial level remained strong.

There was a special procedure for bringing government officials to justice. Before the reform, the highest officials were investigated by the College of Justice and tried by the Senate, whose decisions required Imperial confirmation. Officials appointed by the Senate were investigated by governors or college chairman and tried in the College of Justice, with sentences confirmed by the Senate. After the reform, all officials were investigated by the relevant provincial criminal chamber and then tried by the Senate either in Moscow or in St. Petersburg, with confirmation by the ruler of any resultant sentences. The gravest criminal cases involving officials were tried directly by the combined Senate and Holy Synod as a high court. Thus, bringing to account official malfeasance and criminal activity remained outside the judicial system and fully under the control of the executive branch. For although the Senate employed well-trained jurists, it remained an administrative organ answering solely to the monarch.

In her Instruction and in many other decrees, Catherine often emphasized compassion. There is some evidence that she set a tone that led to somewhat more lenient sentencing. The mandate of the conscience courts to consider extenuating circumstances and of reserving to the criminal chambers, the Senate, and the ruler the right to impose the harshest sentences surely resulted in some softening of the penal regime. Similarly, a decree of 1781 defined various types of theft in terms of violence employed and value of articles stolen.[35] For nonviolent theft under 20 rubles in value, no form of corporal punishment should be used, irrespective of social status. For second offenses, two lashes were the prescribed punishment; and for third offenses, three lashes. This was the first time in Russian law that the number of lashes was specified. Moreover, the number in each case was extremely low given the historical context.

The new judicial system was supervised by an expanded Procuracy functioning at the local, intermediate, and provincial levels.[36] The entire hierarchy answered to the provincial procurators, who were directly subordinated to the procurator general in St. Petersburg. Their purview was not limited to judicial matters but extended to ensuring the legality of all acts of the entire bureaucratic machine. At the same time, however, the provincial procurator needed to get along with the local governor, who inevitably had a higher rank and therefore more authority. He also, as noted above, exercised broad supervision over the judicial process in his province. Most important, he could refuse to confirm any criminal sentence and send it up for review to the Senate. Governors in this regard often acted like the conscience courts; whereas judges were required to apply the law in all its severity, governors could take extenuating circumstances into account and show mercy. Also important, governors were in charge of the police, who alone bore responsibility for investigating crimes. Finally, governors had the authority to exile persons administratively and to confirm sentences of exile imposed by peasant and urban communities. An ethos of arbitrary social control thus was at the very heart of the administrative system, control enforced by a punishment that in modern political systems is typically imposed only by judicial institutions. In Russia, at this time and to some extent right down to the present time, the lines between administration and judiciary were blurred.

The court reform resulted in much better record keeping, thus permitting researchers for the first time to access relatively detailed statistics about crime and punishment in Russia. One scholar has found, for example, that in cases involving domestic violence, spousal murders were more frequent than other intra-family killing and that men killed their wives far more often than the reverse. Moreover, women who killed their husbands—typically in self-defense—were punished more severely than men who killed their spouses—typically not in self-defense. The author concludes that high levels of domestic violence in Russia reflected the "privatization" of violence in the private sphere as the state grew more capable of interdicting it in public spaces, in a historical development analogous to one then unfolding also in Europe.[37]

Although the reformed judicial system remained firmly under the purview of the executive branch, the devolution of authority from the central administration to locally elected representatives was a novel and even radical departure from traditional bureaucratic oversight in Russia. The fact, however, that neither the nobility nor the merchantry constituted a self-consciously autonomous and self-assertive social estate pursuing common interests, much less the common good, meant that in practice the bureaucracy remained in charge.

The new court system, moreover, seems not to have dramatically improved the dispensing of justice in Russia. The availability of trained jurists remained small in the face of the massive number of cases—a total of 53,868 came before the courts in 1786 alone.[38] Enormous backlogs were common, such that cases often took years to reach resolution. They also typically had to be considered for approval or appeal at two or more levels within the judicial hierarchy. The absence of reliable legal compendia much less an up-to-date law code made it hard for judges to reach clean decisions. Simply to ensure the proper completion of adjudication, many participants in the legal system felt compelled to offer bribes, even though this was a criminal offense. Court officials were sometimes punished for corruption, but rarely, and most people did not seem to consider bribe-taking or bribe-giving terribly objectionable. A knowledgeable scholar has concluded that even the reformed criminal justice system provoked "constant calls from the public for reform on the grounds of the high volume of appeals and procedural delays."[39]

Partly to remedy such problems, Catherine issued a Police Ordinance in 1782, drawing upon European practical and theoretical writings of the time. Felonies were now defined much more expansively, to include larceny, fraud, and violations of regulations concerning public order. The purpose of "police" in the contemporary interpretation was to maintain good order and decency. As such, new police organs (*upravy blagochiniia*), instituted in all towns, were empowered to impose fines or brief jail time for infractions of the detailed regulations of urban life set out in the Ordinance. For more serious crimes, the police were entrusted with placing suspects in custody and carrying out criminal investigation. The Ordinance also formulated the principle according to which everything not forbidden by law was allowed, and also that parents and children were not to be held responsible for crimes committed by each other. Throughout the second half of the eighteenth century, denunciations by private individuals as a source of information leading to criminal investigations declined and continued to decline throughout the nineteenth century. Improved police work probably contributed both to this decline and to growing social stability.

The provincial reform of 1775 required each province to establish and maintain houses of correction for the temporary detention of persons exhibiting antisocial behavior and workhouses for the indigent and petty criminals needing to work off fines and other penalties. Taken together, the various monastery prisons, fortresses, hard-labor prisons, provincial jails, and penitentiaries in Moscow, St. Petersburg, and other big cities probably held at most several thousand inmates at any given time.[40] Certainly, far more people suffered exile in Catherine's reign than were imprisoned. According to one estimate, 35,000 males were exiled to Siberia between 1761 and 1781 (not counting family members probably totaling around 60,000).[41] Prisons were a costly and quite modern innovation. Even most European countries did not yet have extensive prison systems. For Russia in particular, with its vast and underpopulated territory, exile to remote locations, as a means of internal colonization, was presumably the most sensible penal strategy.

Catherine reached her high point of liberality with her proclamation of the Charter on the Rights, Freedoms, and Privileges of the Nobility of April 1785. This decree conferred upon nobles "inalienable, inheritable, and hereditary" dignity, which they could lose only through the commission of such grave crimes as treason, robbery, and those entailing the loss of honor and the imposition of corporal punishment and only following a trial of their peers. Henceforth, Russian nobles, possessed rights that could be defended in court. Nevertheless, judges, both military and civilian, had significant discretion in determining which crimes should be considered "dishonoring." Political climate could also influence whether members of the nobility enjoyed true exemption from corporal punishment, the death penalty, and the confiscation of their property. The final arbiter of the status of a noble, as before, remained the ruler. The more honorable urban dwellers received a similar charter of exemptions also in 1785.

The two Charters of 1785 were of utmost importance for four principal reasons. First, they laid the groundwork for the eventual emergence of a civil society—a bulwark of resistance to state power in Western societies—though this was a long way off (Russia's urban dwellers constituted no more than 4 percent of the total population in the 1790s.) Second, the Charters placed the responsibility for crime on individuals—at the elite level of society—rather than on collectives as had been the tradition in Russian law. Collective responsibility for ordinary people, however, remained the norm. Third, the Charters established and guaranteed certain civil rights for certain categories of the Russian population for the first time in its history. Fourth, the Charters were granted by autocratic fiat and at the good pleasure of the empress. Once again, in Russia the ruler was dramatically out ahead of society. Rights were not being demanded or extracted, as they had been, for example, in the lead-up to Magna Carta (1215) or the Petition of Right (1628) in England. Had they been, it seems likely they would have had more staying power than they ultimately did in Russia.

Catherine's response to the French Revolution, moreover, made clear the limits to her tolerance of public activism. Russian newspapers reported openly and objectively on the fall of the Bastille in July 1789. At that time, the war with Turkey was going well. Over the next several months, however, tensions with Britain, Sweden, and Prussia increased. Thus, when Alexander

Radishchev (1749–1802) came out with his *Journey from St. Petersburg to Moscow* in June 1790—which vehemently denounced serfdom, despotism, favoritism, corruption, war making, and the existing order in Russia generally—Catherine was not well disposed to receive it. She concluded that Radishchev was worse than Pugachev, inciting not only peasants but the entire Russian people to revolt. Radishchev was soon arrested, incarcerated in the Peter and Paul Fortress, and interrogated though apparently without any harsh methods. He appealed to Catherine for mercy but was still condemned to death. Catherine then commuted his sentence to loss of noble status and ten years of Siberian exile. Thanks to the solicitude of a well-placed patron, his passage out East was relatively comfortable. Again, personal connections, getting around the letter of the law, monarchical mercy, and other arbitrary principles were at work in the outcome.

The institution tasked with rooting out sedition and state crime was the Secret Expedition of the Senate, which was subordinated to the procurator general. It investigated many frivolous cases, often involving drunken outbursts against the monarch, but typically dealt with them leniently. Although Catherine personally issued numerous instructions to officials within this institution against the use of torture, in practice beatings were routinely applied, though not against well-known members of the nobility. In fact, such elites were typically detained in comfortable circumstances. The number of people punished for political offenses during the late reign of Catherine nevertheless remained quite small—dozens or at most a few hundred.

A key element of Catherine's political philosophy was the centrality of the monarch. It was she who permitted private printing presses in 1783, and she herself who revoked that permission in 1796. The idea of inalienable rights held by all her subjects, over which she could have no influence, for all her Enlightenment ideals, was foreign to her. One can argue that the personal and the charismatic trumped the legal and the rational aspects of governance in her reign. Since the time of Peter the Great, there had been steady movement toward recognizing the importance of the law, rendering criminal justice less draconian, and attempting to invest persons with rights. Such developments would continue throughout the nineteenth century, though as the subsequent reign demonstrated reversals in all these areas were not impossible.

2

Nineteenth-Century Russia before the Emancipation

By the early 1800s, Russia was one of the great military powers of Europe. The machinery of government had become more regular and rational. A uniform hierarchy of courts had emerged. Yet there was still no separation of powers, no independent judiciary. The monarchical authority was all but unlimited, at least in law. Throughout the administrative hierarchy, and indeed throughout society, officials and elites continued to wield unconstrained power. The development of the rule of law was further hampered by the lack of legal codification. There had been no compilation of the thousands of laws issued since the adoption of the law code of 1649. Even legal experts found it difficult to assert with certainty what was lawful and what was not. Resolving this problem was one of the most important accomplishments in the first half of the nineteenth century in Russia.

The interlude of Paul I

In 1796, Catherine died and her son Paul came to the throne. She had kept him away from power and would have preferred that the succession pass over him because he did not share her reformist ideals. Paul was an extremely activist monarch, issuing thousands of decrees. Worried about foreign ideas, he prohibited the import of all printed matter, including musical scores. He rescinded some of the rights granted in the Charter to the Nobility of 1785, including the right to travel abroad unhindered and exemption from corporal punishment. An enthusiast of the parade ground, he insisted on harsh punishments even against officers and often inflicted them himself personally and arbitrarily.

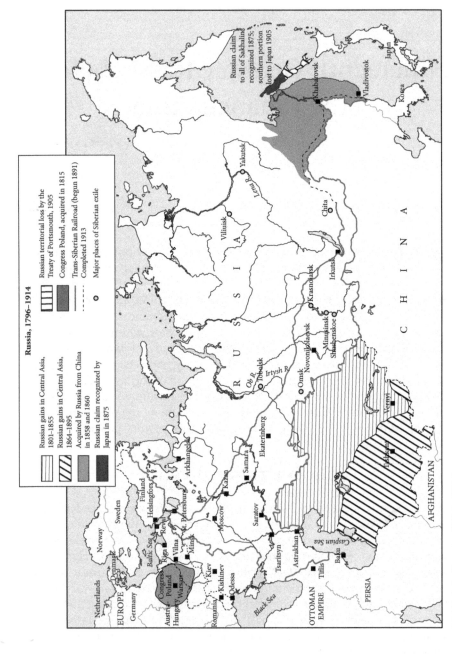

MAP 2.1 *Russia, 1796–1914.*

[handwritten margin note: among Classes? Surely not across Classes]

Paul was also committed to increasing orderliness, rationality, and equality before the law in his realm and to rooting out widespread corruption in the civil service. He thus strengthened the Procuracy and directed it to ferret out government impropriety. Yet he also laid a wide range of burdens upon that institution and its head, the procurator general. Such a concentration of executive functions in the hands of what should have been a judicial functionary resulted in increased arbitrary governance.[1] Similarly, Paul's reorganization of the judicial system, while aimed at streamlining its highly cumbersome functioning, resulted in further centralization and control by the bureaucracy.[2] It also had the effect of reducing local self-government and gentry participation in the judicial system. Nevertheless, except in the case of felonies and high crimes, the peasant world remained judicially self-contained.

Although Paul wished to strengthen respect for the law and legality throughout the bureaucracy, like his predecessors he himself could not conceive of the law limiting his own decision-making. Moreover, his harsh and often arbitrary treatment of members of the nobility, and especially officers, was not accompanied by a clear expansion of procedurally uniform treatment of others. On the contrary, mistreated elites presumably often meted out the same to their subordinates who were largely at their mercy and had been since Muscovite times.

A deeply suspicious man, and not without reason given his unpopular policies, Paul directed the Secret Expedition of the Senate to conduct widespread investigations, which resulted in thousands of arrests, especially among the social elites. The climate of fear was intensified by rumors of the use of torture during secret investigations. Members of the nobility were outraged and longed for a return to the rights given to them by Catherine. They also feared the creeping bureaucratization Paul's reforms gave rise to. Their watchword was often "Constitution" or "fundamental laws." Leading guard officers plotted against Paul and, having secured his son Alexander's willingness to take power, murdered Paul on the night of March 11, 1801.

Russia under Alexander I

Upon acceding to the throne, according to the law of male primogeniture adopted by his father, Alexander I promised to rule "according to the spirit and laws" of Catherine.[3] Several of his first actions reaffirmed such of her important decrees as the Charters to the Nobility and to the Towns, and overturned decrees of his father. In 1801, Alexander abolished the Secret Expedition, which had been unrestricted by legal norms and procedures, and ordered police and judicial institutions to refrain from the use of torture to extract information during criminal investigations.[4] In this regard, Russia was clearly within the European intellectual orbit in a way that China was not. Catherine had demanded the curtailment of judicial torture as early as 1767, and consequently its use gradually waned. Thanks to Alexander's decree, torture was officially abolished in the Imperial Russian criminal justice system. As late as 1905, by contrast, a Chinese official opined that "If we were to prohibit torture, then there would be no terror and who would be willing to disclose the facts?"[5]

Thousands of prisoners arrested during the time of Paul were liberated. Alexander also amnestied dozens of convicted officers, and the auditor-general's office was charged with reviewing all military court sentences. Alexander decreed an end to "merciless" and "cruel" punishments in the military, but the cruelest punishment of all, running the gauntlet, was retained. Like his father, Alexander was closely involved with military justice. In general, the system remained arbitrary, because everything depended on the will of the monarch, who could intervene in any case however he liked.

In June 1801, Alexander established a commission to draft a new law code and appointed Radishchev as a member. The last codification of laws had occurred in 1649, and since that time thousands of decrees had been issued. Some contradicted each other, often unbeknownst to officials, scattered as they were throughout the bureaucracy. Clerks in the various agencies often compiled lists of statutes, but they were rarely available outside those offices. Even judges were often ignorant of pertinent legislation, passing judgment as best they could. A huge number of questionable cases ended up in the Senate for review.

In late 1801, Alexander commenced a reorganization of the judicial system in order to return it to the status quo ante (see Figure 2.1). Several abolished courts were restored, including the conscience courts; elected estate representatives were again allowed to take part in adjudication at the district and provincial levels; and the powers given to governors in the 1775 provincial reform to supervise the entire judicial process at the provincial and district levels, including the confirmation of all court sentences, were restored. At the same time, elected representatives of the social estates (noble, peasant, urban) were given leading roles in local courts. Overall, the judicial system became more cumbersome and more decentralized. Aside from partially returning to the judicial structure set in place by his grandmother, Alexander's core motivation seems to have been his preference to trust administrators rather than institutions and trained jurists.

Alexander had gathered an "unofficial committee" of young aristocratic advisors who proposed thoroughgoing constitutional reforms, including mandatory ratification of all new laws by the Senate and guarantees of civil and property rights for elites. Alexander, who did not believe in the idea of inalienable rights for his people or of limiting his autocratic authority, however, gradually removed these advisors from positions of influence. He certainly believed in respect for the law and opposed governmental arbitrariness, but he held firmly that all sovereignty rested with him and not with the people. Therefore, any reforms could only emanate from

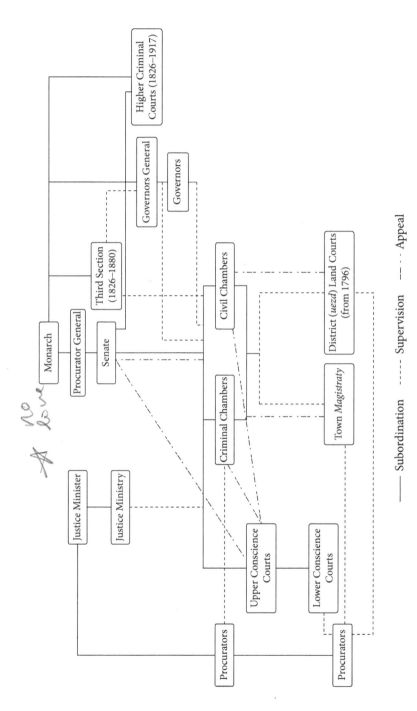

FIGURE 2.1 *Judicial organization from 1801 to 1864. Paul I abolished most of Catherine's lower courts, but his reorganization was rescinded in 1801. A Justice Ministry created in 1802 supervised the judicial system. The justice minister exercised the functions of the procurator general. In 1826, the Third Section, a political police, was instituted with powers of judicial investigation and punishment. Senior administrative officials continued to interfere in judicial affairs.*

his will. The term "Constitution" meant to him not a means to achieve limited government but government based on law. Constitutionally limited government, in his view, could make sense only in polities with politically mature populations. Such was not the case, he thought, in Russia.

Alexander's conflicted goals of reforming the political system and retaining full autocratic power are well illustrated in his policy regarding the Senate. In September 1802, he confirmed the authority of the Senate to ensure proper legal functioning of the government. Yet Alexander simultaneously decreed the establishment of eight ministries for all the main functions of government, which came directly under the authority of the emperor and not the Senate. (The eight ministers were ex officio members of the Senate.) The Ministry of Justice was given authority over all judicial institutions and personnel, including public procurators. In fact, the minister of justice bore the title of procurator general, which made him the head of the chancellery of the Senate. Rather than creating a system of checks and balances by separating judicial from executive power, Alexander kept himself at the center of the entire system and divided institutions with similar governmental functions in order to control them more effectively. Likewise, at the provincial level the justice minister had to compete for authority with the "masters of the provinces," the governors, who reported directly to Alexander himself just like the ministers. Alexander formed a Committee of Ministers but did not encourage them to coordinate their work. The Russian monarchy remained undivided though not entirely unlimited. Alexander opposed the institution of serfdom, as had his grandmother, but the entrenched noble landowning elites prevented any serious movement for improving their lot.

With the rise of Napoleon to power in France and the commencement of the Napoleonic Wars in 1803, Alexander turned his attention for several years almost exclusively to foreign affairs. In this connection, in 1805 he set up a special committee, made up of the ministers of war, interior, and justice, to combat political sedition. In early 1807, he ordered the creation of a permanent committee to establish surveillance over suspicious activities, especially those of Masonic and other covert organizations.[6]

For the next few years, Alexander entrusted numerous domestic reform projects to Michael Speransky, who first worked on improving education and state finances. In 1808, he joined the commission on the codification of laws. He directed the commission to draft the new code not from a careful study of all existing legislation, but rather upon a framework drawn from Napoleon's Civil Code of 1804. (This codification work was later suspended and bore no fruit).

Meanwhile, in 1809, Speransky sketched out a radical overhaul of the entire apparatus of government, with a proposed separation of powers, a four-tiered structure of representative assemblies called dumas, and a State Council headed by the emperor overseeing the entire system. In his conception of the separation of powers, the Senate would oversee the judicial branch, the ministries the executive branch, and the representative assemblies the legislative branch. Judges, he proposed, should be elected by the people. He also advocated the abolition of serfdom, governmental accountability, and the granting of broad-based civil rights throughout society. One scholar has, in fact, concluded that "The clear-cut theme of the 1809 plan is that the autocracy and the rule of law are incompatible, that the autocracy must in time convert itself into a constitutional monarchy."[7] Alexander was opposed to such radical change. From these ambitious plans, only the State Council as a supreme advisory body emerged in 1810. It gradually evolved into a court of appeal along with the Senate and the Committee of Ministers. Again, it was not the various functions of government that were divided to create checks and balances, but rather each function was severally divided. The result was weak institutions and unchecked autocratic power of the monarch.

As noted in Chapter 1, the Military Code of 1715 and other laws issued by Peter the Great reconfirmed inquisitorial procedure for criminal trials. This approach placed the written case report and the judge at the center of the judicial process. Since the most compelling form of proof remained a confession, police officials continued to exert strong pressure to wring one out, despite the formal abolition of torture. The judicial system functioned in a bureaucratic manner, so written documentation, rather than oral testimony, was presented to the court. It is obvious, therefore, that the most important procedural stage was the investigation, which was conducted by police officials who compiled a written record and sent it to the courts. At the provincial level, such investigations were overseen by the provincial governors.

Municipal police officials were either appointed at the recommendation of the governor or temporarily sent to him from St. Petersburg, at his request. Investigators and supervisory investigators were also appointed by the governor and reported to the local senior police official who reported to the governor. The actual administration of justice, following the investigation, was conducted by a judicial board of six men, elected by the townsmen. In the countryside, things were different. There at the district (*uezd*) level, the number of officials was even smaller, consisting of a police official (*ispravnik*), appointed by the governor, and two assessors elected by representatives of the nobility and two others elected by state peasants in localities where they comprised a significant proportion of the population. Here again, the cardinal importance of governors, the police, and indeed administrative officials generally within the judicial system is clear.

Speransky fell from grace in March 1812. On June 23–24, 1812, Napoleon's Grande Armée of a half-million men entered Russian territory. During the war, the treatment of military personnel grew harsher, thanks to a set of field regulations, which provided for depriving officers of their rank and even executing them within forty-eight hours for serious crimes. Under the regulations, many such crimes could be punished with death by shooting within twenty-four hours.[8] Although supposedly a temporary measure, these rules remained in force for several decades, even after the victorious end to the war in 1814, mostly in emergency situations like the Polish rebellion of 1830–1831.

Capital punishment remained off the books during the reign of Alexander, and no civilian-court-imposed death sentences were issued. Reinstituting the measure was discussed in 1813 and again in 1824 in the State Council, but in each case, the proposal was rejected. By contrast, in England and Wales during the same two decades, many hundreds of people were executed each year, often for petty crimes,[9] with a population (11 million people) nearly four times smaller than Russia's. Of course, flogging with the knout could and sometimes did result in death, though throughout these decades it was imposed less and less often by the courts as a punishment. Flogging in England and Wales also declined in the second quarter of the 1800s, but then enjoyed a resurgence in later decades.[10]

In 1815, Alexander granted a liberal Constitution to Congress Poland. It guaranteed an elective bicameral legislature, freedom of religion and the press, the use of Polish for official business, and the right of habeas corpus.[11] (Russians gained such a right only in 1992.) This was a slap in the face to many educated Russians, for it showed that Alexander considered them undeserving of such rights. Abroad, Alexander was even more animated by feelings of idealism. His concept of the Holy Alliance aimed at conforming international relations to the Christian principles of justice and love. It seems unlikely, however, that Alexander gave careful thought to the ideal of justice that should guide geopolitics in Europe or the judicial system in his own country. In Russia, as in Europe, order was maintained through force by largely unaccountable actors.

Again in 1818, Alexander returned to the idea of radical governmental reform. His trusted confidant Nikolai Novosil'tsev proposed the creation of regional (consultative) and central bicameral assemblies without whose consent no law could be promulgated. Most important from the point of view of criminal justice, the Constitution would have instituted the principles of habeas corpus, equality before the law, and freedom from arbitrary arrest. Nothing came of any of these proposals. Despite his commitment to reform, Alexander I remained an autocrat. He insisted that he alone could issue laws.

Alexander's absolutist and idealistic tendencies even led him to imagine that he could radically transform his people. That was clearly the aim of his 1816 plan to create "military colonies," combining state peasants and soldiers in roughly equal proportions in model communities with hospitals, schools, and orderly village planning in the western and southern borderlands. The peasants were exempted from taxation, but many had to serve in the military. All were subjected solely to military justice. Obligatory uniforms, military discipline, and bureaucratic interference alienated most peasant colonists, some of whom rebelled. The project was gradually abandoned, but it testified to the preference for control and the discomfort with even local self-government exhibited by the Russian ruler reputed among the most reformist and liberal.

Alexander was not opposed to piecemeal and concrete improvements, though neither he nor his senior officials felt passionate about implementing them. The case of prison reform is an interesting example. The English prison reformer, Walter Venning, requested official permission in 1817 to inspect Russian prisons.[12] Walter and his brother John found widespread corruption, overcrowding, the mixing together of men and women convicts and those awaiting trial, horrific filth, and an extraordinary profusion of vermin. Walter's report, which contained harrowing descriptions of prison conditions, was given to Alexander, who encouraged him to continue his efforts. A philanthropic prison supervisory organization was established with Alexander's blessing in October 1819. The St. Petersburg Society and others soon created in the provinces sometimes managed to separate prisoners by sex and to introduce vocational labor. But Alexander gradually lost interest, and the relevant senior officials were less than enthusiastic. There were still a few (often temporary) victories. In January 1924, John Venning obtained an order that exiles should not be sent to Siberia without an official medical certification of their fitness to travel. But problems of corruption, mistreatment, overcrowding, and the mixing of diverse categories of prisoner remained.

As in the eighteenth century, far more criminals suffered exile than imprisonment. Prisons were costly and lacked the capacity to house most convicts. Russian officials also still viewed exile as a means to settle and develop sparsely populated regions. In 1819, Speransky was made governor general of Siberia.[13] (He had been brought back into favor in 1816.) When he returned to St. Petersburg in 1821, he was put in charge of drafting reforms for Siberian governance. Among them was a detailed regulation on Siberian exile. Focusing on hard labor and exile to settlement, he established a system of documentation to keep track of exiles and rules on the transport and supervision of convicts.

The Russian bureaucracy, especially since the creation of ministries at the start of the century, had been collecting data somewhat systematically. Thus, only beginning in Alexander's reign does it become possible to present relatively detailed statistics on various aspects of criminal justice. In 1823, there were some 49,600 male exiles in Siberia or 5.69 percent of the total male population. Over the following thirty-seven years, an average of 7,719 exiles (8,335 if one adds the family members who voluntarily accompanied them) were sent to Siberia each year. In the years 1823–1845, Russian government officials counted 202,348 exiles sent to Siberia alone, along with 22,764 accompanying family members.[14] By contrast, in 1820, Russian jails and prisons housed a total of 51,198 prisoners, each for an average of about thirty-five days; therefore, roughly 5,000 people were incarcerated in hundreds of jails and prisons throughout the country at any given time.[15]

An unusual feature of the Russian penal exile system was the fact that a significant, but undetermined, proportion of all the exiles to Siberia were sent by landlords, peasant communes, or urban communities, since each of them had the power (beginning in 1760 as noted in Chapter 1) to recommend to government officials the exile, by administrative procedure, of seriously misbehaving members in their jurisdictions. In all such cases, as a series of government decrees made clear, only healthy and able-bodied people were to be exiled in this manner, because from the government's point of view, the primary reason for permitting such a punishment was to help populate far-flung regions of the empire and to develop agriculture in them. Such persons administratively exiled by their communities could return after five years with their communes' permission, though in practice most communes refused to take the former exiles back.[16] Usually, this meant a return trip to Siberia.

In the last years of his reign, Alexander became suspicious of foreigners and revolutionary activists, which he tended to conflate into a set of secret conspiracies. The thousands of young Russian officers who took part in their country's defeat of France witnessed firsthand the achievements of Western European societies. They expected their heroism to result in an improvement of their status, the securing of more political rights, and the achievement of political and economic reforms. Although Alexander proclaimed to believe in the rule of law and abhorred the institution of serfdom, his failure to carry forward his promises of constitutional change deeply alienated prominent elements of elite society. Many joined Masonic lodges and other secret societies. Political rebellions in Spain, Italy, and Greece, in 1820–1821, suggested that dramatic political change might come to Russia as well. Alexander was forewarned about the activities of the underground associations. Thus, he directed senior officials to increase surveillance over the guard regiments. In August 1822, all secret organizations, especially Masonic lodges, were prohibited.

Russia of Nicholas I

Alexander died in 1825. His brother Constantine was the next in line. He had declined the throne for personal reasons, yet this decision had been kept secret, sowing confusion. The next brother, Nicholas, demanded that the army swear allegiance to himself. Leading officers, who had been plotting for the past few years, rebelled but without a detailed plan. Most of the army remained loyal and crushed the uprising.

Nicholas personally interrogated many of the rebels and took seriously their criticism of major defects in Russian governance—such as widespread corruption, arbitrary power wielding, a cumbersome judicial system, and insufficiently developed respect for the law. Following the investigation of 579 people, a specially instituted higher criminal court judged the Decembrists. In all, it found 289 men guilty of complicity in the uprising. Five of them were sentenced to death by hanging and 116 to Siberian exile.[17] Much of high society, many of whose members were directly related to the rebels, viewed every aspect of their punishment as an outrage, though in comparison with Western European practice at the time, the Decembrists suffered relatively lenient treatment.

The disloyalty of so many scions of aristocratic families, which enjoyed great privileges in exchange for faithful service to the Romanov dynasty, undermined Nicholas's faith in Russia's traditional servitors. Throughout his thirty-year reign, he preferred therefore to rely on loyal adjutants, ad hoc committees, and specialized offices separate from the regular bureaucracy. As noted above, this was a common tendency of Russia's rulers, but it reached an apogee during this reign.

The most important special office was the Third Section of His Imperial Majesty's Own Chancellery, created on July 3, 1826, as a political police. It was a modest institution, starting out with sixteen officials. A year later, on April 28, 1827, a Continental-style gendarmerie, made up of four thousand paramilitary personnel, was instituted as its "eyes and ears."[18] The Third Section oversaw and implemented administrative exile, enforced censorship, monitored people on police probation, sounded the public mood, and investigated religious sects, among other tasks. Its primary function was the preservation of state security. The gendarmes acted largely as local civil police; they took part in pretrial investigations in cases of the murder of landlords by their serfs and kept tabs on "various nonpolitical undesirables, such as gamblers, swindlers, and userers."[19]

State control of Russia's peasants was extensive. Of course, serfs were under the jurisdiction of their masters. But even state peasants' travel of more than 30 *versty* (roughly 32 km) from home required purchase of a domestic passport (or if the departure was for less than six months, they could obtain a less-expensive *bilet*, thanks to a law of 1827). Such persons caught without the required documentation were legally supposed to be returned to their legal domicile or, if they refused to divulge it, branded on their lower right arm and sent to the army or saddled with some labor or settlement obligation. Frequent peasant unrest and rebellions, such as the military colony revolt of 1831 and the so-called Potato Uprisings of 1834 and 1841–1843, were suppressed with great violence by military forces.[20]

Military justice was also used very widely. Since the time of Peter the Great, a wide range of civilians could be brought before military courts. They had fewer safeguards, more streamlined procedure, fewer opportunities for review, and even stronger administrative control than the regular civilian courts. The punishments they imposed were also potentially harsher, specifically running the gauntlet and the death penalty, neither of which was available to civilian judges. In fact, it seems that running the gauntlet—often past 1,000 or more men armed with thick rods—was more likely to result in death than flogging with the knout.

During the reign of Nicholas I, the application of military justice to civilians expanded dramatically, often with the personal involvement of the emperor himself. He personally decided roughly two such cases each week during a twenty-five-year period.[21] In addition, he reviewed all sentences resulting in loss of officer rank or noble status and all cases handled by military courts concerning apostasy from Russian Orthodoxy, insults to the monarch, and diverse other offenses. Many classes of people could be or routinely were tried in military courts, including administrative personnel in the various military branches and institutions, employees of factories and other emporia producing for the military, smugglers who resisted arrest, convicts transferred to military control for building fortresses and other installations, persons accused of theft of military property and valuable state-owned natural resources, mining personnel in the Urals region, counterfeiters, ringleaders of popular rebellions crushed by military forces, peasants who poached wood from state forests, violators of quarantine regulation, and arsonists starting fires during peasant uprisings, among many others.[22] Military courts were furthermore deployed to help crush the massive Polish uprising of 1830–1831, and they operated even more extensively against civilians in the borderlands. Finally, Nicholas selectively decreed the trial by military court of persons whose crimes he considered especially grievous. As an autocratic ruler, there were no limits on his ability to transfer civilians to military justice. It was to some extent his personal purview in a way that the civilian courts were not. Finally, the resort to military justice probably reflected the emperor's impatience with ordinary judicial procedure and his faith in military personnel and ethos.

A momentous achievement of the reign of Nicholas was the publication in 48 large volumes in 1830 of the Complete Collection of Laws of the Russian Empire, encompassing over 30,000 legal enactments issued from 1649 to 1825. A systematic Digest of Laws, which organized legislation still in force, came out two years later in fifteen volumes. (It became operational in 1835.) Volume 15 comprehended all the laws relating to criminal justice. It established a precise ladder of ten forms of punishment of decreasing severity. Starting with capital punishment, the lawmakers followed up with political execution, deprivation of rights, corporal punishment, forced labor, exile, forced conscription, imprisonment, fines, and ecclesiastical punishment. Capital punishment was prescribed for state crimes, military crimes (violations of military discipline, military service obligations, and military statutes), and offenses against the rules of quarantine (including during epidemics)—but not crimes like murder and armed robbery, which were capital offenses in Western countries. The Digest also defined incarceration, rather than exile, as the primary means of punishment.

Unfortunately, Russia still lacked sufficient prison space to incarcerate most lawbreakers, even if one added up all the penal battalions, lockup centers (which had been established in 1827 to provide a source of labor for improvements in provincial administrative towns), houses of correction, fortresses (which housed convicts who did nothing dishonorable), forced labor prisons, and prisons. Most people sentenced to incarceration were held in prisons, but far more had to be built if the Russian government was going to live up to its stated intention.

Why, then, did the legal experts who drafted the Digest propose to shift the center of gravity of the Russian penal system from exile to prisons, if insufficient prison space was available? Throughout the nineteenth century, Russian officials were constantly watching European policymaking and statecraft to get ideas for reform, to see how their own policies compared, and to avoid "falling behind." The European countries and the United States since the late eighteenth century had been building prisons and devoting enormous efforts to improving them. Even the United Kingdom, which "transported" some 164,000 convicts to its Australian colonies in the years 1788–1868, actively built and renovated penitentiaries.[23] Most European countries did not exile convicts, and therefore the entire focus of their penal policies was on prisons. It seems that Russian officials wanted to fit within that framework of policy, even if for the time being they lacked the resources to do so. As during the reign of Alexander, most prisoners were detained in common cells often without distinction as to the severity of their crimes, however, so Russia remained behind European best incarceration practices.

As before, many more convicts were sent into exile than incarcerated. In 1835, the total exile population was 97,121. Of these, government statisticians counted 9,667 exiles in penal servitude, most of whom were not engaged in labor.[24] A high proportion of exiles of all kinds managed to escape throughout the nineteenth century. The proportion of fugitives was typically at least one-third. Most exiles were sent to Siberia, though a minority was remanded to the Caucasus region and distant localities of European Russia, typically in the far north. Throughout the nineteenth century, exile served as a means of colonization, a relatively inexpensive method of punishment, and one that was often more humane than imprisonment. Roughly half of all exiles were peasants excluded from their rural communities because of perceived misbehavior. For most exiles, the harshest aspect of the punishment was the voyage to the place of exile, since before the railroad network was built, one had to travel mostly by foot.

Although murder was not a capital offense in Russia, whereas it was in most European countries, the murder rate in Russia during these years was in line with those Western countries. In 1839, for example, the murder rate was 4.98 murders per hundred thousand persons throughout the empire, but much higher in Siberia, ranging from 11.74 in Irkutsk province to 47.58 in Eniseisk province, apparently because of the high concentration of convicts and especially escaped convicts in these regions.[25] In comparison, in the years 1825–1849, the rate in Scandinavia hovered around 1.4 but in Italy stood at 15, thus a figure worse than for Irkutsk province.[26] (Presumably, a region-by-region breakdown for Italy or any country would yield a similar statistical disparity.)

Volume 15 of the Digest spelled out refined legal concepts. First and foremost, it defined a crime as an illegal action, not some vague offense against the social or political order. From this notion derived gradations of culpability. Previously, any connection with a crime was interpreted as equally culpable. Henceforth, the law distinguished between instigators, accomplices, secondary participants, and primary culprits. Each distinct offender now faced separate and specified punishments. The Digest also distinguished between crimes and infractions. Many more specific crimes were identified and classified. Importantly, the concept of collective culpability was abandoned (although it had been in decline for a couple of decades), and individual responsibility for participation in collective crimes was formally expounded. In general, culpability had to be established in order for any act to be considered a crime. (There were some glaring exceptions in the peasant world, where members of rural communes bore collective responsibility for the collection and payment of taxes.)

In order to train more experts in the law, in 1835 Nicholas decreed the foundation of the Imperial School of Jurisprudence. In December of that year, following intensive work overseen by Speransky, it opened under the auspices of the Ministry of Justice.[27] Combining a classical education for younger pupils and intensive legal training for the older ones, the school started out with 150 students in all seven grade levels. It was a highly elite institution, with the main purpose of preparing officials for service in the Senate and Ministry of Justice.

Speransky died in 1839, but the codification and revision of penal Russian law continued. Among the most important later accomplishments in this work was the 1845 Penal Code. This legislation defined all punishments as either criminal or correctional. The criminal punishments were death, hard labor, exile to Siberia, and exile to the Caucasus. Each was accompanied by the forfeiture of estate, family, and property rights, as well as loss of rank, honor, one's good name, all awards and medals for distinguished service, and all personal certificates and diplomas. This meant the loss of political and civil status. Nonprivileged convicts also suffered flogging. Correctional punishments divided into exile to Siberia or to distant provinces other than Siberia; detention in a workhouse (*rabochii dom*), a fortress, or a forced-labor jail (*smiritel'nyi dom*); imprisonment; short-term detention (*arest*); official reprimands; and fines—along with, in most cases, some loss of rights for the privileged and corporal punishment for the nonprivileged. Each punishment was further subdivided by severity of sentence; thus, exile to Siberia could be imposed on five different levels, depending on the place of exile and length of term.

The 1845 code defined children under age 10 as not responsible for their actions and those aged 10–14 as conditionally responsible (though underage repeat offenders were to be held to the same level of accountability as adults). Mitigating circumstances conferring nonaccountability could result from various forms of mental illness, physical impairments, and senility. Such provisions resulted in expert testimony gradually replacing inquiries into the assessments of a suspect's neighbors in cases lacking more compelling forms of proof. The modern criminal law principle that intent to commit crime is not in and of itself a punishable offense was also recognized in Russian criminal law beginning in the 1845 code. This principle was sometimes violated in practice in regard to regular crime, but state crime was another matter (see below). The 1845 code affirmed in principle freedom of religion for the first time in Russian history. At the same time, however, conversion to any faith other than Russian Orthodoxy and proselytizing on behalf of any other faith remained serious crimes.

The code lessened the punishments for suicide and attempted suicide. From the time of Peter the Great, suicide and attempted suicide (without mitigating circumstances) were viewed as forms of murder and attempted murder. Beginning with the 1845 Penal Code, these definitions fell away. The act was still defined as shameful, but attempted suicide was no longer punished. The code also foresaw circumstances in which suicide could be honorable, for example, if it were deemed necessary to protect state secrets or for a woman to preserve her chastity. Such conceptual modalities of taking one's life did not suggest ascribing individual agency to persons, but rather the upholding of submission to the state, on the one hand, and to one's husband, on the other. The code also added penalties for persons encouraging or driving another person to suicide, defining such persons as accessories to murder. In other words, according to Susan K. Morrissey, "Liberalism was thus counteracted by the expansion of administrative authority."[28]

The Penal Code abolished the knout as a criminal punishment, replacing it with flogging with a whip (*pleti*) and birch rods (*rozgi*). The whip differed from the knout in that it was tipped with pleated leather rather than metal talons. For the first time in Russian jurisprudence, the maximum number of lashes to be endured as a corporal punishment was set at 100. Exceptions also began to be made for the sick and the elderly. (Beginning in 1851, a physician had to monitor the implementation of corporal punishment.) Like the Digest, the code prescribed sentences of death solely for violent attacks on the sovereign, for conspiring against the state order, for treason, or for breach of quarantine. Again, unlike most of Western Europe, such grave crimes as murder, rape, armed robbery, and arson were not capital offenses. Over the next 30 years, Russian courts sentenced 50 people to death, and of these 20 were executed. Most of the sentences were handed down by military and not civilian courts. Those executed had nearly all organized or sought to organize armed insurrections. During the same years, in comparison, 620 criminals in France, 271 in Prussia, 360 in England and Wales, and 1,325 in the United States were executed by court sentence.[29]

The 1845 Penal Code carefully defined the rules under which convicts were to serve sentences of hard labor. Because of a shortage of forced-labor prisons and workhouses, many prisoners sentenced to terms of confinement in such facilities under the 1845 code were incarcerated mainly in regular prisons and in lockup centers. Hard-labor convicts who displayed good behavior for specified numbers of years were graduated to correctional punishment status and henceforth enjoyed such privileges as eligibility for living outside of prison, marrying, and extra holidays. Between 1846 and 1860, official statistics indicate that 974 people were sentenced to hard labor each year.[30] The work of many of those employed in hard-labor enterprises profited government agencies and contractors.

The right to administratively exile ill-behaved persons was confirmed and expanded by the Penal Code. Not only serf masters and peasant communes wielded this power but also owners of private mining works, proprietors of "possessional factories," and some government agencies.[31] Peasant communes, in fact, had to contend with more red tape than all these other authorities. Even so, there were few impediments to imposing exile in this manner for communities or proprietors with a will to disencumber themselves of unwanted members or employees.

In just under 100 articles contained in two chapters—"On State Crimes" and "On Crimes and Offenses against the Administrative Order"—the 1845 code also carefully and elaborately defined political crimes against the monarch and the state. Here merely intending to harm the emperor, the state, the administration, or the political order was held to be the gravest crime and as such entailed the loss of all rights and the death penalty. Such treatment applied even when the culprit, in the words of Article 264, intended to take part in such an act

> by means of a proposal to another person to take part, or by means of organizing to that end a conspiracy or an organization, or by means of joining such an organization or conspiracy, or by means of verbally or in writing expressing one's idea and proposal, or by any other means engaging in preparations of any kind for such an act.[32]

Moreover, a person who possessed information about such "intentions or criminal actions against the holy person of the sovereign emperor, or against the authority of his sovereign power" but failed to report it to the authorities also faced the death penalty. Because of the extraordinary latitude such formulations conferred on the Russian state for mercilessly rooting out political opposition, Richard Pipes called the Penal Code of 1845 "a milestone in the historical evolution of the police state" and asserted that these particular chapters were "to totalitarianism what the Magna Carta is to liberty."[33] Ironically, in regard to the treatment of ordinary crime, Russian penal law was fairly mild, as foreign commentators often remarked. In Europe and the United States, a murder conviction typically resulted in capital punishment, but not in Russia. This mildness, however, can be viewed as evidence that the Russian government did not consider the life of ordinary people as valuable as the reputation, much less the life, of the ruler, his family, and the church. At the same time, the Russian jurists who had compiled the code had undoubtedly carefully studied European criminal law, conferred with their European colleagues about it, and strived to bring Russian law into general conformity. Thus, in some aspects the code was entirely in line with European practice, such as in regard to suicide. Yet the underlying political culture of Russia made it impossible for the law to bridge the gap completely.

None of these reform efforts altered criminal procedure. The most important stage in any case was still the police investigation, which was entirely under the control of administrative officials and in particular provincial governors and urban police chiefs. None of these personnel boasted specialized legal training. All of them were generalists overburdened with manifold administrative duties. Rarely did a police investigator take into account questions of motivation and criminal psychology. The system of formal proofs remained in place. A confession, on the one hand, and eyewitness testimony, on the other hand, were the most compelling forms of evidence, procedurally speaking. If they were available, and if they basically fit the circumstances of the case, a judge's hands were tied: he had to convict. The written record prepared by police investigators, which required rendering colloquial speech into intelligible prose, was delivered to the court that would consider the case. A clerk prepared a summary (*vypiska*) of the voluminous documentation. This summary would then circulate from office to office and from court to court. If the investigators conceived a suspicion that fell on a particular suspect on the basis of a cursory analysis of material evidence at a crime scene, then that supposition remained in the file and dogged that suspect throughout the proceedings, even in the courts of appeal. The accused was denied defense counsel, since an attorney arguing on behalf of his client in the courtroom implied that the prosecution might be wrong, whereas the inquisitorial procedure presupposed that the administration knew what it was doing and conducted the investigation and prosecution honestly and correctly. It was possible to enjoy the services of a delegate (*deputat*), whose role was to defend the accused against improper procedures. But such defenders could only be provided for a defendant by elites (such as serf masters or government officials) or social estates (of nobles, state peasants, merchants, and the like) interested in defending one of their own. Most judges preferred to convict rather than to acquit, because all acquittals had to be sent to higher courts for review. It was as if a conviction was considered by the system to be the normal result of any criminal trial.

The system overall was highly inefficient and cumbersome. Inadequate training of police investigators resulted in frequent requests by court officials for clarifications, which slowed down the progress of many cases. So did the requirement to commence judicial proceedings in courts of lower instance (94 percent of all criminal cases), because a significant proportion (39 percent) then moved on to the appellate level for review. There were also many different courts of first instance, especially in urban areas. Backlogs built up between the 1830s and the 1850s from 9 to 22 percent of cases. Even when Emperor Nicholas I intervened personally—an average of 172 times each year throughout the 1830s—he managed to stimulate the movement of cases through the judicial system within the calendar year in which they were introduced only 61 percent of the time.[34]

For over three decades after the Decembrist Uprising, Russia witnessed few instances of serious political subversion, aside from frequent peasant rebellions and the dramatic but failed Polish Insurrection of 1830–1831. The harsh reprisals against the Polish insurgents, including thousands sent to Siberia and exile, surely deterred other potential political dissidents from open activism. Instead, critically and imaginatively minded intellectuals turned inward, exploring German idealistic philosophy and French "utopian socialist" thought, or contributed to the flowering of prose and poetry of what was later dubbed Russia's Golden Age. Some "state crimes," such as distributing subversive poems, were prosecuted, though rather leniently. Alexander Herzen, for example, spent the years 1835–1839 and 1841–1842 in administrative exile (employed as a civil servant in a series of provincial capitals, presumably because of a lack of coordination among the various police and administrative authorities) for what in the major European countries would have been considered harmless political remarks or writings. This general tendency toward punitive and arbitrary treatment of political dissidents combined with inefficient follow-through remained a feature of Russian political repression right down to 1917. It was often sufficiently unpleasant to radicalize discontented intellectuals but rarely so draconian, even despite periodic crackdowns, as to deter continued political engagement.

The February 1848 Revolution in Paris and subsequent revolutions across Europe triggered a high point of political repression in Russia. Nicholas created a committee to tighten censorship and ordered the Third Section to intensify surveillance over the population and to seal off the country against foreign influences. The increased vigilance led, a year later, to the arrest of forty intellectuals gathered around the socialist Mikhail Petrashevsky, a junior official in the Ministry of Foreign Affairs. Some of them advocated conspiracy and revolution but none had engaged in revolutionary violence. One of the Petrashevtsy was Fedor Dostoevsky. A secret investigating commission was instituted to examine the case. A special mixed military court condemned fifteen to death on the basis of the military field regulations of 1812. They were reprieved by Nicholas, as they faced the firing squad— and exiled to Siberia. Dostoevsky himself was then sent on to four years of hard labor followed by five years of exile in Siberia. Political and intellectual oppression remained heavy until the end of Nicholas's reign. In 1852, for example, the novelist Ivan Turgenev spent a month in jail followed by several months in house arrest on his country estate for having published a brief but praiseful obituary of Gogol in Moscow that had been rejected by the censors in St. Petersburg (Gogol had fallen into official disfavor).

In the context of the government's close regulation of and efforts to control intellectuals in this era, it is worth mentioning its hands-off approach toward the legal profession. Trained jurists and those with practical legal knowledge were not allowed to form professional organizations in Russia. (Such associations had long existed in Poland and the Baltic provinces.) The obvious reason was the hostile attitude of the ruling elite toward private associations with the potential for political influence in general and toward the legal profession in particular. Yet the unregulated nature of that profession in Russia may have been a partial blessing in disguise. Politically organized legal experts could have contributed toward limiting autocratic power. More of them would undoubtedly have acquired standardized legal training. But professionalization in this manner might well have invited increased government meddling. Instead, a wide variety of legal advocates were able to ply their trade, typically based on practical experience, often very successfully, in the sphere of civil law.[35]

Russians could not hire legal advocates to defend them in criminal cases, though of course they could engage their services concerning how to behave during questioning, what evidence to present or not to present, and the like. Overall, the system could and did function effectively and fairly, at least some of the time, and it seems to have been slowly growing more effective. Police investigators could be diligent and imaginative, questioning many witnesses, gathering expert opinion, compiling and analyzing physical evidence, and employing sophisticated reasoning skills. The panels of judges at the first judicial level could carefully and imaginatively interpret the evidence presented to them and could request clarifications. Individual judges on the panel could write dissenting opinions. Procurators and judges could send any case to the next level in the judicial hierarchy, typically the Chamber of Criminal Justice, which routinely reviewed all important criminal cases. Here, the university-trained judges could request additional information from all witnesses and parties to a given case. Judges could overrule a previous decision or let it stand. Again, dissenting opinions could be written. After the provincial governor signed off on the decision, it would be sent on to the Senate, which would review the case yet again and impose its final judgment.[36] The process was formal, often rigid, closely supervised by the executive branch, and inquisitorial: defendants had no right to defense counsel during their trial. There was no lay participation of jurors and no appeals at the behest of those convicted, but the system worked, at least sometimes, intelligently and fairly.

In 1853, war broke out with the Ottoman Empire. Fearing an overly powerful Russia, France and Britain joined forces with the Turks. Russia's defeat in the war was a crushing and humiliating blow to a country that had seemed the greatest continental European power since the Napoleonic Wars. After all, the Revolutions of 1848 had broken out in every major European country except Russia and Great Britain. Toward the end of the war, in 1855, Nicholas died and his son Alexander came to the throne. Russian public opinion judged the regime harshly. Its repressive nature had been taken as the price to be paid for maintaining a strong geopolitical position. But if the autocratic government could not even win a war fought largely on its own territory, then perhaps the lack of political and civil rights was also unnecessary. In any event, Alexander II found himself under great pressure to yield dramatic concessions to society and ultimately to radically transform the criminal justice system.

3

From Great Reforms to Revolution

Following defeat in the Crimean War, intellectuals of many political perspectives educated people generally, and even government officials in Russia clambered above all for an end to serfdom. How could Russia continue evolving into a modern country with tens of millions of people born into and living out their lives in servitude? Could Russia stand up to developed European countries with citizen armies? Could it compete economically with free societies?

Alexander II and the Great Reforms

The emancipation, proclaimed in February 1861, was not all the serfs had hoped for. They were granted land, but had to pay for it for forty-nine years. The more than one million domestic serfs who had worked in their masters' households received no land allotment at all. The government kept the liberated peasants bound to their communes, as a means of social and fiscal control. The passport system continued to function as before.

Judicially, the peasants remained subject to customary law and, except for certain serious offenses, were not tried within the regular courts. Heads of household and village elders now directly exercised the power (no longer in consultation with landlords' representatives) to recommend banishment of the recalcitrant, to refuse to readmit any member who had served time in jail or exile or had merely been tried for a serious crime, and to grant—or deny—the issuance of passports.[1] Yet increased outmigration of younger peasants in search of work slowly weakened the patriarchal system, while strengthening the communal principle.

Peasants accused of crimes could be tried either in the traditional village courts or in the township (*volost'*) courts, which had been established in 1839 for state peasants but now were to be created throughout the country.

These courts were adversarial but without lawyers. Plaintiff and defendant both had to attend in person but could send a relative in case of illness. Township courts could impose sentences of up to thirty days' detention, fines of three rubles, or twenty blows with a birch switch.[2] At first, most peasants preferred the traditional courts, in which village elders and other elected representatives adjudicated, as quicker and fairer than the official township courts. The procedures were age-old and simple, according to customary law.[3]

As discussed in the Introduction, customary law regarded crimes chiefly as personal offenses, as violations of the moral and not the legal order. Crimes, in this conception, could not be victimless. Real harm was an essential attribute of crime. The peasant mind could not interpret the state or wealthy landlords as harmed by wood-poaching or kindred forms of petty theft. Likewise, a stolen object returned to its rightful owner blotted out both guilt and criminal damage. Committing an offense against an outsider or in a state of inebriation or for what could be seen as valid reasons (for example, taking food when hungry or committing homicide while trying to exorcise a demon) mitigated culpability. Every offense was considered in isolation, as an individual act and not falling under a general rubric or law. Customary law, therefore, was not law at all but rather mores, norms, morality, or what scholars call "the moral economy." Both guilt and punishment could be collective, as could the meting out of justice and penalties. The primary goal was to restore moral equilibrium and harmony.

Such subjective and intuitive features of customary law did not prevent judicial procedure from being systematic and extensive. All the houses of a village might be searched for stolen property. Eyewitnesses would be questioned. Yet the process remained informal. The plaintiff often determined the penalty, which might involve a blow to the face. Once the punishment had been administered, harmony was usually restored, and a drinking bout might occur. Appeals were often made to supernatural powers for help in solving puzzling cases, though such methods gradually died out, with more attention paid to circumstantial evidence. By the end of the century, many peasants preferred the township courts.

Emancipation coincided with and probably contributed to a decline of the harshest form of punishment outside of the death penalty: hard-labor exile. This form of punishment was associated with labor exploitation, and consequently hard-labor exiles had a status akin to that of serfs. With the abolition of serfdom, the exploitation of convict labor in mines, distilleries, and factories gradually diminished, as did the number of sentences to hard-labor exile.[4] The number of hard-labor convicts fell from 26,162 in 1852[5] to 8,068 in 1884.[6] The vast majority were of the lower social estates, though some 4,000 inmates exiled in the 1860s were participants in the Polish rebellion of 1863. Bouts of unrest in Siberian hard-labor camps in the later 1860s precipitated a government investigation in 1868. Its final report pointed to gross malfeasance, including filthy living conditions, careless oversight, and widespread escapes. Consequently, Alexander II approved a plan to establish a system of hard-labor exile on the Island of Sakhalin. Although officials found geographic conditions highly inhospitable, it was hoped the penal colonies would become self-sufficient from agriculture. (Conditions turned out worse than in Eastern Siberia, and the entire experiment was abandoned during the Russo-Japanese War of 1904–1905.)[7]

At the other end of the social hierarchy, prisoners of conscience (for both "political" and "religious" crimes) typically enjoyed better treatment. The Third Section was beginning to inspire dread, but it still was not an efficient security police institution. It had little experience in combating political crime, which remained a rare phenomenon before the 1860s. Justice Minister D. M. Zamiatnin, for example, began only in 1861 to keep a separate list of state crimes. His more careful record-keeping stemmed in large part because of radical political tracts that appeared, beginning that summer, with names like *Great Russia*, *To the Young Generation*, and *Young Russia*. The latter was written by a university student, Peter Zaichnevsky, while in prison for revolutionary activity. Similarly Nicholas Chernyshevsky composed and arranged to publish *What Is to Be Done* (1863) while in prison. It exerted a greater influence on the next generations of revolutionaries than any other single book in the second half of the nineteenth century. Such unevenness of repression was typical of the Russian who government. Here, it incarcerated a man who advocated organizing for a future revolution, yet permitted him a forum from which to broadcast his call to revolt.

The reforms continued as well. Censorship was relaxed somewhat in 1862. A statute of June 1863 expanded university autonomy. April 1863 legislation drastically curtailed the use of corporal punishment. All methods except birching were abolished. Women were completely exempted. Township courts could impose sentences of flogging with birch rods against peasants, but they did so less and less in the years that followed. Hard-labor exiles also faced birching as a punishment, but in practice, many avoided it by paying bribes. There was an unintended consequence in the abolition of the harsher forms of corporal punishment: it caused Russia's prisons to grow more crowded and therefore less humane.

Beginning in 1863, a series of commissions met to study Russia's prisons and to recommend how to reform them.[8] As usual, a few of the commissioners made obligatory pilgrimages to Western Europe and inevitably their colleagues voted to adopt Western European and American models. During Imperial Russia's final half-century, enthusiastic government reformers advocated the centralization of Russia's prison system, the building of new model prisons with isolation wings and universal labor duties, the abolition of penal exile, and the adoption of regimes of parole and probation for convicted criminals. The major stumbling block to implementing many of these reforms was the inelasticity of Russia's state budget. Obliging all prisoners to work, for example, was intended first to reform them (in the Victorian era, idleness was conceived as the root of all evil) and second to help pay for running the prisons. Yet Russia's Finance Ministry doled out miserly start-up capital necessary for putting prisoners to work. Also problematic was the slowness with which Russian officialdom proceeded with the reforms and the doubts Western penologists were having about their own systems of punishment by the time the Russians got around to trying to implement them.

A second Polish rebellion broke out in January 1863, as noted above, and lasted a year but ultimately was crushed by the Russian military, and thousands of Polish rebels were sentenced to hard-labor exile. Such a challenge to Russian Imperial rule might have halted the urge to reform, but it did not. By a decree of February 1864, institutions of local self-government, called zemstvos, were established in twenty-seven provinces (and soon thereafter in seven more) at both the district and provincial levels. Their role was to organize services for the rural population. (In 1870, town councils, or dumas, were instituted to perform the same task in urban centers.)

A far more important—and successful—reform transformed the judicial system. Drawing on a careful study of European legal institutions, a committee of jurists drafted legislation adopted in November 1864.[9] The legislation comprised four statutes, setting out rules for a new configuration of judicial institutions, for criminal procedure, for civil procedure, and for punishments to be imposed by justices of the peace for lesser crimes.

Alexander II thus created an independent judiciary, separating one of the main branches of government from his control. Judges were appointed for life by the Ministry of Justice. A simplified hierarchy of courts was established, rising from dozens of circuit courts (okruzhnye sudy), each of which administered justice in several districts (uezdy) but typically not in an entire province and tried criminal cases by jury; to the fourteen regional Chambers of Justice (sudebnye palaty), which served as courts of first instance for cases of official malfeasance and crimes against the state, as well as courts of appeal for most other crimes; and finally, the highest appeals court, the Senate (see Figure 3.1). The peasantry also had access to an entirely new judicial institution, justices of the peace. Intended to bridge the gap between customary law and statute law, they were elected by district-level zemstvos to try offenses, the punishment for which could not exceed a fine of 300 rubles or imprisonment for a year. The justices of the peace were supposed to apply newly formulated statute law, though many of them found themselves striving to apply customary law at the request of peasants. (The 1845 Code of Punishments, severally revised, remained in force for more serious crimes.)

One of the most significant elements of the judicial reform was the introduction of trial by jury. Many conservatives within officialdom had resisted the idea, arguing that Russian people were not sufficiently developed morally and intellectually to shoulder such responsibility.[10] Most reformers had argued in favor of the English and American principle of unanimity of

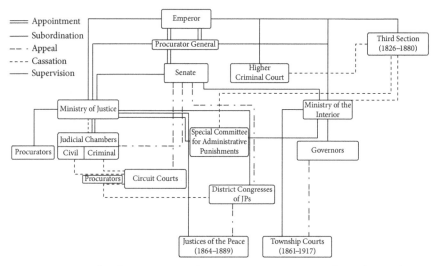

FIGURE 3.1 *Judicial organization from 1864 to 1880. An independent judiciary was created. The emperor appointed senators; the Ministry of Justice appointed all other judges (though not justices of the peace, who were elected), but neither could remove them. Trial by jury was instituted along with an adversarial system of procedure and an independent Bar.*

decision, but the statute adopted required only that a majority agree on a verdict, as was the practice in France. Since peasants made up at least 85 percent of the population, most jurors hailed from that social estate. Typical jurors were staunch upholders of private property, but indulgent toward white-collar crime. The right to a jury trial was gradually extended from the central Russian provinces in 1866 to large swaths of Western Siberia in 1909. Many provinces of the empire, including Poland, the Caucasus region, Central Asia, and most of Siberia and the Far East, never gained the right to jury trials. Although government officials in Russia often remained mistrustful of the public and typically felt themselves to be above the law, the institution of jury trials, albeit only in most provinces of European Russia, was an important advance on the path toward popular participation in governance.

Criminal procedure and the administration of justice were also overhauled.[11] Members of each estate were made equal before the law. Estate-based courts were abolished except for peasants at the township level. An office of public procurator was created and subordinated to the minister of justice. (It is preferable to continue to use the term "procurator," since his authority and influence remained greater than implied in the Western term "prosecutor.") The procurator oversaw the work of judicial investigators. The police no longer compiled the official record of criminal investigations for the courts. Yet the police were required to participate in judicial investigations, especially before the arrival of a judicial investigator, to whom they had to hand over all relevant materials. Not surprisingly, tensions between these officials often broke out. Judges and judicial investigators, though not justices of the peace, were required to be trained in the law. The courts and judicial investigators were made fully separate from the administration, which no longer had the right—in principle—to interfere with its operations, though in practice, officials often attempted to do so. (Government officials also remained completely outside the purview of the courts. One could seek redress against them only by appealing to their superiors.) Trials henceforth became adversarial and open to the public, although criminal trials still involved some elements of inquisitorial procedure, including a weakened presumption of guilt. Oral proceedings replaced the hierarchy of formal proofs of guilt. A trial could result only in conviction or acquittal and no longer in the status of "under suspicion." State crimes were handled in much the same manner as regular crimes, though without juries. The new system also ended the Third Section's role as a judicial arbiter.

Although the reformers aimed to replace Russia's inquisitorial judicial procedure with an adversarial approach, in practice important elements of the old system remained in place. The investigation of crimes was conducted under the supervision and indeed control of the executive branch. Procurators answered first and foremost to the Ministry of Justice. The written record of the investigation was still the central focus of most trials. The presiding judge was still concerned to achieve convictions and to find guilt. At the same time, judges often encouraged free-ranging debate within the courtroom among the main participants. The result was a sui generis mix of adversarialism and inquisitorialism.

A further innovation of the reform was the establishment of the Bar, which united attorneys, or advocates, in a single corporation. This organization insured a high level of professional standards. The Bar grew rapidly into a highly influential and self-consciously important institution, probably because a critical mass of legal experts was by then available and because the legal profession was the only venue in which independent actors could enjoy significant authority, sometimes even at the national level. Lawyers arguing a case in court enjoyed complete freedom of speech, a unique civil right in Russia at that time. Here again, this was a far from insignificant development in a polity where critical opinion could express itself for the most part only indirectly.

Judicial openness meant that journalists could report, and sometimes did in detail depending on the importance of the case, on trial proceedings.[12] In turn, the reading public could closely follow the arguments of the prosecution and defense, the testimony of witnesses, and other elements of the contest. The reformers' goal of using the reformed courts as a "school of citizenship" thus had a very concrete and successful outcome. The public discussed the major cases, and writers incorporated scenarios from crime and judicial reporting in their stories and novels—none more than Fyodor Dostoevsky. The trials themselves became events of great public interest, with ordinary members of the public eagerly seeking admission to these spectacles.

The most talented defense advocates gained empire-wide recognition and some made substantial fortunes. The most successful melded together logical argumentation, verbal eloquence, and theatrics. Russian intellectuals wrestled with the problem of advocates knowingly defending criminals of whose guilt they were certain. Some Bar associations forbade their members' participation in trials of especially disreputable persons, like prostitutes, unless they were certain of their innocence. Public perceptions of charlatanism and the view of lawyers as threatening to absolutist governance combined to undermine the prestige of the profession, which nevertheless steadily grew influential and materially successful.

In addition to the professions of defense advocate and public procurator, the new adversarial judicial system fostered the emergence of a third indispensable actor: the forensic specialist or expert witness. Psychologists, graphologists, medical personnel, chemists, and many other experts played leading roles in the reformed judicial proceedings. They made it possible to zero in on the details of the circumstances of the crime and then to expand the focus to the personality and character of the criminal. All such professionals, because of their importance in determining guilt or innocence within the new system, gained substantially in status and contributed to the development of civil society in Russia.

Before the judicial reform, juvenile lawbreakers were treated like adult criminals, despite some provisions in the law for treating them differently. The legal experts who drafted the statutes held that the punishment of adolescent offenders should serve above all to reform them.[13] A law of 1897 went further, providing for the release of juvenile offenders to the custody of parents or guardians or for their confinement in special detention facilities. The law also granted defense counsel the right to participate in the preliminary investigation of cases involving minors.[14] (Adults did not gain this right until 1917, briefly, and then again in the post-Soviet era.) The trial of adolescents was to take place in closed session but with the participation of parents or guardians.

The Russian Empire was a traditional multinational polity comprised of over 100 ethnic and national groups. It had developed gradually over the centuries according to a model of difference rather than sameness, as was common for the traditional amalgamation of empires from conquered territories. As new peoples were added to the empire, each was granted a "separate deal," negotiated in each case as if there were no such thing as universal rules for members of the society.[15] The judicial reform in Poland involved imposing the Russian language for official business in the regular courts (though not the village courts) and abolishing the Napoleonic code. Jury trials were not introduced, but the Polish villages were integrated into the reformed judicial system, whereas the Russian villages were not. Jury

trials were established among the Tatars in Kazan. In the Baltic region, they were not, nor were justices of the peace instituted. The insufficiency of Russian speakers in Transcaucasia (in 1912, only 10 percent of males could speak Russian) made it difficult to establish the new courts successfully in that region. Jury trials were not even considered. It goes without saying that the nomadic peoples of Central Asia were completely untouched by the reformed judicial system.[16] Only in 1907 was that system imposed, in modified form, in all the distant non-Russian corners of the empire. It is unclear whether the reformed justice system helped integrate national minorities politically and culturally or tended to alienate them.

Many factors tempered the scope, functioning, and reach of the reform. Juries, in which peasants were preponderant, often adjudicated in ways the reformers did not approve, for example, extremely harshly in case of horse-theft and sacrilege, but leniently in cases of crimes against women. Ordinary people sometimes took the law into their own hands with vigilante justice (*samosud*), especially in cases of horse-theft, which government officials often failed to prosecute vigorously.[17] Administrative officials retained the power to exile criminal suspects to prevent the potential commission of crimes. Rural and urban communities also retained the power to arrange for the exile to Siberia of ill-behaved members. Officials could still not be indicted, without the consent of their superior, for criminal acts perpetrated in the course of duty.

Moreover, several independent courts remained outside the jurisdiction of the reformed judiciary, including ecclesiastical, military, and township courts. These latter courts still kept the peasantry isolated from the regular judicial system, unless their conflicts involved members of the elite or grave crimes. The divergence of elites from ordinary people, which intensified with Peter the Great's Europeanization program, now reached its apogee. Some of the most heinous crimes—such as murder and arson—were still handled by military courts but much less than before 1864.[18] The statutes on military courts permitted capital punishment for a wide range of crimes, including rape and robbery, but persons convicted of such crimes by military courts did not always receive the death penalty.

Despite these reservations, the judicial reform limited the power of the monarchy, curbed the arbitrary and discretionary authority of government officials, and strengthened the rule of law. Indeed, the reform set Russia firmly on the path toward constitutionalism.

An unintended consequence of the reforms was an increase in both the crime rate and general criminality. For example, 1,154 accused killers (not counting those whose victims were infants) were tried in 1880, but 1,302 in 1890, 1,640 in 1900, and 2,244 in 1904—almost a doubling in a quarter-century.[19] Why? It seems that more people filed crime reports, thanks to the growing realization among ordinary people that they could complain about mistreatment and that they had dignity and rights. The fact that appeals in criminal cases also surged seems to bear out the supposition. It seems that people were less afraid of going to court and more confident about the possible outcomes. Women understood that they no longer had to quietly endure beatings from their husbands. Workers grasped that they deserved fair treatment by their employers. At the same time, it seems likely that increased criminality stemmed largely from a weakening of traditional social control, especially among peasant migrants to cities. Criminality among young people expanded dramatically. Minors—anyone under twenty-one years of age—committed 21 percent of all crimes by 1913, up from 7 percent in 1834. Crime was most pervasive in urban areas—cities and towns accounted for 24.7 percent of all convicted persons but only 8.4 percent of the country's total population. The social segment at the end of the century most likely to commit crimes were industrial workers. In other words, peasants committed nineteen times fewer crimes than workers, as a proportion of population.[20]

A dramatic example of how well the new courts functioned, from the point of view of equality before the law, is the spectacular trial in 1874 of Mother Superior Mitrofaniia of the Vladichnii Convent in Serpukhov not far south of Moscow.[21] A baroness in secular life, a former lady-in-waiting at the Imperial court, a protégé of Empress Maria Aleksandrovna, and a dynamic organizer of charitable work, she was charged with forgery, fraud, extortion, embezzlement, and other means of stealing over a million rubles—money she apparently used to fund philanthropic endeavors. It was the first time in Russian history that such a high-ranking person was tried before the public and the first time a member of the clergy had been hauled before a secular criminal court. Crowds pressed to catch a glimpse of the illustrious defendant and to gain entry to the courtroom. The major newspapers, including the official government daily, printed transcripts of the proceedings, as they did for all major trials. Commentators had feared that influential persons might try to interfere, but they did not. The jury found Abbess Mitrofaniia guilty. She was to be stripped of her corporate rights and exiled to Eastern Siberia for three years, followed by eleven more in a closer province. At this point, well-placed individuals interceded, and she spent the rest of her life banished to a series of convents in the far south. Both senior officials and the Imperial family apparently wanted to demonstrate that no one was above the law and that the new courts were truly independent not only of the administration but also of the emperor himself. The fact that the abbess received some clemency, secretly and after the trial, shows that arbitrary power at the highest levels had not been fully given up.

Another sensational trial unfolded from February 8 to March 5, 1877. The trial involved forty-eight criminal defendants and hundreds of witnesses. The defendants were accused of dozens of instances of fraud, extortion, forgery, and other crimes committed during the previous decade. The government organized the trial around a loosely associated network of con artists whom journalists labelled the "Jacks of Hearts Club."[22] As in the case of Mitrofaniia, many alleged members of the "Jacks of Hearts" were part of high society. As their trial seemingly demonstrated, they too, although exploiting their privileged status to swindle often-naive victims, were not above the law. Like her, they were tried in the Moscow Circuit Court.

The procurator, Nikolai Muraviev, explicitly brought out the elite status of most defendants and argued that vestiges of the serf-owning mentality, including overweening greed and sloth, influenced their evil deeds. His basic argument was that the inequities of the old social system had corrupted the defendants. To the old evils, he claimed that modern society as it was evolving in Russia contributed other causal factors, such as extensive access to credit, excessive freedom, and mass entertainment "catering to the baser human instincts." The effect was a general criticism of Russian society, both its preemancipation domination by aristocrats and the rising domination by money and capitalism.

Sergei Antonov argues that the judicial proceeding was a show trial staged to discipline the emerging world of entrepreneurship and business by means of a completely fabricated congeries of cases with very little relationship to each other and certainly not the conspiracy they were presented as. The trial was also somewhat related to the almost simultaneous "Trial of the 50," occurring in St. Petersburg from February 21 to March 14 and involving political defendants. In both cases, a major goal seems to have been to push members of the elite into the bounds of acceptable behavior. Another similarity seems to have been the conflation of promoting political and ideological goals with the pursuit of truth and justice. In the Moscow trial, the procurator devoted much effort to denouncing past and present Russian society; in the St. Petersburg trial, the defense attorneys exerted similar efforts (see below). The net effect of both trials may have been to undermine faith in Russia's political institutions as much as to promote faith in its judiciary.

Arbitrary administrative power was wielded most pervasively in regard to political or state crime. In April 1866, Dmitrii Karakozov attempted to kill Alexander II with a point-blank pistol shot. The following month, special bureaus for security policing (*Okhrannoe otdelenie*) and regular criminal investigation (*Sysknoe otdelenie*) were instituted in St. Petersburg. The robust development of radical political activism drove the administration to emphasize fighting political crime. Over the next several decades, the lion's share of resources available for policing flowed to the security service. In July 1866, governors were empowered to close any public meeting, club, or cooperative association deemed a threat to state order or public security and morality. The following year, in March, all societies of political, nihilistic, or atheistic tendencies were outlawed, and membership in any secret society was defined as a criminal act.

One such secret society was People's Revenge, formed by Sergei Nechaev in 1869. Its manifesto, "Catechism of a Revolutionary," was apparently co-authored over the summer by Nechaev and the anarchist Michael Bakunin. It advocated absolute devotion and a willingness to sacrifice oneself to the revolutionary cause of overthrowing and annihilating the existing political order. In November, he and other members murdered one of their fellows as an alleged traitor to the organization (an event that inspired Dostoevsky's *Possessed*). The police arrested 152 Nechaev "conspirators."[23] The St. Petersburg Judicial Chamber applying the new judicial statutes for the first time to a political case, tried eighty-seven of them from July to September 1871. By transforming themselves into accusers of the government, however, the defendants won the sympathy of the jury, the judge, and the broader public. Most of the defendants avoided conviction but subsequently were administratively exiled. Here is a prime example of the politicization of justice in Russia. Alexander and his administration were clearly unwilling to respect the decision of the judicial system. Indeed, throughout the remaining decades of the Imperial era, administrative officials retained the power to impose extrajudicial punishment.

Administrative control over political dissidence was anchored in myriad legislation. On the eve of the trial, by a law of May 1871, gendarmes were made the primary investigators in state-crime cases.[24] These investigations were always conducted under the direction of procurators. The result was a definite compromise between the Third Section and the Justice Ministry. A second element of this compromise was a mechanism for bypassing the courts. Henceforth, the justice minister analyzed the results of each gendarme investigation and, in consultation with the director of the Third Section, either sent the case to a court investigator or, with the emperor's permission, dropped it. The law authorized the justice minister to propose to the emperor, again in consultation with the director of the Third Section, to punish state-crime suspects with exile, probation, and fines by administrative fiat. Until 1904, when the law was rescinded, nearly all state-crime cases were handled administratively. For example, from 1872 to 1877, the courts tried 140 state-crime cases and convicted only 100 people. During the same period, 5,129 such cases were handled administratively on the authority of the 1871 law.[25]

In summer 1874, thousands of young idealists, dressed as peasants and some even trained in rustic craft and skills, set out to the countryside to bring light to, and learn from, the peasantry. They fanned out across thirty-seven provinces, many hoping to ignite a rebellion. Radical Russian youth had "gone to the people." The government investigated 770 "Populists" (*narodniki*). Of these, 265 were detained for three years, in extremely harsh conditions, pending trial. During their confinement as many as eighty died, provoking public outrage. The remainder was finally tried, in February–March 1877 and October 1877–January 1878, respectively, in the famous "Trial of the 50" (as noted above) and "Trial of the 193."[26] The defendants used both trials to make political arguments and criticize the government. A small number received prison sentences, but many of those acquitted were subsequently exiled by administrative process.

The day after the "Trial of the 193" ended, a young noblewoman, Vera Zasulich, shot and wounded St. Petersburg city governor Fedor Trepov, because he had ordered the flogging of an imprisoned student, merely for failing to doff his cap. Her deed was an act of social vengeance, she claimed. The government assumed that the case was open and shut: Zasulich had openly confessed to the crime. Officials decided therefore to try the case as an ordinary instance of attempted murder. The prosecution, however, was weak. In Russian law, jurors had the authority to judge cases on moral grounds and not solely according to the evidence of guilt or innocence. Zasulich's brilliant lawyer spoke to the jurors' moral sense, arguing that the political system was unjust and that the assailant had acted as a crusader for justice. The jury was moved and exonerated the accused. The police had intended to arrest Zasulich after the trial and to punish her administratively, but she managed to escape abroad. Her acquittal provoked the adoption of a law depriving of the right to a jury trial persons accused of committing attacks on, or even resistance to, government officials. Over the following month, coincidentally, two separate assailants attempted to kill the German Kaiser. The antisocialist law, adopted in October by parliament, dramatically expanded police powers in Germany. Clearly, radical political activism was not unique to Russia at this time, nor was governmental recourse to extrajudicial punishments and emergency legislation. Both phenomena were more extreme in Russia, however, presumably because of arbitrary governance, an unwillingness of the authorities to recognize the dignity and rights of persons, and the weaker entrenchment of the respect for law of both rulers and ruled.

Following the assassination of the chief of gendarmes, Nikolai Mezentsev, in August 1878, the government decreed the systematic transfer of cases involving violent attacks on government officials to military courts. In September, the government issued an unpublished decree empowering gendarmes, or police officials in their absence, to verify the "political reliability" (*politicheskaia blagonadezhnost'*) of any person and to propose the administrative exile of the "unreliable" (such a sentence rested with the interior minister in consultation with the gendarme chief). The decree also provided for the arrest of anyone suspected of having committed a political crime or having participated in a political demonstration or disorder. No length of detention or exile was prescribed. With these extrajudicial weapons, administrative Russia expanded its ability to bypass the courts in the struggle against radical activists. Such arbitrary state policies tended to alienate educated people, especially those trained in the law, many of whom sympathized with and abetted the radicals.

Meanwhile, efforts to improve the criminal justice system continued, demonstrating the government's commitment to reform, despite its tepid support for the strengthening of the rule of law. In 1878, a Main Prison Administration was instituted, with subordination to the Interior Ministry. For the first time, accurate statistics relating to prisoners were compiled, efforts to improve prison conditions were systematically undertaken, more prisons were built, older prisons were renovated, and Western penal techniques and methods—like isolation cells—were implemented. Lack of funds and increasing criminality, however, hampered but did not stall progress in these areas.

An attempt on the life of Alexander in early April 1879 provoked the government to empower governors general to transfer to military courts any persons whose actions were deemed potentially harmful to public order and tranquility, to arrest or banish any person, to close any periodical publication, and to take any measures whatsoever to maintain public order. Three temporary governors general (in St. Petersburg, Khar'kov, and Odessa) were added to the existing three (in Moscow, Kiev, and Warsaw); together they held sway over twenty-one of the fifty provinces of European Russia, plus the Polish Kingdom. In less than a year, they exiled 575 people.

By this time, the world's first political terrorist organization, People's Will (*Narodnaia volia*), had been formed. In August, its leaders resolved to assassinate Alexander II, ultimately planning nine attempts. The most sensational failed attempt involved a bomb detonated in the Winter Palace in February 1880. Over the next several months, senior officials scrambled to strengthen the security apparatus (see Figure 3.2). In August, the Third Section was replaced by a central police institution, the Department of Police, subordinated to Ministry of the Interior. In October, a security bureau was set up in Moscow. This office and its counterpart in St. Petersburg would

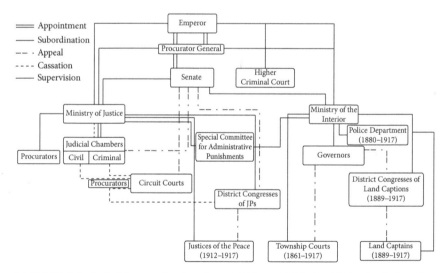

FIGURE 3.2 *Judicial organization from 1880 to 1917. In 1880, the Police Department replaced the Third Section. The Security Law of 1881 formally imparted judicial functions to administrative officials. Thus, a special committee (Osoboe soveshchanie) was created to impose administrative punishments, including exile for up to five years. A law of 1889 abolished justices of the peace in most places and created the office of land captain, administrative officials with judicial functions. The JPs were restored in 1912.*

serve as the chief nerve centers for struggle against revolutionary activism until 1917. From this time, security policing in Russia became gradually more sophisticated and professional.

Over the next several months, the reformed police had arrested nearly all of the members of People's Will. Alexander and his government had regained such confidence that the indiscriminate use of administrative measures was gradually curtailed. In fact, Alexander had agreed to implement a package of further reforms, including the creation of a consultative representative assembly, when the last remaining members of People's Will assassinated him on March 1, 1881. A special commission of the Senate tried six participants in the crime and condemned all of them to death (Gesia Gel'fman, who was pregnant, had her sentence commuted to penal servitude for life; she died in prison after having given birth). Five were hanged. These were the last public executions in Imperial Russia. (Public executions had been abolished in England in 1868.)

Alexander III and the counter reforms

The next tsar, Alexander III, staunchly opposed political reform. He shelved the idea of a consultative assembly. In August, he signed into law a measure, which systematized but also limited the scope of the welter of existing emergency laws. Confirmed by the Senate in September as "temporary," the Security Law established three sets of rules governing administrative power: "reinforced security" (*usilennaia okhrana*), "extraordinary security" (*chrezvychainaia okhrana*), and "rules for places not declared in a state of emergency." The latter, although incorporated into a "temporary law," established what became in late Imperial Russia "normal" administrative prerogative. These rules (arts. 28–31) empowered *all* police and gendarme authorities: (a) to search, arrest, and detain for up to seven days persons suspected of involvement in the planning or perpetration of state crimes, or of belonging to illegal organizations; and (b) to propose the exile of such persons for up to five years (arts. 29 and 32–36). In places under the higher levels of "emergency," nearly always a minority of provinces, administrative officials wielded still greater powers.

The Security Law did not introduce administrative exile, which had long existed, but for the first time it limited the term of exile to five years. The process functioned in the following way. Governors sent petitions to the minister of interior and he submitted them to an ad hoc committee on administrative exile (*Osoboe soveshchanie*) composed of two representatives of the Justice Ministry and three of the Interior Ministry. Between 1881 and 1904, this committee met 153 times and considered 7,159 cases, as a result of which it subjected 11,879 people to administrative exile. Of these, fully 4,424 (37 percent) were peasants exiled at the request of their communes for "reprehensible" (*porochnoe*) behavior. Twenty percent were exiled by governors for social disobedience, including involvement in factory disturbances (1,891) and agrarian disorders (733). Only about one-third (4,077) were being punished for their "political unreliability."[27] In 1888, the State Council overwhelmingly recommended stripping peasants (and urban communities) of the right to propose the exile of their members. However, Alexander III sided with the minority, who argued that this power was necessary given the insufficiency of police forces in the empire. The government, in their view, could not ensure public order without recourse to emergency measures.

Administrative punishments and emergency legislation were far from unique to Imperial Russia. In addition to the antisocialist law mentioned above, France was under a state of siege, following the Franco-Prussian War, from 1871 to 1873 (and in a few places until 1876). The major difference between Russia and its European counterparts was the former's suspension of the normal guarantees of due process for so many years. The principle of due process had not had a chance to put down roots in Russia before it was curtailed. By the same token, the Western European colonial powers ruled their empires by means of similarly arbitrary authority.

Throughout the 1880s, the Russian police systematically repressed radicals, especially activists striving to rebuild People's Will. The organization undertook one last major political assault, a plot to kill Alexander III in March 1887. It failed, and five of the plotters (including Vladimir Lenin's older brother) were hanged. In all, 175 members of the People's Will organization were brought to trial between 1880 and 1890. About one-half received death sentences; only 11 percent of those thus condemned were put to death.[28] By early 1888, People's Will had all but collapsed.

Now might have been a good time to reform the penal system. Government officials, who on a regular basis attended international conferences on criminology and penology, debated the merits of penal exile. Those in favor pointed to the various functions it fulfilled, such as punitive, socially protective, correctional, and colonizational. Detractors noted that it was hard to find appropriate locations for exile, transportation to the places of exile was often arduous, keeping track of the exiles was difficult, and there were always many more males than females. The obvious alternative was to build more prisons. Prison construction and renovation continued apace, and after the turn of the century, Russia's places of incarceration began to meet the needs of the penal system, though both administrative and judicially imposed exile persisted in Russia.

Historians have called the reign of Alexander III an age of "counter-reforms." Several such changes affected criminal justice. In 1884, new rules were adopted to increase the proportion of educated people in jury pools. The number of acquittals handed down by juries over the next several years dropped from 43 to 36 percent. (The proportion of acquittals in jury trials in Western countries ranged between 15 and 25 percent).[29] In 1889, a major judicial overhaul occurred. The office of elected justice of the peace was abolished everywhere, except in the two Imperial capitals and six other major cities. In the remaining urban areas, the judicial functions of the JPs' work were given to city judges appointed by the Ministry of Justice. In rural areas, they were shared by the relevant district member of the circuit courts and a newly created official, the land captain. Most land captains were members of the nobility and former military officers, who wielded great discretionary power, both administrative and judicial. They could overturn any village court decision, could impose fines up to six rubles and incarceration for up to three days with no possibility of appeal, had to approve decisions of rural communities to propose the exile of undesirable members, and exercised extensive supervision over local judicial institutions, including the township courts. The land captains also adopted a paternalistic attitude. In dealing with peasants, they shifted from the polite form of address used by justices of the peace to the familiar form typically used when speaking to children and social inferiors. The arbitrary and domineering power of land captains undoubtedly reinforced the peasants' understanding of authority as personal.

Such an understanding combined well with the peasant conception of justice. Despite government regulations requiring the township courts, when judging criminal cases, to apply only official and not customary law, the system remained quite informal. Even most criminal cases were considered personal matters—there were no public procurators—and could be withdrawn at any point. The peasant judges gradually gained a practical understanding of the legal system. And peasants in general became more and more comfortable with these courts.[30]

Overall, despite a number of minor victories, conservatives within the government failed to curtail the autonomy of the judiciary. Most notably the lifetime tenure of judges remained in place, as did the right to a trial by jury. The main obstacle to rolling back the judicial reform was the professionalized bureaucracy, key members of which were trained in the law and dedicated to upholding legal principles and the independent judiciary.[31] Most would have been loath to turn their backs on the ideals of the rule of law and the independence of the judiciary, however much in practice they may have undermined them.

Nicholas II: The last tsar

In 1894, the vigorous and physically powerful Alexander III died unexpectedly at the age of 49. His eldest son, Nicholas, psychologically insecure and physically slight, had received an excellent education and was being groomed to succeed his father, but at age 26, he did not feel sufficiently prepared to rule the world's largest country. As his father lay dying, however, Nicholas promised he would uphold the autocratic principle of government. This attitude, expressed publicly in many ways, alienated educated Russians from the government. Nicholas intended to carry on the policies of his father, but circumstances drove him in other directions.

In the 1890s, the government handled an ever-dwindling number of state-crime cases in the courts. Whereas the civilian courts tried 369 of 5,851 state-crime cases from 1881 to 1894, they heard not a single such case from 1894 to 1901; and administrative authorities transferred fewer than eleven nonespionage, state-crime cases to military courts between 1885 and 1903, largely because it was easier simply to exile the politically "unreliable," suspected radical activists, and alleged state criminals administratively.[32] Such procedures were so convenient for overextended police officials that they routinely applied them to behaviors that had no political aspect, for example, to regulate prostitution. In such instances, banishment, that is, the removal of persons from major cities without specifying where they should go, was more often used than exile.

After a spike in the late 1870s and early 1880s, the incidence of capital punishment also declined. From 1866 to 1891, the courts sentenced 134 people to death (including 16 women), of whom 44 were executed (including 1 woman). The worst year for executions was 1879, when sixteen people were put to death. Most of these cases were decided by military courts, which in the years 1876–1882 had thirty-nine people executed. From 1891 through 1902, the regular civilian courts sentenced not a single person to death.[33]

The general census of the Russian Empire conducted in 1897 and 1898, combined with the work of the Main Prison Administration, gives one a clearer sense of penal statistics than at any other time in prerevolutionary Russian history. Between 1807 and 1898, an estimated 876,500 persons were exiled to Siberia alone; among these, approximately 118,500, or nearly one-seventh of the total, were exiled to hard labor. In 1897, some 298,600 people were in exile (not counting hard-labor convicts) and made up 5.2 percent of the entire Siberian population.[34] Roughly half of these were administrative exiles, nearly all of them recalcitrant members of peasant communities shipped off by their fellows. A law of June 1900 rescinded the right of urban communities to recommend the exile of their members and made it more difficult for rural communities to do so. The incidence of exile, both court-ordered and administrative, had been in decline, and now fell off more swiftly. Here is yet more evidence of government officials actively seeking to curtail arbitrary punitive methods and to bring Russia into closer alignment with European best practices.

Legislation in 1903 brought further important changes to the criminal justice system. Corporal punishment with birch switches was abolished for hard-labor convicts (and the following year for all peasants, soldiers, sailors, and all other members of the population hitherto not exempted). Most important, a new Criminal Code was promulgated. First, the new code reinterpreted criminal action. Civil servants were henceforth required to protect the interests of private individuals and society, under penalty of law. It also became a criminal offense to fail to report crimes against private individuals or outbreaks of disease and other phenomena harmful to society. Second, it specified several conditions—primarily mental illness—under which the culpability of defendants was mitigated. Third, hundreds of crimes listed in the Penal Code of 1845 (revised in 1857 and 1866) were no longer considered criminal acts in the 1903 statute. In other words, the Russian government was moving away from using criminal law to micromanage society. It was also moving toward a conception of criminal justice oriented toward protecting society. Whereas the earlier code had devoted only 15.7 percent of its articles defending private individuals from criminal actions, the new code doubled that proportion to 32.7 percent.[35] Furthermore, the hierarchy of punishments was simplified, the division between criminal and correctional punishments was abolished, capital punishment was retained only for military and state crimes, and terms of penal servitude were lessened to an average of four years. Several rarely used punishments that had been on the books were discontinued, including the privileged form of exile (*na zhit'e*), forced conscription, and obligatory repentance in church. The 1903 code came into force in 1904 and then only partially. No wonder: it was as advanced as any such legislation worldwide. Probably the jurists who drafted the code, in their desire to impose in Russia criminological best practices, made impossible the code's full implementation. Treating crimes against private persons as equally harmful to the social order as crimes against the state and its officials was something most Russian administrators could not readily accommodate themselves to.

Russia under Nicholas had pursued an aggressive policy in the Far East and in early 1904 became embroiled in a war with Japan. The war went badly from beginning to end. In January 1905, government troops in St. Petersburg fired on thousands of peacefully demonstrating workers, attempting to deliver a petition to the emperor. Some 150 died, and hundreds more were wounded in events that came to be known as Bloody Sunday. Over the next several months, hundreds of thousands of workers struck, radical activists organized protests, political terrorists attacked government officials, and peasants rebelled. Government troops came to the aid of civil authorities over 2,000 times, mostly in rural areas.[36]

In mid-October, a general strike all but shut down the Russian economy. Nicholas felt he had no choice but to issue the October Manifesto, which promised expanded civil rights and government by an elected parliament. He also amnestied all persons punished administratively before the issuance of the manifesto. Many opposition leaders and activists accepted the promises and were ready to work with the government or to go about their lives peacefully. Others continued the fight. An armed uprising broke out in Moscow in December and was crushed with military force. Hundreds were killed. Rebellions in the borderlands and along the trans-Siberian railroad were quashed, resulting in thousands of deaths, in the early months of 1906 by "punitive expeditions." Supporters of the autocracy who opposed the Manifesto as incompatible with the traditional Russian political order organized associations, like the Union of Russian People. Some turned violent, attacking what they took to be enemies of that order: revolutionaries, students, intellectuals, Jews, and other national minorities. While local officials occasionally turned a blind eye to them, and senior officials sympathized with their values, the government strongly disapproved of disorder and violence of any kind. When it broke out, officials typically prosecuted the culprits vigorously.[37]

In April, Fundamental Laws established a bicameral legislature, whose approval was necessary for the adoption of any law, though it had no means for checking the power of the executive branch, aside from the right to question senior officials about their policies. Temporary rules on the press and associations expanded freedom in these areas but left much room for administrative discretion. The government and the legislature spent the next several years discussing ways to expand civil rights and to limit the arbitrary power of officials, especially their right to impose punishments administratively, but to little avail. One can argue that, henceforth, Russia was a state governed de jure, though not entirely de facto, by the rule of law. Not only did many government officials disdain the law in practice, believing themselves to some extent above it, but the mass of the population—the peasantry—had little respect for formal legal norms.

Agrarian unrest continued to break out in 1906–1907—apparently because of poor harvests, sporadic agrarian hardship, hostility toward the loss of traditions, and declining respect for government authority—with nearly 4,000 incidents occurring throughout the country. The government crushed these actions with troop deployments and massive repression. Governors were authorized to exile peasants suspected of involvement in agrarian disorders. Martial law and extraordinary security were declared in dozens of localities. In urban areas during these two years, political terrorists carried out several thousand acts of violence, mostly against lower-level government officials and resulting in many hundreds of dead.[38]

Government repression and punishments jumped dramatically. After a steady program of construction, Russian prisons and jails had finally achieved sufficient space to house roughly 70,000 prisoners (including 30,000 merely under investigation) relatively humanely in 1905, with one of the lowest prisoner-mortality rates in Europe. By 1909, however, the total number had shot up to over 135,000, including 60,000 under investigation, resulting in massive overcrowding and a spike in the prisoner-mortality rate. Lack of prison space naturally led to heavier resort to exile. The number of hard-labor convicts increased from 6,123 in 1905 to 31,836 in 1912, before slowly declining. The number of other exiles similarly spiked from 6,699 in 1905 to 32,549 in 1912.[39] The annual number of executions also surged. In the years 1906–1908, 2,215 people (apparently mostly civilians) were executed by military-court sentence (no one was executed by a sentence of civilian courts in these years).[40] Following the August 1906 terrorist bombing of the official summer residence of Prime Minister Peter Stolypin, in which dozens of government employees and bystanders were killed or wounded, the emperor issued a temporary decree creating military-field courts with even less procedural specificity than normal military courts. Over the next several months, these courts, operating mostly in the borderlands, sentenced over a thousand people to death, nearly all of whom were executed.[41]

The total number of people killed by government forces in 1906–1908 exceeded 5,000 and may have reached 8,000. This was a shocking deviation from Russia's path of the previous decades. One must recall, however, the final week of May 1871, when French government troops massacred as many as 20,000 Communards. France's population at that time was only about one-third of Russia's in 1905. Thus, the French government in quashing the Commune killed proportionately six times more people, and in a much shorter period, than Russia's did in suppressing the Revolution of 1905. Both episodes appear to be gross aberrations, however, brought about by the desperation of governments struggling to survive in the face of broad-based popular disorder.

Much of educated Russian opinion vehemently opposed capital punishment. In June 1906, the First Duma voted without a single dissenting vote to abolish it. Although the bill never became law owing to the dissolution of the Duma, intellectuals, public figures, clergymen, and professionals continued to agitate for an end to the death penalty. Even the justice minister admitted publicly that capital punishment should not be used to punish regular crimes. Yet, this was a time when regular and political crimes were blending together in something like an orgy of criminality. Although capital punishment remained on the books, it was resorted to less and less frequently, with the annual number of executions falling to 129 in 1910 and 25 in 1913.[42]

As the revolutionary movement and political violence wound down, the government might have worked to rescind the Security Law or at the very least to curtail or abolish administrative political exile. Either reform would have won considerable goodwill from Russia's educated elites. One can argue that the Imperial regime, by failing to guarantee full civil rights, to draw educated elites into the government, and to curtail recourse to harsh repressive measures, drove them toward the radical opposition, thus helping to polarize Russian state and society.

Following an unconstitutional change in the electoral law in 1907, which drastically reduced popular representation, the Third Duma was willing to work with the government to achieve significant criminal justice reform. For example, a system of parole, first advocated by Russian penologists and government reformers in 1882, was made law in 1909. The new law was intended to take pressure off the prison and exile systems. A further draft-bill aimed at creating a system of probation, however, was not adopted, because the upper chamber, or State Council, rejected it. Many conservatives in the body could not conceptualize a punishment with so little bite.

Both law projects stemmed from direct influence of the leading Western European countries, which had adopted such penal methods not long before. Legislative action made it possible to establish Russia's first juvenile court, which opened in St. Petersburg in January 1910; two years later, a similar court opened in Moscow. By 1917, nine juvenile courts functioned in various cities of Russia. In 1912, the legislature passed a bill, signed by the emperor, revoking the judicial authority of land captains and restoring the elective office of justice of the peace. The JPs were placed at the head of a newly created higher rural court. In 1913, the courts were empowered to absolve an accused person of legal culpability, if that person displayed specified personal characteristics. In other words, Russian officials quickly snapped back, following the turmoil of revolution, to their default position of pressing for further reforms inspired by Western best practices.

Even after the waning of radical activism from 1909, the ordinary crime indices remained high. From 1803–1808 to 1911–1913, the number of crimes per hundred thousand population rose 2.9 times. Punishments were for the most part, however, not draconian. In 1911–1913, just over half of all punishments involved no loss of social or other rights; of these, 35 percent involved incarceration for one year or less.[43] During the same time frame, the nature of criminality also changed. At mid-century, most offenses affected state property and the administrative order. After the turn of the century, by contrast, private individuals and their property were the primary target of most crime. This trend indicates that the relative importance of society and the individual had dramatically increased—and that of the state had declined concomitantly—in Russia.

The police had also grown in professionalism during these years, apprehending a higher proportion of criminal perpetrators in the early twentieth century as compared to mid-century. Of course, since the crime rate had gone up (though it remained about half as high as in France or Germany in these years), this greater efficiency of the police did not mean the population was significantly safer. Nevertheless, the criminal justice system was growing more responsive to society.

Following the Revolution of 1905, hooliganism became a frequent occurrence, both in urban and apparently especially in rural areas. Young men seem to have felt even less inhibited by rules of propriety than before. Such behavior was now more than ever targeted at figures and objects of authority, especially clergy, social elites, and government officials.[44] The phenomenon largely manifested itself in central Russia—not in the borderlands—and most frequently in villages with close ties to urban, industrialized areas. Seasonal industrial workers were among the most numerous perpetrators. Criminal activity in rural areas apparently rose significantly in the years 1908–1913, though accurate statistics are hard to come by, given the reluctance of peasants to report on their fellow peasants. It seems that even elected peasant officials often turned a blind eye to hooligan activity. Political conservatives and government officials worried about what they believed was the dramatic growth of such activity, though even many liberals considered hooliganism a serious problem.

The main cause of the trouble seems not to have been rural impoverishment. On the contrary, Russia's economy, both urban and rural, grew rapidly after the turbulence of 1905–1907. The countryside also fared quite well in general. Most peasants experienced a rising standard of living, better health, and improved nutrition, though pockets of poverty, even desperate ones in some places, continued to plague prewar Russia. So, if poverty does not explain most increased criminality, what does? Arguably unmet expectations of becoming better off drove some people to criminal activity.

In fact, Russia seemed largely stable socially and politically. The economy was booming. Rural areas—most of the country—were tranquil. The radical political parties suffered declining membership. Civil society was thriving. Huge numbers of people, especially in the towns and cities, were joining voluntary associations and going to the theater and the cinema. Literacy was increasing, and people were reading the surging output of periodicals and books. True, the assassination of Prime Minister Peter Stolypin in 1911 by a revolutionary activist and one-time police informant not only deprived Russia of its last great statesman. Stolypin had strived to build bridges between political moderates in the Duma and the emperor who apparently always regretted having created the institution. Now tensions between the ruler and the legislature festered. In April 1912, troops fired on hundreds of Siberian mineworkers, who had been protesting their working conditions. The resultant carnage set off a spate of strikes and breathed new life into the labor movement. Intermittent strikes continued for the next two years culminating in the Petrograd general strike in the summer of 1914. But few would have predicted the collapse of the monarchy less than three years later.

In late summer 1914, war broke out between Russia and its allies— France and Great Britain—and Austria-Hungary, Germany, and the Ottoman Empire. For a while, Russian society, the main political parties, and the tsar seemed united by a shared desire to fight and win the war. Most of the empire's eastern and southern provinces (twenty-six in all) were declared in a state of martial law, and in the rest of the country, a state of extraordinary security was imposed. Presumably at least in part because of the extraordinary powers invested in government officials, criminality dramatically fell during the first two years of the war. Because of police repression and probably also a surge of patriotism, the strike movement collapsed, and the revolutionary parties were driven underground.

Yet from the start, the war went badly. Russia was the biggest and most populous of the great powers, but also the least developed economically with the smallest industrial base (aside from Austria-Hungary) and the weakest and least politically integrated civil society. In summer 1915, Russia abandoned most of Poland, including Warsaw. A successful offensive against Austria in summer 1916 was the country's only major triumph, but it soon collapsed. People's experience of the war was mostly

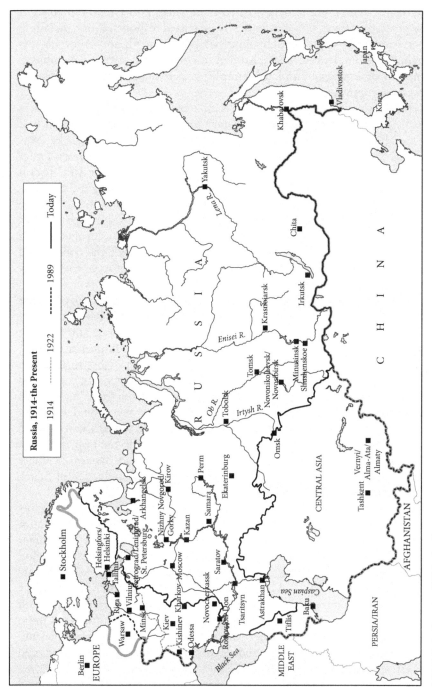

MAP 3.1 *Russia, 1914–the Present.*

negative. Police and land captains were drafted in great number, leaving the countryside even more undergoverned than usual. Police who remained at their posts, moreover, bore dramatically increased responsibilities, including supervising draft stations, tightening passport control, and enforcing the wartime ban on alcohol. They also had to compile lists of foreign subjects suspected of espionage and to carefully watch thousands of potentially subversive enemy aliens.

The Russian military authorities went much further; they gave orders to exile "enemy-subject males of military service age"—first Germans and Austro-Hungarians (often excepting Slavs) and, after war with Turkey was declared in October, Turks also—from the vast swath of territory under direct military rule east of the front lines to locations in the Ural region and the far north. Gradually, such operations affected women and children, Russian subjects of German and Jewish heritage, and Roma. Roughly 256,000 "enemy subjects" were thus deported by train during the war.[45] Several more hundred thousand Russian subjects of German and Jewish origin were also exiled into the interior. Civilian officials often complained about what they considered the excessive application of exile by military authorities and their disregard for procedural norms, but to no avail. This was arbitrary power at its most egregious, shocking even to government officials entirely accustomed to arbitrary power-wielding in Russia.

Inflation began galloping in 1915. In May, devastating anti-German pogroms broke out in Moscow and other cities. That summer a crisis of confidence seized public activists and Duma deputies who formed the reform-minded Progressive Bloc. In September, Nicholas made the fateful decision to assume personal command of the army at the front lines, which left his wife, Empress Alexandra, in Petrograd (as the capital city was renamed during the war), and under increasing influence of the self-styled holy man, Grigorii Rasputin. His apparent easy access to the Imperial court undermined public confidence in both government and dynasty. Rumors of administrative corruption, official malfeasance, the influence of "dark forces," and treason in high places circulated widely.

At the end of 1915, a strike movement recommenced. Conscription riots also broke out. Shortages of food and fuel affected urban areas sporadically. With industrial production focused on the war effort, ordinary consumer goods, like tools and boots, grew harder to come by. The popular mood soured. In 1916, the crime rate began to rise. While the execution rate seems not to have increased dramatically during the World War, summary executions by military authorities were presumably more frequent. Although the political police continuously arrested radical activists, thousands more spread antigovernment messages in the military ranks, in Siberian exile, and in factories. Agitation, anxiety, and hostility in both popular quarters and elite circles intensified throughout fall and winter 1916.

In December, a coterie of conservatives and monarchists murdered Rasputin, hoping his death would heal the rift between Nicholas and high society. It did not. In the new year, the strike movement swelled, troops mutinied, and in late February and early March 1917, the government and the dynasty collapsed.

During the February Days in Petrograd, crowds ransacked police stations, pillaged court records, destroyed most of the Main Prison Administration's records, hunted down and killed policemen, and stormed jails and prisons, freeing tens of thousands of prisoners. The newly formed Provisional Government abolished all police institutions and dismissed all governors and vice-governors, appointing local political activists as their replacements. The death penalty was repealed. Thousands of regular criminals were amnestied. Radical activists flooded back from distant exile. A popular militia, under the auspices of the Petrograd City Duma, was instituted on March 3, but functioned poorly and only at the local level. Violence and crime gripped the streets of Petrograd, as well as of Moscow and other cities. The sharp spike in criminality shocked and frightened the population.[46]

The Provisional Government, under the leadership of Justice Minister Alexander Kerensky, a leading socialist lawyer, abolished most special courts, introduced jury trials into military courts, and expanded further the civil system of trial by jury. The eligibility for jury duty expanded to include women if they expressed a desire to be included in jury lists, and the property qualification was abolished. The Provisional Government also liberalized criminal procedure. For example, attorneys were henceforth allowed to participate in the pretrial investigation. Likewise, all estate-based distinctions in the criminal justice system were done away with. The restrictions on, and distortions of, the judicial statutes of 1864 were rescinded. Trials were to be open and public and juries were to try all important cases, including offenses against the state. Thus reformed, the judicial system continued to function, but it was unable to cope with the rise in criminality.

In a new departure, a law promulgated in December 1916 was to institute a system of administrative justice, under the purview of the Senate, for hearing cases brought against government officials. The law entered force on June 1, 1917, with the full support of the Provisional Government. Although the system began functioning slowly and only partially, for the first time in Russian history citizens had a means to seek redress for mistreatment at the hands of government officials.[47]

The Petrograd Soviet also emerged as a tribune of the popular masses. Its first legislative act, Order Number One, drastically reduced the authority of military officers, thus undermining the only remaining arm of executive power. Soviets, or councils, sprang up throughout the country in factories, military units, and villages. Russian society organized itself from the grassroots up. Even parishes and other religious communities thirsted after autonomy, as did many national minorities.

A criminal investigation project on which both the Provisional Government and the Petrograd Soviet collaborated aimed to uncover abuse of power and official malfeasance at the highest levels of the prerevolutionary state. The Extraordinary Investigating Commission arrested and interrogated former officials, worked systematically through police archives, and built up several big criminal cases. Most of the charges involved the interception of mail and the deployment of secret informants. Yet it turned out that, according to Russian law, such activities were not in fact illegal and not a single official was ever brought to trial.[48]

As crime surged, workers formed red guard brigades and worker militias for self-defense. Ordinary people took the law into their own hands, murdering thieves and other malefactors in the traditional *samosud*. Peasants chopped down millions of trees on private and state property, seized landed estates, and attacked authority figures throughout the countryside. Troops mutinied and deserted their posts. Liberals and moderate socialists viewed all such activities as evidence of an anarchic breakdown of order. In this context, the Provisional Government tried to reassert its authority. In July, capital punishment was restored at the front lines. In late summer, administrative officials were empowered to search, arrest, imprison, and expel from Russia anyone threatening national defense, internal security, and the liberty secured by the revolution. Such powers were apparently not used vigorously. An attempted military coup in August was put down by armed workers. By fall, central authority had all but collapsed and public disorder helped win support for the Bolsheviks—the only political leaders who seemed ready to impose a new order. On October 16, the Petrograd Soviet voted to create a Military Revolutionary Committee to defend the capital, following a plan drafted by Leon Trotsky. The Bolsheviks would use the MRC to seize power ten days later. Once in power, they moved quickly to radically transform criminal justice in Russia.

4

The Era of Lenin

The Bolsheviks came to power with a radical notion of law, governance, and criminal justice. Although many moderate socialists conceptualized the law and the judicial system as instruments of class oppression, they nevertheless shared with liberals a view of these institutions in "bourgeois" societies as fundamental bulwarks of order that simply needed to be reformed and made more inclusive. The Bolsheviks, by contrast, viewed prerevolutionary criminal law as hopelessly integrated with structures of class exploitation, the whole of which needed to be jettisoned and rebuilt from the ground up. In this way, leading Bolsheviks turned their backs on several hundreds of years of Western political theory, whose main achievement was an understanding of undivided and unlimited power as a grave political threat. "Power corrupts and absolute power corrupts absolutely," argued the liberal theorist Lord Acton. Checks and balances and the separation of powers were the only hope for avoiding tyranny. An independent judiciary, as a separate branch of government, was one key element in this gradually emerging classically liberal conceptualization of good governance. Russia in the late Imperial era had been moving slowly and tentatively in this direction. For the Bolsheviks, by contrast, true law was a self-evident manifestation of good judgment guided by "revolutionary consciousness." Institutions were unnecessary.

In *State and Revolution*, which Lenin wrote in summer 1917 while evading the Provisional Government's warrant for his arrest for alleged treason, he argued that no special officials or institutions would be necessary to regulate relations among people under communism. Quoting from Engels, he argued that order and social harmony would be maintained by a "self-acting armed organization of the population."[1] The police, the law courts, lawyers, prisons, criminal investigators—the tasks of all such officials and institutions would be handled by the conscious masses. James Madison proclaimed that "if men were angels no government would be necessary." Lenin either disagreed or thought that proletarians were angels.

The earliest Bolshevik institutions of criminal justice were inspired by this political philosophy. A People's Militia and People's Courts were to be staffed by ordinary people without any training, as were revolutionary tribunals. Proletarian consciousness would guide all their actions and deliberations. Soon, however, repressive agencies emerged and were gradually endowed with far more unchecked power than their prerevolutionary counterparts. To be sure, the new rulers completely repudiated the old regime and fully intended to break with its old repressive ways. Carrying forward the achievements of the Provisional Government, the Bolshevik leadership quickly made women fully equal before the law, legalized abortion, and decriminalized homosexual acts between consenting adults.

Nevertheless, they built a system of government whose arbitrariness, personalized authority, and paternalism were all strengthened, as if Russia had returned to an earlier form of rule. The Bolsheviks effected a radical break—not with Russian traditions so much as with the more shallowly rooted legal westernization. In the process, the lines between prosecution and persecution and between reprisals and justice blurred to the point of becoming effaced. It is hard to avoid the impression that, during the Civil War and especially during high Stalinism, the era of Russian history that early Bolshevism most resembled was the time of the Oprichnina of Ivan the Terrible.

The Bolsheviks come to power

In late October, the Bolsheviks seized power in the name of worker and soldier councils, or soviets. They immediately proclaimed an end to the war, abolished private property in land, set up and empowered a new government (the Council of People's Commissars, or SNK) to legislate by decree, outlawed the liberal press, established an eight-hour working day, guaranteed the self-determination of national minorities, and nationalized all banks, among much other radical legislation. The new government appointed a commissar of justice, whose main task was to dismantle the former Ministry of Justice. Another early act was the Decree on Courts, issued on November 22. As the Provisional Government abolished the entire prerevolutionary apparatus of repression, by this early decree the Bolsheviks dismantled the entire prerevolutionary judicial system: the procurator's office, the Bar, the office of judicial investigators, the district courts, trial by jury, the judicial chambers, the fledgling system of administrative justice, and the Senate, as well as most remaining specialized courts, such as the military courts and those dealing with commercial matters.[2] The office of justices of the peace was suspended, existing justices retired, and democratic elections held to replace them.

The decree (with more detail spelled out in a second Decree on Courts of February 15, 1918) also urged the establishment of new local courts for deciding criminal cases liable to sentences up to two years' imprisonment and of revolutionary tribunals to judge more serious crimes, especially those harmful to the state, such as speculation (profiteering) and sabotage (see Figure 4.1). In other words, the interpretation of offenses against the political order as more dangerous than those against ordinary persons was to be dramatically strengthened. In practice, however, both types of court exceeded their mandates by deciding cases beyond those limits. Any citizen without a criminal record and with full political rights—excluding "former people" like clergy, wealthy merchants and financiers, prerevolutionary political policemen and military officers, and other categories of "anti-proletarian" persons—was authorized to serve in any capacity in the new courts. No legal training or experience was needed, though lower-level staff of the old courts were required to continue to serve in the new ones. Judges and their assistants were to be democratically elected, though initially they were chosen by the executive committees of local Soviets. In practice, this turned out to be the permanent recruitment method. This typically meant that local political officials exercised strong control over the courts, sometimes insisting on reviewing their decisions. Preliminary investigations were to be conducted by the judges who eventually would try the cases themselves. These plans for radical judicial reform obviously contained deep tensions between the political order, which was viewed as most deserving

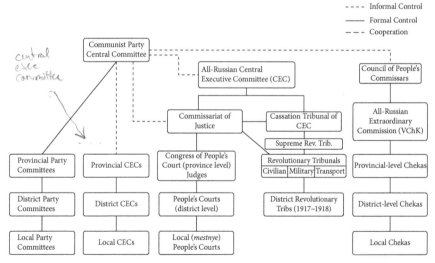

FIGURE 4.1 *Judicial organization of the RSFSR, 1918–1921. Officially, the justice system answered to the Council of People's Commissars and the All-Russian Central Executive Committee. In practice, however, the supreme authority was the Russian Communist Party. The political police, or Cheka, wielded broad judicial power as well. Military revolutionary tribunals, during the Civil War years (1918–1920), tried more civilians than the regular revolutionary tribunals.*

of protection, on the one hand, and untrained, ordinary people, who were conceived as its guardians, on the other hand.

The decree did not abolish existing law, or require the firing of existing clerical staff or even judicial personnel, but instructed judges in the new courts to disregard any law that had been abrogated by the SNK or that contradicted the programs of the Russian Social Democratic and Socialist-Revolutionary Parties, decrees issued by the new government, revolutionary conscience, and the revolutionary sense of legality. It is unclear how most judges, who were drawn from the working masses and therefore had no legal training and often very little education, decided cases.

In practice, some senior judicial officials attempted to remain in office, for example, the entire general assembly of senators, but they were removed by force when necessary. Members of the Bar in Moscow and Petrograd continued to function for nearly a year before those organizations, too, were fully abolished.[3] Before any new courts could be instituted, the Military Revolutionary Council created an investigating commission, which for a time was virtually the only judicial institution in Russia. People accused of various crimes were sent to it from all over the country, often without any supporting documentation.[4]

People's courts spontaneously sprang up, in some cases even before the November decree, beginning with such Petrograd districts as Vyborg, ever a radical workers' hotbed. Factory committees and trade unions also formed early people's courts, often in makeshift quarters and conducting sessions on the fly. Some sprang up in villages as well, though in most places, people's courts were not instituted until at least midsummer 1918. In many regions, moreover, township courts continued to function for months. In the people's courts, anyone present could spontaneously act as either a prosecutor or a defense attorney. The courts issued mostly lenient sentences, a significant proportion of them suspended, and were expected to adopt a class-based approach.[5] This meant that members of the lower classes should be judged more leniently and members of the upper classes more harshly.

Lenin was enthusiastic about such popular initiatives and for some time seemed to expect Soviet justice to emerge from the grassroots. The radical writer, Maxim Gorky, by contrast, believed that destroying the old judicial system strengthened the traditional Russian tendency to vigilante justice, the popular sense of one's right to engage in *samosud*. Rare was the case in which specific articles and paragraphs of laws or codes—or even laws—were referenced. In such instances, inaccuracies often cropped up, as though the laws were being cited from hearsay.[6] Witnesses typically gave muddled testimony.[7] Government officials generally considered rural courts inefficient and unable to uphold revolutionary justice. Indeed, some local courts exhibited distinctly non-Bolshevik attitudes, for example, in defense of the church. Others preserved elements of the old judicial system. It seemed to the political leaders that few peasants were ready and able to serve as defenders of the law, as the Bolsheviks conceived it. Therefore, a decree of

November 1918 required rural judges to be selected from lists of candidates prepared by local Soviets. Here, the tension between the state, as deserving utmost protection, and ordinary people, as its protectors, began to dissolve. In other words, the leadership quickly began to subordinate society to the interests of the state, as conceived of by the party leaders.

The term "revolutionary tribunal" was borrowed from the French Revolution.[8] The Bolshevik version had broad discretion to determine the character of trials, whether they would be public or closed, whether there would be witnesses, and whether the accused would have defenders. They were created to handle offenses considered dangerous to the new Soviet order, including treason, financial and commercial speculation (or profiteering), and sabotage. Yet the tribunals soon found themselves judging much less spectacular cases, including the misappropriation of funds, petty swindling, bribe-taking, robbery, murder, and censorship cases.[9] Nearly all trials in these institutions proceeded with neither defense nor prosecution. The tribunals' sentences could not be appealed, except on procedural grounds via the Commissariat of Justice. Those sentences, as confirmed in a decree of December 19, could not exceed four years' imprisonment. The Bolsheviks clearly wanted to project an image of moderation, the more so as the abolition of capital punishment had been a cardinal popular demand since the Revolution of 1905. None of the new courts conducted jury trials.

The tribunals were to be founded by local soviets but under the jurisdiction of the People's Commissar of Justice. Petrograd's Soviet established the first one, on December 3, 1917, and Moscow followed suit on December 5. The first trial conducted by a revolutionary tribunal was that of Countess Sofia Panina (1871–1956).[10] It took place on December 10 in Petrograd. Panina, a leading member of the liberal Kadet Party, had served as deputy minister of education under the Provisional Government. (On the night of her arrest, on November 28, the Bolshevik government issued a decree outlawing leading members of the Kadet Party as "enemies of the people.") When the Bolsheviks seized power, she refused to hand over her ministry's cash and securities on hand, worth 93,000 rubles, declaring that the new government was not legitimate. Charging her with criminal sabotage, the tribunal expected that her wealth and high social status would make a guilty verdict a foregone conclusion. But Panina's main occupation had been philanthropy, and in particular the founding and maintenance of a settlement house outside the capital, which had provided a variety of social and educational services for the poor.

The auditorium in the former palace of Grand Duke Nikolai Nikolaevich, now outfitted to accommodate the revolutionary tribunal, was filled to overflowing, primarily by professionals and public activists but also a contingent of soldiers and workers. The seven judges consisted of two soldiers and five factory workers. Six were Bolsheviks. The trial had not been staged, and at first members of the audience sang Panina's praise, including a Socialist-Revolutionary factory worker, who gushed about her work among the people. Scrambling, the court called upon another worker. This one denounced her as a representative of her class. A witness for the government accused Panina of withholding employees' wages. In her concluding statement, she claimed she would return the 93,000 rubles only to the democratically elected Constituent Assembly (to which free elections had begun). After an hour of deliberations, the court found her guilty of "opposition to the people's authority" but also decreed that so long as she gave the money back there would be no punishment other than "public censure." Panina and her liberal allies considered the verdict a triumph of legality. In reality, legality as predictable, procedurally governed, impartial, and fair justice, especially in regard to a "political" case, had just reached its high point. The prospect of a fair trial for opponents of Bolshevism dramatically receded in the coming months and years.

Indeed, after a few more such unanticipated and unfavorable outcomes, as the Panina trial was from the point of view of the Bolsheviks, the authorities took better control of judicial proceedings. Henceforth, most trials took place behind closed doors, audiences were carefully selected, and the right of advocates to speak on behalf of defendants was restricted. In May 1918, a Supreme Revolutionary Tribunal was instituted for handling the most serious political crimes. All such changes were somewhat beside the point, since the revolutionary tribunals were soon eclipsed by the political police as the main agency for punishing perceived opponents of the new order.

The Bolsheviks did not initially have a police apparatus. In fact, they ordered the disbandment of city militia organizations and advocated the creation of a Workers' and Peasants' Militia. Yet criminality continued to rise. Immediately after the Bolsheviks seized power in October 1917, Petrograd soldiers went on a rampage, looting shops and wine stores for weeks. From late November, a commission was instituted for "combating drunkenness and pogroms." On December 5, the Bolsheviks abolished the Military Revolutionary Committee and two days later replaced it with the All-Russian Extraordinary Commission for Combating Counter-Revolution and Sabotage, or Cheka.[11] Felix Dzerzhinskii, a tough Bolshevik of Polish origin, was placed in charge of this political police institution. Given the lack of other well-organized police forces in Soviet Russia, for many months the Cheka investigated regular crime, in addition to political crime, and meted out punishments to regular criminals. In principle, the Cheka was supposed to conduct investigations and then transfer the resulting documentation to the revolutionary tribunals. In practice, it both dictated sentences to them, took cases away from them, and applied punishments administratively on its own authority. The Bolshevik political police, which punished and applied terror rather than sought justice, became a mainstay of Soviet governance.

During the first months of Soviet power, institutional chaos reigned. The democratically elected Constituent Assembly was shut down at gunpoint in early January 1918. That month and the next, vigilante groups of soldiers massacred hundreds of officers in many garrison towns. Local Bolshevik officials set up three-person teams (troikas) with broad administrative power and the authority to shoot alleged criminals on the spot to root out crime. Such bodies mirrored the high-level troika of senior Cheka officials with the countrywide power of life and death. On February 21, with the German army penetrating Russian territory, the Bolsheviks declared the "socialist fatherland in danger," temporarily authorizing unconstrained summary executions by the Cheka. In early March, the seat of government was transferred to Moscow and the Treaty of Brest-Litovsk put an end to the war but required giving up 1.3 million square miles of territory and 62 million people. Almost immediately Allied forces began to land in the far north—initially with the approval of the Bolshevik leaders, who wanted help in building a new military force—to protect stores of war material provided to Russia by the Allied governments and to continue the fight against the Central Powers. Many national-minority regions broke away from Russia, including Finland, Poland, and the Baltic lands.

Conditions in prisons were especially bad. Many prisons, which had been damaged during the revolution, were shut down because of official neglect and for lack of resources to repair them. As of January 1, 1918, there were 606 jails of all kinds (*mesta zakliucheniia*); but as of October 1, only around half that many were functioning.[12] In February 1918, severe food shortages forced the authorities to transfer many prisoners from Petrograd to provincial lockups. It seems probable that dealing with criminals via summary executions was in part a means to address the problem of insufficient places of confinement. Periodic amnesties, beginning on May 1, were proclaimed apparently also for this reason. The frequency and the fanfare with which amnesties were decreed as well as their broad scope suggest that their purpose was not merely expediency. It also seems likely that the authorities wished to use them to demonstrate the mercy and benevolence of their rule.[13] It is also quite possible that—probably unconsciously—blanket amnesties served to reinforce a sense of complete dependence on the regime. Just as one could end up in prison or exile for relatively arbitrary reasons, so one could owe one's liberation to the arbitrary and all-powerful judgment of Soviet power.

Many political activists who spent time in prisons both before and after 1917 later described the conditions in the early Bolshevik era as deplorable by comparison. One factor that worsened them was the policy of giving tough regular criminals significant authority over other prisoners. Moreover, beginning in May 1918, more and more prisoners were held by central and local Cheka offices, where conditions were especially bad. As before the revolution, however, political activists occasionally staged protests and hunger strikes against the conditions of their confinement. The results were often similar, as well: various improvements in food, creature comforts, access to books and writing materials, more frequent baths, permission to receive visitors, and kindred concessions.[14] Such ploys continued to bear fruit through the 1920s.

In April and May 1918, the government adopted several measures aimed at socializing the economy, including a prohibition on buying or leasing commercial and industrial businesses (they were nationalized in June), making it unlawful to pass on significant wealth to one's heirs, and launching a systematic campaign to confiscate grain from the peasantry. Such actions took state economic intervention to such a high level as to criminalize many ordinary economic activities. In fact, during the Civil War trading grain and other foodstuffs, instead of handing them over to the government at low fixed prices, became a crime punishable by death. The totality of these policies was called War Communism and was intended to transform Russia into a socialist society. In this context, a centralized, professional regular police force, still called the militia, also began to take shape.

Criminal justice during the Civil War

In May, a contingent of roughly 60,000 Czechoslovak troops, which had been making their way from the Eastern front across Russia in order to travel around the world and join the Allied fight in France, refused to surrender their weapons to Bolshevik forces, a requirement imposed on Soviet Russia by the victorious German military. As a highly trained military force, the Czechoslovaks easily bested the disorganized Bolshevik units and quickly took control of several Eastern cities, beginning with Samara on the Volga River, and soon the entire Trans-Siberian Railroad. In late May, martial law was imposed in localities on the Volga River and in Moscow.[15] Thus began the Russian Civil War. It also involved peasant resistance to grain confiscation and the so-called White Armies commanded by prerevolutionary officers and operating along the country's borderlands. This struggle continued until late 1919 and early 1920. The Bolsheviks ultimately triumphed because of superior military organization, unified political and military leadership, control of the Russian heartland and the main transportation hubs, a more compelling vision of the future, better strategic communication, and the fear of most peasants that the anti-Bolshevik coalition might return private estates to the landlords.

On June 15, a central Cheka "troika" headed by Dzerzhinskii was given the power to authorize the execution of criminal suspects.[16] Also in the first half of June, the powers of the revolutionary tribunals to impose sanctions for cases of sabotage and counterrevolution were expanded to include capital punishment. The first victim of these new judicial powers, in this case wielded by the newly created Supreme Revolutionary Tribunal, was Aleksei Shchastnyi, the commander of the Baltic Fleet, who in April had saved the fleet from capture by the German Navy. At his trial on June 20–21, he was accused of counterrevolution and was shot the following day. Thus began the Soviet policy of legal executions. It continued virtually throughout the entire Soviet era. (On the first day of the trial, V. Volodarsky, the commissar for propaganda and agitation in Petrograd, was assassinated by a Socialist-Revolutionary.) On July 20, a further Decree on Courts empowered local courts to impose punishments up to five years' incarceration.

The Bolsheviks imposed a form of punishment on an entire population category, which they called "the bourgeois classes." Such class-based prejudgment was part of the Bolshevik outlook from before the revolution, but it was established in the highest law of the land on July 10, when the Fifth All-Russian Congress of Soviets approved the Constitution of the Russian Socialist Republic of 1918. According to this document, merchants, clergy, former policeman, anti-Bolshevik military personnel, and persons who lived off unearned income, among others, were denied voting rights, social services, and other state benefits. Such disabilities affected millions of people and, during times of political tension, often resulted in far severer penalties, including exile and death.[17]

Also in July, the Cheka began to establish more places of confinement under its jurisdiction for isolating people considered to be a threat to state security. Such facilities, like the Cheka itself, were not defined by law or regulated by any statutes. In August, at the time of a peasant uprising in the Ural area of Penza, Lenin recommended incarcerating the rebels in concentration camps to be constructed in each province of the country.[18] In early September, a decree required isolating "class enemies" in concentration camps. Throughout the Civil War their number and capacity steadily expanded. A parallel criminal justice system with separate agents and institutions of investigation, sentencing, and punishment thus emerged.

Extrajudicial executions also continued, for both regular and political crimes. In fact, most alleged counterrevolutionaries were repressed by the Cheka. During the summer, as anti-Bolshevik forces gathered strength and seized positions along the Volga and in the south, Socialist-Revolutionaries rebelled in Moscow and in Iaroslavl to the north, peasants resisted grain confiscation, and the rhetoric and practice of extrajudicial violence heated up. Orders went out from Moscow to crush counterrevolution "with merciless means" and to apply "steely and pitiless" terror. It seems that within a couple of weeks hundreds of people had been summarily shot.[19] Among them were a dozen members of the former Imperial family (including Nicholas and his wife and children).

On August 30, left-wing terrorists assassinated the Petrograd Cheka chief M. S. Uritskii and attempted to kill Lenin himself. Decrees of September 2 and 5 declared Russia a single military camp and proclaimed mass terror against "class enemies." Thus began the Red Terror. A party instruction of September 17 ordered Cheka authorities to "shoot all counterrevolutionaries."[20] They indeed shot hundreds and hundreds of people. The Cheka also began systematically to take hostages from among people related to alleged counterrevolutionaries—a policy that persisted and intensified during the Civil War—with the explicit threat to kill them for potential misdeeds of family members. Over the next few months, thousands of people were taken as hostages and housed in makeshift concentration camps. This was a return to the sort of traditional Russian collective responsibility that had been declining for decades and had been all but abandoned in the official criminal justice system. It continued under various guises throughout the Soviet era. Neither the Commissariat of Interior nor the Commissariat of Justice was involved with these measures of repression. The rhetoric of violence in the state-controlled press was bloodcurdling throughout the month of September.

A flurry of decrees empowered provincial chekas to impose summary executions on their own authority and district chekas to do so with approval at the provincial level, though it seems in practice they often shot first and reported later.[21] Many hundreds and probably even several thousands of people were executed summarily in the fall. Part of the carnage was brought about by the Military Revolutionary Tribunal of the Republic created under the authority of the Revolutionary Military Council, of which Leon Trotsky was the chairman. Numerous local and mostly autonomous military revolutionary tribunals were also active at the various fronts and eventually in all large military units, beginning in late June 1918. By fall 1920, throughout the country 150 to 160 military tribunals were operating.[22]

Far from all Communist Party activists and local soviet leaders were happy with the arbitrary and extrajudicial violence. Many of them complained to the central authorities. So much so that the Extraordinary Sixth All-Russia Congress of Soviets, which convened on November 6–9, 1918, felt compelled to affirm that the Cheka was required to operate within the bounds of law "except under extraordinary conditions of Civil War and counterrevolution."[23] Of course, that formulation left a lot of leeway for arbitrary action. The political police overstepped the politically tolerable balance, however, when, in mid-October, its weekly newspaper published an article, submitted by local officials, praising torture without any editorial comment. The party leadership abruptly shut down the newspaper and ordered an investigation into the activities of the Cheka. The Red Terror tapered off in November, but the Cheka retained the power to carry out uncontrolled capital punishment.

Other institutions of criminal justice and law enforcement also continued to function. The criminal detective system was centralized and expanded in October 1918 under the auspices of the militia.[24] A decree of November 30, 1918, abolished the distinction between local and district courts and created a uniform judicial system with people's courts as the first instance and cassation courts for appeals, which could vacate but not lessen sentences. The decree also prohibited applying laws from the pre-October-1917 era. The Bolshevik leadership was obviously attempting to move as radically away from the Imperial criminal justice system as possible. The fact that so much of that system was influenced and inspired by European and broader Western principles and practices means that the new system was intended to move in a starkly new direction.

A criminal-law handbook of 1919 defined crime as conditioned by social relations in a class-based society. Criminals were not individually responsible, it asserted, but rather crime is conditioned by social status. The proletariat, therefore, needed no codes or rules to deal with its oppressors. Instead, new laws would be borne out of the experience of repressing the oppressors. It was as if the Bolsheviks were trying to create an entirely new society with new principles—one that had never existed before. Indeed, that was exactly their hope.

One part of that expected transformation was the complete abolition of both private property and the free market, as well as the rooting out of such key elements of market economics as the price mechanism in the law of supply and demand. By now, nearly all private economic initiatives had been criminalized, and on October 21, 1918, it was made a crime for able-bodied citizens not to register with government employment agencies. Then on December 10, a new Labor Code established a universal labor obligation for people aged 16–50. In other words, society was intended to become regimented like a military force. Yet with a twist. Decrees issued in February and March 1920 empowered the central and provincial chekas to incarcerate violators of labor discipline and "parasites" in concentration camps for up to five years. The Bolsheviks were creating a hybrid regime combining elements of traditional, paternalistic, and authoritarian governance along with modern techniques of social control. The result was a society in which nearly any act could be deemed criminal and result in serious punishment.

Revolutionary tribunals continued to handle cases far beyond acts of counterrevolution. An inspection of thirty-two revolutionary tribunals in November 1918 indicated that they had deliberated on over 12,000 cases during the previous several months. Of these, only 38 percent involved counterrevolution, while 32 percent concerned "speculation," or profiteering (which typically meant buying and selling ordinary products for more than fixed state prices); 19 percent, bribery or improper use of documents; 7 percent, pogroms; 6 percent, "sabotage"; and 1 percent, espionage. The most common punishment meted out by the tribunals was incarceration with obligatory public works. Only 14 people were executed, 12 of them for counterrevolutionary activity.[25]

The most spectacular case before a revolutionary tribunal in the fall involved Roman Malinovskii. A leading Bolshevik activist who doubled as a police spy and was elected as a deputy to the Fourth Duma in 1912, Malinovskii had proletarian origins and was a favorite of Lenin himself. Malinovskii apparently thought these characteristics might save his life. Although the procedure adhered to Western jurisprudential norms, with the calling of witnesses and a relatively unfettered defense, the sentence was apparently a foregone conclusion. The trial lasted only two days (October 27–28). The court retired only briefly and returned a sentence of death, to be carried out within twenty-four hours. The former double agent's crime was betrayal of the revolutionary cause and for that he could not be pardoned.

In November, Germany lost the war and had to return conquered Russian territory. Now, the Civil War spilled over into Ukraine and other regions. Special sections (*osobye otdely*) of the Cheka were created for surveillance in the military. A burst of directives empowered government agencies to execute people for such infractions as failing to clear snow from railroad tracks, damaging telegraph lines, and stealing state property.[26] From the point of view of the Bolshevik leaders, defending the first truly socialist government in history was the most sacred goal of their work. All the resources and people of the country should be bent to that objective.

In early December 1918, the Council of Labor and Defense issued a ruling limiting the power of the Cheka to arrest senior government officials. Henceforth, they could be arrested only with full knowledge of their superiors. If such prior notification was not possible, given the sensitivity of the case, responsible officials had to be notified within forty-eight hours. Moreover, party and state officials had the right to be present during any criminal investigation of their subordinates. If two members of the provincial or city party or state leadership should vouch for an employee, he or she had to be set free, unless the political police insisted on transferring the case to a higher level of government. Such a political immunity continued throughout the Soviet era. This was the beginning of the *nomenklatura* system of special privileges and access to power of senior officials. Among the privileges was standing above the law. Prerevolutionary officials also enjoyed a similar extralegal status, but it became much more expansive under the Bolsheviks.

When the tide of the Civil War seemed to turn in favor of the Bolsheviks in early 1919, the top leadership reorganized the revolutionary tribunals, giving them simplified and expedited procedure, but restricting the extrajudicial power of other agencies. By a decree of February 17, only the tribunals were to have unimpeded authority to impose death sentences; the chekas could do so only in cases of armed uprising and in regions under martial law where specific crimes were defined by statute as capital offenses. There were now hundreds of revolutionary tribunals—and hundreds of chekas—right down to the district level. In March, however, because of a major offensive of anti-Bolshevik forces from the east, the restrictions on imposing extrajudicial punishments were lifted.

Alter Litvin, a professor at the University of Kazan, has calculated from archival documents that in the first seven months of 1919, the Kazan provincial Cheka put 117 people to death. Since there were 40 provincial chekas throughout the country at that time, along with 335 district chekas, 49 special military sections of the Cheka, hundreds of revolutionary military tribunals, and hundreds more township chekas, by extrapolation one can assume that these institutions, taken together, executed thousands of people summarily. This was in addition to the roughly 400 death sentences issued by the thirteen central-level revolutionary tribunals in 1919.[27]

A government decree of April 11, 1919, spelled out rules on organizing forced-labor camps. Chekas, revolutionary tribunals, people's courts, and kindred institutions were authorized to designate people for incarceration in them. A further decree, of May 17, specified a requirement to set up a forced-labor camp (or concentration camp) with a capacity of 300 persons in every provincial capital. Smaller towns could also set up such camps with the permission of the People's Commissariat of Internal Affairs or NKVD. All inmates were required to labor within the camps and could be detailed for labor to any Soviet institution. The inmates were to toil physically but could perform intellectual work with special permission. Separate camps were created under the purview of the Cheka for the most dangerous prisoners. The number of camps throughout the Russian Republic alone increased rapidly from 21 camps at the end of 1919 to 122 camps in November 1921. In 1920, some 25,000 people were held in these camps, not counting prisoners taken in the Civil War.[28] Such camps during the Civil War were not located in remote locations, as they later would be under Stalin. The living conditions were apparently also vastly better, as they had been before 1917. People in exile in the Imperial era, except those serving sentences of penal servitude, lived autonomously, though under police supervision.

The Bolsheviks were aiming at fine-grained social control. In May 1919, the Petrograd authorities ordered housing committees to organize twenty-four-hour security for all apartment buildings with "universal participation" of the residents. The effect apparently was to dramatically diminish criminality.[29] Yet the authorities' hope was also to create a completely new society that eventually would not need criminal law at all. Crime, according to the Bolshevik Party platform adopted in summer 1919, was interpreted as a vestige of prerevolutionary capitalist society. With the final destruction of the bourgeoisie and allied hostile classes, both the state as a coercive institution and the law as an emanation of the state would wither away.

One of the crimes most frequently prosecuted during the Civil War was military desertion, a capital offense. Throughout the country, in the first seven months of 1919, roughly 95,000 deserters were sentenced, and 600 of them were executed. The government furthermore threatened with forced labor entire villages whose members had fled from military service. In this way, many tens of thousands of deserters gave themselves up so as not to cause trouble for their family members and neighbors.[30] This policy was another example of the resurgence of the traditional Russian notion of collective responsibility.

Because the Bolsheviks sought to abolish private initiative—in business, labor organization, voluntary association, publishing, and professional life—the ranks of the bureaucracy swelled dramatically. For example, roughly 7 percent of employed people in Moscow and St. Petersburg worked for government agencies before the war, but the proportion had spiked to 40 percent in 1920.[31] Even considering the drastic decline of the populations of those two cities owing to economic collapse, those are telling statistics. Indeed, the bureaucracy at all levels continued to grow as the state attempted to control and administer nearly every aspect of society, including the entire economy.

Lenin and other Bolshevik leaders anxiously watched the growing bureaucratization of Soviet Russia. They had not expected the state to wither immediately; but, in the meantime, they had envisioned direct popular administration of the machinery of government. The expanding red tape, graft, self-serving officials, inefficiency, and other elements of the swelling state apparatus lacking an ethos of professionalism and accountability often led them to the brink of despair. On October 21, 1919, a separate revolutionary tribunal was established under the auspices of the Cheka to try various grave crimes, including bribery and abuse of office. This judicial body was to be guided solely by a consideration of the interests of the revolution, without any procedural norms. Nor were appeals permitted. On February 7, 1920, the Worker-Peasant Inspectorate (*Rabkrin*) was created to supervise the functioning of all government institutions (except the political police)—yet another layer of bureaucracy. As of November 1, 1920, from one set of data on persons sent to forced-labor camps, 2,036 out of 16,967, or roughly 12 percent, were serving terms for crimes in office.[32] Obviously, with officialdom growing so robustly but also haphazardly, official malfeasance and corruption could not but swell also—a perennial Soviet problem.

Throughout this period, regular crimes were investigated and handled indiscriminately by the militia, the political police, and military agencies. According to law, any defendant brought before a revolutionary tribunal or a people's court had a right to a defense advocate, but there were too few available and therefore in 1920 this right was dropped. The developing criminal justice system had no presumption of innocence, though defendants could refuse to testify. On October 21, 1920, an office of people's investigators was instituted to regularize criminal investigations. Yet the system remained arbitrary. Witnesses or even plaintiffs were sometimes treated as defendants and found guilty in the course of a trial, as had also frequently occurred in the Muscovite era. Judges and indeed the entire judicial system were not independent of the executive branch. In fact, judges were considered rank-and-file members of the state apparatus.

Yet the judicial system exhibited paternalistic tendencies, at least toward members of the lower classes. A consideration of class origin was expected to influence the measure of punishment—with workers and peasants receiving lighter sentences—though not the determination of guilt. Progressive-minded social scientists exerted a strong influence on judicial thinking in the early years of Soviet power. Drawing on some of the latest European social theory, many attributed a powerful corrupting role to the social environment. The criminal acts of persons of lower-class social background were often justified or explained by poor upbringing or harsh living conditions.[33]

Moreover, in contrast with the treatment of so-called political criminals, which gradually became harsher beginning in 1920, regular criminals were handled relatively leniently. The people's courts in 1920 sentenced 582,571 people to various punishments, the vast majority for regular crimes. Of these, 199,182 received jail time, nearly 80,000 on suspended sentences. The remainder, some 400,000, were punished with fines, social work, reprimands, and other lesser penalties.[34] The new Soviet courts were especially supportive of women, typically finding in their favor against abusive family members.

The ideological retreat

The Civil War was over by early 1920; during the summer, war broke out with Poland. By early fall, the Bolshevik regime was free of foreign threats. The human toll had been great. In addition to hundreds of thousands of lives lost in combat, many thousands—probably tens of thousands—of civilians were executed both extra-judicially and by sentence of the revolutionary tribunals. For example, in 1920, according to one reckoning, 5,757 people were shot by court-imposed verdicts.[35] Moreover, the economy lay in ruins. Industrial output had fallen to 13 percent of the prewar level. Heavy industry had completely collapsed, with iron production plummeting to 2 percent of the output before 1914. Major cities had lost half or more of their population. Livestock production had shrunk drastically. The leadership above all wanted to return the country to work and to focus on economic growth.

Yet open rebellion was soon a big problem. In January 1921, factory workers struck in Petrograd. The communist leadership brought the workers to heel with both repression and more food and clothing. Simultaneously, the authorities sought to return to the hoped-for mass-based support of the criminal justice system from among the lower classes. A commission was formed on January 13 to promote the formation in trade unions of commissions tasked with reviewing all criminal cases of persons of peasant and worker origin. The broader goal was to draw the masses into fighting crime within the working-class milieu and to convince them that Soviet criminal justice was but an extension of the proletarian dictatorship—their proletarian dictatorship.

Harder to satisfy were the thousands of sailors at the nearby fortress of Kronstadt who rebelled in March, demanding freedom of speech, assembly, and labor organization. Hundreds if not thousands were shot on the spot or left to die. Subsequently, some 2,103 alleged rebels were sentenced to execution, and thousands more were exiled to labor camps in the north and south.[36]

Meanwhile, peasant uprisings continued to break out south and east of Moscow. Since the Civil War was over and the anti-Bolshevik military forces had been defeated, the peasants had little fear of the landlords coming back. In March through May, the Bolshevik authorities imposed a state of siege in many of these areas, which empowered the Cheka and other armed forces to shoot suspected rebels on the spot. In addition to massive punitive measures, local authorities carefully orchestrated show trials, such as one in Ishim, in the Omsk region of Siberia, in February 1921. Local party officials thought it would be clever to put on trial simultaneously a half-dozen civil servants who had mistreated peasants and nearly 100 peasant rebels fighting against the Soviet regime.[37] The authorities planned out in advance who would receive harsh sentences and who lenient ones. The purpose was to show the benevolence and the might of Soviet power.

Simultaneously, the Party proclaimed a New Economic Policy (NEP), which embodied some of the demands of discontented workers, soldiers, and peasants. In a "retreat on the economic front," the government halted forced grain confiscations and decriminalized the retail trade in agricultural and other products. The retreat was to be temporary, because for Marxists not only private property but also free economic exchange had to be eradicated in order to build socialism.

The struggle against peasant rebels and "bandits" continued into 1922 and at times resulted in terrible carnage. A government order of June 11, 1921, prescribed execution "on the spot without trial" for suspected rebels who refused to identify themselves, for those who failed to surrender weapons, and for family members hiding "bandits." In the case of the escape of a family of "bandits," their property should be confiscated and redistributed to peasants loyal to Soviet power and their houses burned down. Troops, artillery, and poison gas were also used to crush the rebellions, especially the massive one in Tambov province southeast of Moscow.[38]

Tragically, the widespread confiscation of grain, which had depressed planting, was exacerbated by an intensive dry spell. A horrific famine resulted. By the end of 1922, at least 1.5 million people had died from starvation and disease. The government itself supplied little support to the hunger victims, nor did it allow civic organizations to help, except foreign agencies like the American Relief Administration. This assistance was decisive, however: without it, millions more would have died.

The retreat on the "economic front" was accompanied by an offensive on the political and ideological fronts, because the Bolshevik leaders did not want to give up too much or to stop building socialism. They were also afraid of resurgent counterrevolution. The same Party Congress that adopted the NEP also imposed a ban on factions within the Communist Party. Not only were no other political parties allowed to take part in government, but even within the ruling Communist Party, it became illegal to form coalitions or groupings. A series of show trials against political and cultural activists took place as well, beginning with one in August 1921 against the "Petrograd Fighting Organization," supposedly led by a geography professor, V. N. Tagantsev. He and over 800 others—nearly all of them intellectuals, scholars, scientists, and students—were arrested, investigated, and tried. Their political convictions ranged from socialist to monarchist. Sixty-one were shot, including the Silver Age poet Nikolai Gumilev. Well over 100 were incarcerated in concentration camps and prisons. It seems that they did not constitute a unified political organization, much less a movement, and had posed next to no threat to the Bolshevik regime.[39]

Also in August 1921, a decree was adopted allowing for the banishment abroad of "citizens whose way of life was incompatible with the principles and way of life of the worker-peasant state."[40] This authority was applied from time to time against political dissidents throughout the history of Soviet Russia, for example, beginning with numerous anarchist leaders in January and Menshevik leaders in February 1922. In the most spectacular instance, in late summer and throughout the fall, this policy affected between 160 and 400 leading intellectuals, scientists, scholars, and engineers, who were rounded up and shipped off to Europe with a prohibition on ever returning home.[41]

In the context of the NEP, the Bolshevik leadership talked a lot about reinforcing the principle of "revolutionary legality." They meant increasing respect for the law of both citizens and government officials. In November and December, a series of decisions, some adopted at the Ninth Congress of Soviets, in December 23–28, 1921, aimed at strengthening the courts, limiting the power of the political police, and increasing sanctions against false denunciations and false testimony by expert witnesses in judicial investigations and in court. A decree of November 30 provided a full amnesty for lower-rank fighters in the anti-Bolshevik military forces, though participants in "banditism," counterrevolutionary plots, espionage, armed rebellion, and anti-Soviet activism were not eligible.[42] The Commissariat of Justice strongly advocated abolishing the 117 functioning concentration camps, but other senior government officials rejected the proposal. The camps were maintained under the control of the People's Commissariat of Internal Affairs, or NKVD.

As part of the official campaign against lawlessness, the central leadership abolished the Cheka in February 1922 and replaced it with the Main Political Administration, or GPU. This new institution was to have no extrajudicial authority for search and arrest, much less for summary executions. Unlike the Cheka, however, its creation was announced as a permanent, legally established institution. All political crime cases discovered and investigated by the GPU were to be transferred to the revolutionary tribunals or people's courts. Over the next several months, however, the GPU's powers expanded, first to include the political security of the borders of the RSFSR, then censorship over all publications, then control over correspondence (save diplomatic), next (in August) administrative exile, and finally (in October) to shoot on the spot people caught in the act of armed robbery.[43] Presumably, the latter power could be applied to anyone caught with a weapon in hand. The GPU also maintained a system of secret detention sites. After the USSR was created in December 1922, the GPU, renamed the OGPU, was given authority over the entire country.

Two big show trials took place in the summer: against Socialist-Revolutionary activists and against Russian Orthodox church leaders. The outcome was a foregone conclusion—the political police were behind both trials. Several death sentences were issued, but, because of international pressure, those against the socialists were commuted; by contrast, four of the religious defendants were executed secretly and for no other reason than their nonviolent resistance to the confiscation of church valuables in the spring. During the trial against Socialist-Revolutionaries, huge crowds allegedly gathered at the courthouse, demanding the death penalty. A couple dozen such agitators were invited into the courtroom. The defense advocate, Nikolai Murav'ev, who had devoted his life to defending radical activists before the revolution, objected that such interventions trampled upon the rules of criminal procedure.[44] The judge rejected this objection on the grounds that the tribunal was being guided by its "revolutionary conscience" and "a revolutionary conception of proletarian law." Murav'ev then refused to continue with the defense. For these actions, he was arrested by the GPU, locked up for several weeks, and then exiled administratively for three years (but allowed to return to Moscow in summer 1923).

At the end of 1921, the Main Administration of Forced Labor held 40,913 prisoners. Of these, 28.5 percent were being held for regular crimes, 18.3 percent for antisocial behavior like drunkenness or prostitution, 18.3 percent for counterrevolution, 8.7 for official crimes, 8.5 percent for desertion from the military, and 1.9 percent for espionage. (The Main Punitive Department also held 73,194 prisoners, but such a breakdown is not available for that institution.)[45] It was not always easy, however, for judicial authorities to distinguish between regular criminal, counterrevolutionary, and antisocial behavior. There were no controlling legal statutes; judges were expected to decide on the basis of revolutionary conscience. Yet, in the context of War Communism, it had been difficult to know what might be viewed as falling under those categories. For example, riding public transportation without a ticket might be considered a counterrevolutionary act and certainly an antisocial one. Even after the adoption of the NEP, such confusion remained.

In forty-one provinces of the Russian Republic, the number of criminal cases increased by roughly 32 percent from 1920 through the first half of 1922.[46] The causes of the rise in criminality were various, including increased economic hardship brought about by the Civil War, inadequate police forces, and a dramatic surge in the number of homeless children and therefore juvenile offenders. Penological reformers developed programs for rehabilitating unattached youth, such as shepherding them into labor communes. In practice, the vast number of homeless children and the meager available government resources rendered the success of such programs something like an impossible dream. The number of militia personnel had increased dramatically during the Civil War but plummeted thereafter. Most of these officers were poorly trained. Nor could the police easily avail itself—for ideological reasons—of the skills of experienced prerevolutionary policemen.

To address such problems, the authorities often continued to deploy two unorthodox crime-fighting methods. First, the political police joined forces with the militia. Second, they applied extrajudicial punishments. Politburo decisions in 1922 empowered both regular and political police in six cities with high rates of crime (Moscow, Leningrad, Kharkov, Odessa, Rostov-on-Don, and Kiev) to submit recommendations for the banishment of repeat offenders for up to three years to a special committee (*Osoboe soveshchanie*—the same name and function as before 1917) of the NKVD.[47]

The share of criminality committed by women dramatically increased. Available statistics indicate that before the First World War women accounted for under 7 percent of all crimes committed in the Russian Empire, but by the end of the 1920s, roughly twice that proportion, or just over 14 percent.[48] Moreover, the range of crimes in which they participated also expanded, to include many crimes of violence. The likely explanation was significant material hardship, the liberation of women from traditional social control and disabilities, looser sexual morality in society generally, and the greater difficulty women encountered in seeking to benefit from opportunities offered by the NEP. At the same time, women received more lenient treatment than men in the criminal justice system, despite the fact that they contributed significantly to some violent crimes. For example, women committed 13.7 percent of assaults in 1922, but 23.4 percent in 1928.

Senior Bolshevik authorities were concerned that Soviet judges often referred in their decisions to prerevolutionary legal codes, including the 1845 Code of Punishments. Already in 1919, jurists at the Commissariat of Justice had begun drafting a new code. They drew heavily on the Imperial Russian 1903 Criminal Code, mostly for crimes against the person; they even borrowed from the 1845 Penal Code for crimes against personal property. The Soviet jurists moved in new directions in the sections regarding economic, official, and counterrevolutionary crimes. Severe penalties were prescribed for "economic crimes," generally meaning unauthorized profiteering, like producing and selling homebrew. "Official crimes," like malfeasance and corruption in office, were also to be punished harshly. Lenin advocated capital punishment for bribe-taking, but such a draconian stance did not make it into the final draft, which was adopted in May. The code defined counterrevolution very broadly. Merely intending to aid the international bourgeoisie in its alleged struggle against communist systems of property was deemed a counterrevolutionary act.[49] Such a broad definition of "state crime" was also reminiscent of the 1845 Penal Code.

Capital punishment was retained for various grave crimes, including counterrevolution, treason, rebellion, and subversion against the Soviet order (arts. 58–63), but only as a temporary measure. The death penalty was, nevertheless, applied frequently for armed robbery in the 1920s. Since most property was owned by the state, this crime was viewed above all as an attack on the state itself and the socialist economic and social system. The number of death sentences issued by revolutionary tribunals fluctuated but basically declined from 1,285 in 1923 and 1,748 in 1924 down to 457 in 1927. About half of these sentences, on average, were commuted.[50] Death statistics for the political police went in the opposite direction. Having declined from at least 10,000 in 1921 to nearly 2,000 in 1922, the number of executions held steady at over 2,000 for most years before spiking to over 20,000 in 1929.[51]

For most ordinary crimes, however, the code was lenient by prerevolutionary standards and closer to Western European practice of the time. The emphasis was on noncustodial punishments (including fines and suspended sentences), shorter prison terms, compulsory work as a means to rehabilitate offenders, and a move away from retribution as the main goal of criminal justice. Compulsory work, a concept devised by German penologists, entailed requiring a convict to work at his or her ordinary job or some other assigned task for less pay than would be normal for that activity. Such a punishment made sense in urban areas for people who already had jobs, but in an era of high unemployment, it was impractical. Following the requirements of the new code, in 1923, only 20 percent of convicts spent time in prison. And the terms of imprisonment were usually short—the vast majority under two years. Even the most serious regular crimes were punished leniently. A conviction for nonpolitical premeditated murder would land one in prison for only three years. The code also gave judges wide latitude in determining punishments. They often imposed the minimum allowable penalty, especially for defendants of lower-class backgrounds. Many prisoners were released early by penal officials and periodic amnesties. Penal reformers were eager to facilitate the rehabilitation of criminals. Educational and cultural opportunities were provided for the first time in Russian prisons. A regimen of progressively more comfortable stages of confinement, dependent on good behavior, was also instituted. The economic devastation brought about by the Civil War and War Communism, however, meant there were never enough funds to pursue reformist goals.[52]

Procedural rules adopted in May 1922 maintained the principle of judicial discretion, to be governed by revolutionary conscience. Purely formal law was to be avoided. The rules also required that whenever a procurator appeared in court, a defense advocate also was required to appear. Given the relative paucity of defense advocates throughout the country, and their primary focus on civil cases, procurators typically did not participate in criminal trials. As before 1917, the Procuracy was intended to ensure the proper adherence to legal principles of the entire bureaucracy. In particular, it supervised most of the criminal investigation work leading up to trials, though the vast majority of criminal cases throughout the 1920s and early 1930s were preceded by no preliminary investigation.[53] In such cases, investigators simply compiled an accusatory act based on the police inquest. All criminal trials handled by the people's courts required the presence of two lay assessors, who functioned somewhat like jurors, in addition to the judge. Ordinary people could also participate as public accusers, though few did.

The Soviet authorities worried about the criminal justice system losing touch with the people and therefore required judges to conduct some of their trials in "visiting sessions." Such sessions were called "show trials" (*pokazatel'nye protsessy*)—using the exact same name as for the political trials mounted against alleged enemies of the Soviet state. In both cases, the purpose was pedagogical and propagandistic much more than to promote justice as such. Whereas the political show trials occurred periodically and in bouts, the regular criminal show trials were a standard feature of Soviet criminal justice in the 1920s and 1930s.

Throughout the Soviet era, personal connections could save one from the harshest forms of criminal justice. Leading Bolsheviks in all walks of life regularly used their personal clout to intercede on behalf of friends, relatives, colleagues, persons they admired, or simply out of compassion. Some intellectuals and cultural figures, like the author Maxim Gorky, made an avocation of such benevolence, but it seems that nearly everyone within the system—that is, all supporters of the Bolshevik regime—did so regularly. After all, the system could be cruel and unpredictable.

The criminal justice system included several other extralegal and subjective elements. Confining people in a concentration camp was not a prescribed form of punishment in the 1922 Criminal Code, yet the GPU retained that authority, giving the judicial system a dual nature: one aspect relatively formal and one highly arbitrary. Class bias was retained: members of the lower classes were supposed to enjoy especial indulgence. The concept of "social danger" was incorporated into the code. "Social defense"— removing or correcting the social danger— was considered a more important goal than punishment. "Socially dangerous" and "parasitical" elements were regularly expelled from Moscow on this basis, mostly via administrative exile.[54] Many unwelcome persons were so-called Nepmen, or private traders allowed to buy and sell goods and services under the NEP, but viewed with deep suspicion by dedicated Bolsheviks. All such mass search operations were the beginning of a mind-set aiming at social control, a mind-set that would result in a frenetic sweep of the country resulting in hundreds of thousands of arrests and executions in 1937 and 1938.

The primary method of dealing with all such "undesirables" was administrative exile, just as it had been before 1917. Under the auspices of the GPU (OGPU from November 1923), the special committee on exile continued to evaluate and essentially rubber-stamp administrative-exile recommendations. The committee assessed and passed judgment on thirty to fifty cases at each session—not a recipe for careful deliberation. In 1924 alone, the OGPU dealt with 8,074 people in this way.[55] For all the differences between the Imperial and the Soviet regimes, they had in common the belief of government officials that they could not fulfill the duties of ordinary administration without recourse to extrajudicial punishments.

The key factor in the recruitment and retention of judicial personnel was their loyalty to the Soviet system. The vast majority were Communist

Party members. Few had legal training or even much general education. This was in keeping with the suspiciousness with which most the leadership of the new regime—like many of their tsarist predecessors—viewed trained jurists. For this reason, during the 1920s, the authorities devoted few resources to legal education. In fact, the number of judicial personnel with formal legal expertise declined.

A further judicial restructuring in November 1922 abolished the revolutionary tribunals and created a unified system of courts, running from people's courts, to provincial courts, to a new Supreme Court (see Figure 4.2). Other tribunals, under the auspices of various government agencies, including the transportation system and the military, continued to function. Military tribunals carried out most of the executions applied in the country during the 1920s.

The first Constitution of the USSR, enacted in January 1924, allowed regional authorities, including constituent "Republics," to adopt specific laws but reserved to the central government authority over the criminal justice system in general. As such, it adopted, also in 1924, the Fundamental Principles of Criminal Law of the USSR. This statute again preserved capital punishment as an exceptional and temporary measure. Local

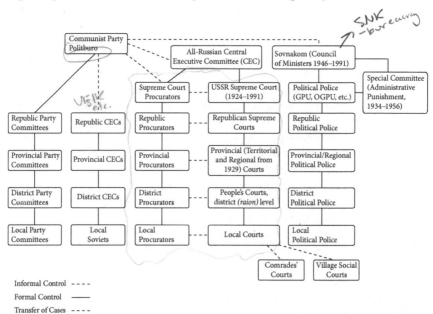

FIGURE 4.2 *Judicial organization of the USSR from 1922 to 1991. Senior government, and especially party officials continued to intervene in criminal justice, though formally the judiciary was independent. The secret police continued to wield significant judicial power. In 1934, a Special Committee (Osoboe soveshchanie) was re-instituted to exile or incarcerate "socially dangerous" persons for up to five years. This institution was abolished in 1953.*

juridical particularities in national minority regions, including separate and autonomous courts and legal rules and practices, persisted at least in some places well into the 1920s.

Nikolai Krylenko, a leading prosecutor, undertook efforts in 1925 to limit the arbitrary power of the OGPU and to subordinate its work in the judicial realm to the Commissariat of Justice. The head of the political police, Dzerzhinskii, argued forcefully that his work was essential for combating counterrevolutionary threats to Soviet power. The Bolshevik leadership were sufficiently frightened of capitalist encirclement, vestiges of the old regime, secret counterrevolutionary activism, and other potential threats to their regime that the political police—whatever the acronym of the day—remained a powerful parallel system of justice for dealing with any alleged offenses that did not fit within the formal criminal justice institutions.

In the 1920s, both the regular nonjudicial state apparatus and the political police deprived tens of thousands of people of their liberty. At this time, the vast majority of the 185,000 inmates in 1927 were held in prisons under the auspices of the prison administration, a department of the People's Commissariat of Internal Affairs (NKVD), yet roughly 30,000 were in the control of the political police, several thousand of them in remote locations like the Solovetsky Monastery on the Solovetsky Islands in the White Sea.[56] Here living conditions were desperate.

After Lenin died in January 1924, a power struggle among possible successors raged. It involved personalities and policies. The main contenders were the charismatic and intellectually brilliant Trotsky and the homely but politically astute and tactically clever Stalin. Others played supporting roles. The policy clashes concerned above all the pace of "building socialism." Trotsky advocated rapid industrialization by squeezing resources to fund it from the peasantry, since the state had already taken all other major sources of wealth. Stalin claimed the mantel of Lenin, seeking to carry forward the NEP.

By 1926–1927, the NEP had enabled the country to return to production levels in agriculture and industry previously achieved only before the revolution. Still, more grain was needed for export and feeding industrial workers. Heavy taxation, confiscation of property for failure to pay, and the high price of manufactured goods sparked rural discontent, even violent attacks against officials. The Bolsheviks blamed such troubles on the better-off peasants, called "kulaks." Yet most peasants only wanted economic freedom, reasonable taxes, fair prices, and the right to benefit from the fruits of their labor. Few peasants had the intellectual ability to formulate a political position much less a program. The party leaders, for their part, were pursuing contradictory goals. They wanted agricultural development but feared the stronger peasant households and the "class warfare" this would bring. Ultimately, Stalin cut the Gordian knot and set Russia on a path toward radical fulfillment of communist ideals—and a dramatic hardening of both criminal justice and political repression.

- 1936-8 — Great Terror

Show trials
 ↳ example
 ↳ Scapegoat for economic problems

5

The Era of Stalin

Stalin outmaneuvered his rivals by pretending to be a team player, controlling patronage jobs within the Communist Party, and formulating a theoretical departure from Leninism already in 1924. Lenin and the other leaders had assumed that backward Russia could not build socialism alone but needed the help of advanced capitalist countries. After Moscow's efforts to promote revolution in Europe failed in 1919–1923, Stalin argued that the Bolsheviks could "build socialism in one country." He and a shifting coalition of allies expelled Trotsky from the Communist Party in 1927 and then turned on other potential rivals, gradually adopting Trotsky's hard-line perspective on squeezing wealth from the countryside. The party leadership hiked the taxes on the peasantry, slashed the official price paid for grain, excluded private traders from grain procurement, and raised the cost of manufactured goods. Many peasants responded by withholding their produce, planting other crops, failing to pay their taxes, lashing out against rural officials, and refusing to buy factory-made merchandise. Gradually, most party leaders advocated an offensive against the "kulaks."

Apparently rising criminality pushed the leadership to launch a campaign against hooliganism in 1926. The following year, the regular courts issued nine times more sentences against such offenders than in 1926. Most such cases were handled extrajudicially by the militia, which issued hundreds of thousands of fines during the campaign. In mid-1927, the Politburo authorized local OGPU institutions to conduct extrajudicial punishment, including the execution, of persons accused of counterrevolution or banditry. International tensions in 1927 provoked a "war scare" that the leadership used to justify more pressure on the countryside.

With tensions mounting both domestically and internationally, in early 1927 the Worker-Peasant Inspectorate investigated the criminal justice system. It found that provincial judges halted 49.3 percent of all serious criminal cases, largely because of inadequate investigatory and other preparatory work. Of those that made it to trial, one quarter ended in acquittal.[1] Other studies indicated that massive corruption, especially of the police but also of judicial personnel, explained part of the failure to reach convictions. These personnel were generally overburdened with paperwork and efforts to enforce an overwhelming thicket of laws. Periodic campaigns against bribery occasionally flared up but with few positive results. The weak—or almost inexistent—legal training and semi-literacy of many judges also contributed to judicial inefficiency. It remained a cardinal point for the Bolshevik leadership, however, that judges should stem from the lower classes and profess allegiance to communist ideology.

In 1927 and 1928, Soviet judicial experts and political leaders debated on how to improve the system. In keeping with the cultural revolution that began in 1928, which promoted radical solutions, village social courts in the countryside and comrades' courts in factories began to develop, where ordinary people could try members of their collectives for minor offenses.[2] The rural courts apparently functioned more successfully, but the goal of unburdening the regular courts of overwhelming dockets of cases failed, because precisely at this time major campaigns against perceived enemies commenced and overloaded the courts anew. New rules adopted in 1929 greatly simplifying judicial procedure were also aimed at unburdening the courts. Henceforth, police inquests were deemed fully adequate pretrial preparation, and for many lesser offenses (such as hooliganism, petty theft, and homebrewing), no lay assessors needed to be present and no appeals were permitted. Such judicial streamlining only increased in the years ahead.

The Great Break

From early 1928, the OGPU became directly involved with grain collection using extrajudicial punishments against "speculators," "kulaks," and others who resisted.[3] The judicial authorities now actively enforced Article 107 of the Criminal Code, an obscure and little-used statute banning speculation, or profiteering. Thousands of officials were also prosecuted for slackness in collecting grain. Many thousands of peasants were arrested for obstructing the collection campaign.

Amid worries about "kulak" terror and foreign threats, on March 10, 1928, sixty engineers, including several German nationals, were arrested in the North Caucasus town of Shakhty and charged, on flimsy evidence, with sabotaging Soviet industry at the behest of Western capitalists. Some of them confessed, though apparently because of harsh interrogation methods and psychological pressure. Many admitted to their defense advocates that their confessions were untrue. Further pressure from the political police, however, induced most of them to return to their original assertions. Brought to trial the following month, thirty-four of the alleged saboteurs were sentenced to prison for up to ten years. Eleven were sentenced to death, but six had their sentences commuted because of their confessions. Five were executed. This was the first major political show trial in a half-dozen years, and the harbinger of many more to come. It also resulted in the prosecution of thousands of technical specialists (2,500 in the third quarter of 1931 alone).[4] Yet Stalin and the party leadership realized they depended too much on such expertise to permit its arbitrary destruction, and therefore such prosecutions slowed to a trickle for a number of years.

By this time, prison overcrowding had reached massive proportions, despite periodic amnesties. The main reason for the rise was a dramatic increase in the number of acts once again defined as criminal, such as producing alcohol for one's own consumption or buying and selling vegetables. Several ultimately vain efforts were undertaken to resolve the problem of overcrowding. The new Criminal Code of 1926 stipulated more lenient sentencing, especially shorter prison terms. Prison officials, for their part, gave many prisoners the right to take temporary absences. A government edict of March 26, 1928, addressed the problem with a recommendation for imposing more sentences of compulsory work. Here was a clash within the government whose leading officials considered themselves standard-bearers of liberation but who at the same time criminalized many ordinary activities and sought to micromanage society minutely.

The shift toward forced collectivization—requiring peasants to pool their resources and labor for the benefit of the state—dramatically altered the trajectory of criminal justice in the USSR. The justice system began to be used much more both to provide a coerced labor force and to punish alleged enemies of Soviet power. A decree of July 11, 1929, directed the ordinary penal system to expand the use of penal colonies for work in industry, agriculture, timber-production, and construction, with the ultimate goal of phasing out prisons entirely.[5] The entire system was, moreover, to become completely self-sufficient, squeezing out as much labor as possible from the inmates. Part of the reason for this turn in policy was the commencement of the First Five-Year Plan, announced the previous year, with the goal of rapidly industrializing the country. Squeezing labor in town and country was meant to fund the whole project.

A series of political moves pointed toward collectivization. In June, Article 61 of the Criminal Code was amended to authorize imposing fivefold tax obligations on peasants who fell behind in their payments to the state. "Kulaks" and "non-laboring elements" also lost their voting rights, which diminished their political influence. Throughout the summer, perhaps 200,000 party activists, Komsomol, trade-union organizers, and factory workers were sent into the countryside to assist with grain collection. A directive of September 9 forbade peasants to sell grain on the free market, even after they had met their delivery quota to the state. Mass arrests of persons engaged in such activity netted 28,344 unfortunates by November 4, according to incomplete data. Hundreds of indictments were brought against officials for inaction and abetting alleged profiteers.[6] A week after

Stalin's "cult of personality" began with his grandiose fiftieth birthday celebration on December 21, 1929, he announced universal collectivization and "liquidation of kulaks as a class." Although Stalin temporarily slowed the onslaught in March 1930, with his "Dizzy with Success" speech, presented in the face of massive peasant unrest, by summer 100,000s of despoiled peasants had been freighted to distant "special settlements" as vast armies of slave labor.

These developments radically affected criminal justice. First, they encouraged officials at all levels of government to disregard the law and normal legal procedure. Second, judicial officials were pressed into the collectivization campaign, thus largely removing them from the ordinary criminal justice system. The courts, police, and judges in the countryside devoted nearly all their time to promoting the collectivization, spring sowing, fall harvesting, and "dekulakization" campaigns. In other words, the criminal justice system was harnessed almost wholly to the perceived needs of agriculture, probably a unique phenomenon in the annals of legal history. Investigations were typically expedited, as were the trials themselves, which often took place in the out-of-doors. One way to make up for the insufficiency of judicial personnel was the recruitment of "socialist substitutes," ordinary people brought in to various government agencies to supplement existing staff. In the years 1930–1933, roughly 40 percent of such laypersons worked within judicial institutions.[7] Naturally, their competence was uneven. Another way to make up for insufficient personnel was the handling of simple and petty cases using rushed procedure. Likewise, many petty crimes, including hooliganism, which was on a rising trend, were handled in large proportion by the police through administrative process.

Third, state resources were diverted away from many ordinary administrative tasks and toward the processing of at least 381,026 families—1,803,392 individuals—exiled as "kulaks" in 1930–1931.[8] Fourth, such actions provoked huge peasant resistance. Throughout 1930, officials counted 13,754 bouts of significant unrest, involving over 3.3 million participants, the largest share concentrated in February–April. Such numbers dwarfed those experienced during the Revolution of 1905–1906.[9] In this context, it is not surprising that the role of the OGPU as both an executive and a judicial arm of government dramatically expanded and indeed became central to Soviet governance and criminal justice.

Many otherwise ordinary activities were criminalized during the era of collectivization, such as the slaughter of one's own livestock and the theft of "socialist property," including gathering grain remnants lying in the fields after the harvest—the traditional poor-person's occupation of gleaning. The latter action was made a capital offense by a law of August 7, 1932. It seems almost inconceivable that stealing a small quantity of grain could earn one the death penalty, yet such was the case. Not surprisingly, many officials turned a blind eye to this "crime," and many judges issued more lenient sentences than required by the letter of the law. Nevertheless, over the next nine months, enforcing the law resulted in 9,163 executions and 152,908 people sentenced to 10 years' "deprivation of freedom."[10] The endless stories of women with children, old people, and the poor suffering heinous punishments merely for such "crimes" as gathering twelve stalks of grain are harrowing. An extreme and tragic irony resides in the fact that over-hasty and slipshod grain collection resulted in significant wastage in these years despite hordes of officials, party activists, and factory workers descending on the villages to ensure the successful harvesting of grain.

The confiscation campaign prompted many peasants to sow less and to tend their crops less conscientiously. If the state was going to take most of the harvest, why bother? Consequently, famine struck the USSR in late 1932 and raged into summer 1933. (Poor weather seems to have played a minor role.) The mortality levels peaked in March–April. Only Moscow and Leningrad mostly escaped its ravages, thanks to large grain reserves.

Rapid industrialization also resulted in big problems in factories and construction sites. The fast tempo and unfeasible targets caused breakdowns, shoddy output, harsh treatment of workers, and inevitable scapegoating. High-handed treatment by managers might have resulted in a flood of prosecutions, but Stalin advocated a policy of protecting technical specialists so necessary for industrialization. Procurators were sent to inspect factories for criminal negligence, abuse of power, accidents on the job, and defective goods.[11] Government officials were especially concerned to ferret out persons suspected of purposely triggering accidents, producing defective output, and causing shortages of goods and food. The prosecution of alleged offenders does not seem to have diminished these problems. Nor, perhaps, were they intended to. Certainly, they shifted the blame from the system itself to specific individuals. Even so, relatively few alleged industrial malefactors suffered prosecution. Moreover, judges in the people's courts tended to avoid imposing harsh sentences. Sometimes senior officials, including Stalin himself, pushed for stiffer laws and sanctions. A decree of December 8, 1933, for example, made factory managers and foremen liable to up to five years' imprisonment for the production of shoddy goods under their watch. Yet a government seeking to control completely and radically transform at the same time one of the biggest economies of the world—without regard to the law of supply and demand, the price mechanism, individual incentives, and other unavoidable principles of economic life—had to result in inefficiency and even chaos. Prosecuting people for such inevitable results was arbitrary and unfair. It also had to result in confusion, discontent, and mistrust of the government.

Instead of trying to make the economy more consumer- and worker-friendly, the government issued a flurry of laws and instructions aimed at further strengthening social control. A decree of November 15, 1932, defined missing work for even one day as grounds for termination and thus loss of ration tickets. Far more significant, a system of internal passports was instituted on December 27, 1932. It was adopted to control migration, to keep track of labor, to filter out the wrong type of people ("kulaks, criminals, and other antisocial elements"), to determine who should live in the major cities, and indirectly to tie down the peasantry. Since peasants did not receive passports, they thus became second-class citizens. A few weeks later, the central authorities forbade the migration of peasants from the grain-producing countryside. The leadership supposedly feared that such human movement was being organized by foreign and domestic enemies of Soviet power, though it was a normal survival strategy traditionally adopted in times of dearth. By early March 1933, the political police had tracked down 219,500 peasants and had sent 186,600 back to their villages and the others to concentration camps.[12]

Amid the starvation, cannibalism was rife. As there was no provision in the Criminal Code against it, police and investigators were instructed to transfer all such cases (even those involving murder) to the political police. Hundreds of accused cannibals were shot or imprisoned.[13]

Scholars still dispute the number of "excess deaths" brought about by the famine, but most reckon the population losses (including children never born because of the harsh conditions) to have ranged from 5.5 to 7 million.[14] The greatest devastation occurred in Ukraine, which lost between 3.5 and 4.5 million people, and Kazakhstan, where some 1.5 million perished. It seems incontestable that this great tragedy was caused largely by government policies. The famine itself, however, was publicly denied and treated as a state secret in the USSR for many years. Merely to have tried to report on it would have landed one in prison or worse.

Since the government and the Communist Party represented themselves to the people as infallible, other causes of people's hardship had to be found. One category of scapegoats that became a major target was ordinary criminals. In January 1933, at a plenary session of the Party's Central Committee, Stalin specifically linked ordinary criminality with class war and counterrevolution. He clearly intended the passport law to serve in this struggle. One can argue that Stalin purposely politicized ordinary crime as the latest "front" on which to fight against the enemies of socialism and Soviet power. That is not to say there was not a problem of crime; the inefficiencies of the system undoubtedly exacerbated it. Official reports revealed widespread criminality throughout the economy. Factory workers pilfered raw materials, supplies, equipment, and output from their factories. White-collar workers embezzled funds from their offices. Purchasing agents and other employees received vast quantities of bribes. One report estimated that in the region and city of Moscow alone, over 25 million rubles of goods were stolen or embezzled in 1933.[15]

Government officials wanted to control all economic activity in the country and considered it a crime to buy and sell goods and services without official permission, no matter how small the scale. Despite harsh laws against such activity, many entrepreneurs managed to earn a decent living making and selling clothing and other goods. Others stood in long lines for scarce consumer goods and resold them for a profit. Still others stole merchandise from state stores, warehouses, and factories and resold it on the black market or in secondhand and consignment shops. These shops did a brisk business off "class-aliens," who often needed to liquidate property quickly and cheaply merely to survive, and people whose property was simply confiscated. All such wheeling and dealing required "cover" typically obtained through bribery of police and other officials. It is not surprising, in fact, that seeking to influence officials with money and gifts flourished. This became a huge problem throughout the Soviet era and beyond. Naturally, both the scarcity of consumer goods and bribery aimed at obtaining them stemmed from the criminalization in the USSR of producing, buying, and selling goods as a private activity.

Upheaval in the countryside gave rise to increased social disorder. Gangs of bandits, often involving "dekulakized" peasants, operated throughout the country, raiding farms, villages, depots, armories, and other emporia likely to contain goods and valuables. Another big source of criminality was the new massive wave of homeless and unsupervised children—hundreds of thousands across the country. Most of them were orphaned during collectivization. Many orphans turned to crime; some joined criminal gangs. All such people were typically categorized as "socially harmful." During the 1930s, this category, like the passport system, was deployed more and more often, by a state that refused to tolerate autonomy and personal liberty, as a handy means of controlling both floating populations and people without fixed means of support or a place of residence. Statistics for 1935 indicate that throughout the country the police punished 1,370,000 people for violating the passport laws, of whom nearly a million were fined; all were expelled from the places where they had been arrested.[16] In a large proportion of cases, the enforcement of the passport regulations enabled the authorities to capture fugitives, ex-convicts, and socially suspect "elements" who were then placed under police surveillance.

It must have been concerning to government officials that the number of regular police, the militia, remained very small throughout the NEP and even into the early 1930s. It seems that in 1930 there were at most 100,000 regular police of all kinds throughout the entire USSR, a number that had increased to some 125,000 in 1935.[17] This was more than twice as many as before the revolution, even considering the increased population, but for a state aiming to control society far more extensively than under the tsars, it was inadequate. In any event, a single policeman might have responsibility for a vast area, both in towns and the countryside. The level of training of the personnel, moreover, as well as their equipment and pay, was poor.[18] Many did not have adequate housing. Few had access to vehicles. Most people were suspicious of the police, as well. Such conditions help explain why many police fell to bribe-taking or even petty crime. Among the forms of corruption they engaged in was selling blank passports, thus undermining the system of social control. The two major cities of the country, Moscow and Leningrad, enjoyed far higher ratios of police to people, yet even there criminality was rife. Crime was especially bad in areas that had received large numbers of exiled "kulaks," like the far north, the Urals region, and Western Siberia.

Starting in late 1930, Stalin and the party leadership began transferring control of the regular police to the OGPU. The militia remained formally subordinated to local Soviets, but the ultimate authority henceforth rested with the political police. The reform placed militia officers under the jurisdiction of military courts for offenses committed in the line of duty. A reason for the transfer of authority was to enlist militia support in collectivizing the peasantry, though many of them proved reluctant to take part.

In order to expand its scope, the militia organized a huge network of voluntary police assistants, essentially vigilante groups, though under the strict control of the state. In spring 1934, there were apparently more than 325,000 such organizations operating in towns and the countryside across the USSR. The political police had another vast army of auxiliary support in its burgeoning informant network. In early 1935, official statistics indicated that some half-million informants throughout society reported to 27,650 case officers.[19] (The comparison with prerevolutionary Russia was stark. The political police in those times never disposed of more than 1,000 informants at any given moment; the total for the years 1880–1917 was roughly 10,000.)[20] Along with an informant network, the political and regular police also maintained detailed card catalogs and registry systems for keeping tabs on suspect populations. In each city of 200,000 or more people, a complement of nine full-time staff were supposed to track them.[21]

The political police were far more numerous than before 1917. The total number of personnel was roughly 21,000 at the start of 1933, not counting OGPU prison guards, border guards, and some 50,000 internal troops. To these forces, in 1933 the regime added another 25,000 officials, all party members, and around 3,000 OGPU staff, who were to be stationed in nearly 3,400 political departments scattered around the countryside to maintain surveillance over the newly formed collective farms.[22] Such statistics bear witness to the far greater political control the Soviet government was seeking to exercise over the population than the rulers of prerevolutionary Russia. The vast size of the political police under Stalin can be largely explained by the politicization and criminalization of what in other societies was ordinary economic behavior.

During this era, harsh and numerous punishments were meted out by the political police. But the courts also issued much harsher sentences, including the death penalty and lengthier prison terms. In 1933, for example, judges condemned three times more people to prison than in 1929, and the average term in 1933 was a few years, as compared to six months in 1928.[23] The number of government officials prosecuted for failures of one kind or another connected with collectivization—ironically, for both doing too much and doing too little—increased. It was hard for officials to know what was expected of them. For example, a largely unspoken demand was the labeling and punishment as a "kulak" of anyone who resisted collectivization. But technically people with a family member in the Red Army and several other categories of citizen were not supposed to suffer that penalty. In practice, many of them did.

At the same time, many ordinary criminals still benefited from the policy of lenient punishments, especially noncustodial obligatory labor. Almost 75 percent of all "hooligans," for example, received noncustodial sentences in 1932. The harshness of one's penalty depended on many factors, however, as the criminal justice system became more and more politicized. Gradually, over the course of the decade, noncustodial sentences declined. Prison sentences, by contrast, increased from 24.7 percent of punishments in 1934 to around 40 percent over the next several years.[24]

By May 1933, the party leadership had concluded that the "war on the peasantry" was over and had been successful. It was now possible, they thought, to curtail "the application of mass exile and harsh forms of repression," including the mass application of the August 7 law. (It was still applied, though more selectively.) A broad discharge of prisoners was immediately undertaken. It seems that none of these prisoners were freed but instead were transferred to other places of confinement, especially OGPU labor camps and special settlements, though also to terms of compulsory labor.[25] Meanwhile, local officials still condemned peasants to relatively harsh punishments for petty theft. (So much so that decrees of June and December 1935 sought to curtail excessive arrests, though apparently without great success.) It is hard to imagine a more contradictory set of policies and attitudes. Prisons were systematically filled because it was hard to survive without engaging in criminal activity. They were then emptied periodically because of insufficient capacity. The leadership considered it imperative to fight mercilessly against the enemies they imagined lurking in every corner, but they also saw themselves as merciful and benevolent toward loyal citizens.

The peasantry had been cowed into submission, its will broken. Food had been and would continue to be used as a weapon. But the regime pulled back and decriminalized many routine activities, like growing vegetables in one's kitchen garden and selling them for profit. In fact, the government created a network of "collective farm" markets. This side labor supplemented the entire country's diet for the next several decades. A variety of material and moral incentives were also offered to promote heroic agricultural output, following the model of Alexey Stakhanov, a coal miner who on August 31, 1935, dramatically exceeded his normal daily quota. Even so, the Soviet agricultural system never functioned well and resulted in periodic food shortages. Any troubles were, moreover, blamed on a variety of scapegoats—like wreckers, squanderers, misappropriators, and other alleged evil-doers, including many Communists and senior government officials—but never the woefully inefficient and wasteful economic system itself, which was largely to blame.

"Stakhanovite"

In June 1934, the government adopted a law defining "betrayal of the motherland," in addition to betrayal of the revolution, as a form of treason. This law incorporated the concept of criminal liability of family members of convicted traitors. Such guilt by association, which had been a cornerstone of Soviet jurisprudence from immediately after the revolution and had influenced the punishment of family members of "kulaks," became a routine feature of Soviet criminal justice. This policy also marked a return to an earlier cultural norm in Russia, which was strong in the early modern era and had gradually lost force toward the end of the Imperial era. By that time, the Western emphasis on individual responsibility had put down strong roots. The return to collective responsibility in Soviet criminal justice was part of a general repudiation of Western values and principles.

In July, the political police were reorganized and renamed the NKVD, with a subordinate state security organ, the GUGB, though this change did not diminish their scope, ubiquity, power, and extrajudicial authority. When, on December 1, the popular Leningrad party boss, Sergei Kirov, was murdered under mysterious circumstances, the NKVD acted with no more inhibition than the OGPU and in fact with much less, thanks to a law drafted by Stalin and adopted that very night to simplify legal procedure. The law required "terrorism" cases to be investigated and tried immediately and death sentences to be carried out upon conviction. The accused were to be informed of the charges against them a mere twenty-four hours before their trial and denied any legal counsel or appeal. Capital punishment, if imposed, was to be carried out at once. Within days, 70 people had been tried for "preparing terrorist actions against Soviet authorities"; 66 were sentenced to death.[26] In 1935 and 1936, roughly 100,000 people were convicted for counterrevolutionary crimes each year. Although they were arrested by the political police, military tribunals and special chambers within the regional courts heard roughly half of these cases. Accusations by the political police were not rubber stamped at this time, however, and many judges issued relatively lenient sentences.[27]

Ironically, 1934 had seen serious efforts to restore the authority of law.[28] Most important were official affirmations that the law was made for everyone, including government agents. Perhaps there was a sense among the party leadership that during the collectivization drive, arbitrary administrative action had got out of control. It was one thing for Stalin and his close associates to ignore the law but quite another for officials up and down the hierarchy to do so. Yet grain collections still seemed to need coercive methods. It was also hard to get officials to hew to the letter and spirit of the law when habits of arbitrary power-wielding had grown deeply ingrained. At the end of 1934, senior officials ceased publicly promoting respect for the law, though behind the scenes such efforts continued.

Stalin and the party leadership undertook a campaign against juvenile crime with an edict dated April 7, 1935, which required trying children aged 12 and over for serious crimes of theft and violence according to adult laws and procedures. Part of the concern of the Soviet leaders was a new wave of "hooliganism"—an offense engaged in primarily by youths—throughout the 1920s and into the 1930s. The edict was part of a campaign against "hooliganism" in 1935 and 1936. Technically, juvenile offenders could even face the death penalty, though in practice it seems rarely to have been applied to them. Judicial authorities moved quickly to create separate juvenile chambers within some people's courts to try young offenders. In most courts, however, they were tried in the same way as adult criminals. Unscrupulous school officials sought to unburden themselves of problem children by sending them to court. Over half of those tried under the new rules, during the first year, received jail time, though typically shorter terms than for adults. They were supposed to be sent to special juvenile corrective-labor colonies, but since few existed, most young offenders were sent to ordinary labor camps of the Gulag.[29] Local judicial officials often tried to soften the treatment of juvenile offenders, but central officials frequently hindered such efforts.

Soviet legal institutions were reorganized in 1936 in a further effort to make them more efficient and effective. The Procuracy, Supreme Court, and Commissariat of Justice were all further centralized. In particular, the Procuracy was given greater power of supervision over questions of legality throughout the governmental apparatus. As before 1917, procurators exercised wide authority over criminal justice. They supervised preliminary investigations, prosecuted cases, monitored the legality of the proceedings, and could appeal any court decisions. In this way, they enjoyed greater power and prestige than trial judges. The power of procurators to oversee the fulfillment of the laws by all commissariats and subordinate agencies was also enhanced. An All-Union Commissariat of Justice was created with authority over "republican" justice commissariats and a supervisory function over all courts throughout the country. The 1936 "Stalin" Constitution confirmed this judicial centralization.

The new Constitution seems to have had more of a propagandistic than a concrete and juridical purpose. The document guaranteed many civil rights cherished in democratic societies such as freedom of speech, press, assembly, and religion, though in practice the citizenry could not exercise them. Presumably, the leadership hoped to use the document to project an image of the USSR as a member of the democratic community of states, in large part to make possible an alliance with them against Nazi Germany. Soviet citizens, one supposes, were also expected to welcome the appearance of the legality and normality of their state, so that no matter what injustices they might suffer or witness in practice at least they could have a favorable impression of the intentions of their government.

In all polities, the letter and spirit of the law and legal institutions never coincide absolutely with day-to-day practice of government officials and citizens. All people cut corners some of the time; some people cut corners all of the time. But such a dualistic functioning of parallel realms of governance and justice loomed especially large in the Soviet Union. For one thing, getting almost anything done in Soviet society required personal connections, informal workarounds, breaking rules, and paying bribes. For another, local officials had an ingrained habit of ignoring directives from the center. This stemmed from something like a tradition of revolutionary anarchism but also from poor legal training, illiteracy, and general incompetence.

To resolve such issues, Stalin and his supporters carried out periodic "purges," that is, systematic and mass replacement of officials. (At this time, purging did not imply severe criminal punishment.) Tens of thousands of investigators, Procuracy staff, and judges, for example, were fired in 1934–1936. Replacing them took time, which of course increased inefficiency. Better legal training of staff was required and provided, though perpetually fell short. It could not have been otherwise, since only 250–300 lawyers were trained each year throughout a country of 160 million people.[30] Even training courses for existing officials, while expanded, could not keep pace with need. Inevitably, insufficiently trained legal officials resulted in inefficient and ineffective legal institutions, leading to more frustration and more purges.

One other major area of criminalizing what had been a legal right was the law of June 27, 1936, forbidding all abortions except those to save the life of the mother and to prevent the birth of babies with congenital disease. Abortion had been made legal in 1920. From that time, free abortions had been provided in hospitals. The purpose of the new law was largely to promote maternity, in order to mitigate the disastrous demographic results of collectivization. Inevitably, illegal abortions proliferated and led to prosecution. In the first quarter of 1937, for example, 1,228 underground practitioners were convicted.[31] There presumably would have been more convictions if not for an unwillingness on the part of judicial officials to apply the full rigor of the law. Ultimately, the law did not increase the birth rate or curtail the number of abortions. Curbing private decisions in this intimate area had shown a limit of Stalinist power.

The Great Terror

If the difficulty of enforcing the antiabortion law showed the limits of Stalin and the communist regime, the Great Terror demonstrated its extraordinary sweep. Several trends combined to produce it. First, an ongoing practice of periodically verifying the loyalty of Communist Party members and officials and removing from office those deemed disloyal or insufficiently dedicated was intensified in September 1936. Second, a campaign of urging the population to watch more vigilantly for hidden enemies began. On July 29, 1936, the Central Committee warned party organizations that terrorists had infiltrated the press, the army, the defense industry, and other institutions. The directive asserted that true Bolsheviks should be able to recognize enemies of the Party no matter the cleverness of their disguises.

In May, thirdly, a campaign to eliminate saboteurs throughout the ruling apparatus, including in factories and other places of employment, also broke out. Finally, a series of "mass operations" commenced in July, targeting a wide variety of alleged threatening persons. Such operations had their origin in mass sweeps of urban areas against dispossessed, criminal, and other marginal populations that had begun following the setting up of the passport system. Despite huge centrally orchestrated operations, the day-to-day policing of "socially dangerous elements" remained sporadic and inefficient. It was to address this problem that the Terror was undertaken. Since the courts, with their relatively slow procedure, could not process the huge upsurge of cases expeditiously, the vast majority were handled through administrative process by troikas of the political and regular police.

Although Genrikh Iagoda had built up the political police as a powerful support of the regime, by September 1936 Stalin had concluded that a tougher head of political operations was necessary and engineered his replacement with Nikolai Yezhov. The latter had emphasized the ongoing political threats of alleged subversives lurking throughout society. What came to be known as the Terror, or the Yezhovshchina, deployed mass repression against allegedly political and social threats beginning in summer 1937. Yezhov himself prepared the ground in April in a letter to Stalin warning of "incorrigible" criminals swarming throughout the USSR.

On July 2, 1937, the Politburo, at Stalin's instigation, directed all regional party organizations to compile lists of "former kulaks, criminals, and other anti-Soviet elements."[32] Stalin was deeply fearful that such people had snaked their way into Soviet institutions, especially collective farms, railroads, and factories. Officials throughout the country were also frightened by the millions of people constantly wandering, moving from job to job, living in temporary circumstances, not fitting into official categories, including the unemployed, orphans, "hooligans," and national minorities. Of course, the collectivization and "dekulakization" drives had uprooted millions and cast them into uncontrolled movement, searching for ways to fit in. On July 30, Yezhov signed Operational Order No. 00447. It became known as the "kulak operation," since it affected them first and foremost. Yezhov proposed that officials arrest 259,450 people and execute 72,950 of these unfortunates.[33] Out of fear of appearing too lenient, nearly all relevant authorities went beyond the required minimum, searching through police, party, and judicial files for potential victims with some stain in their records. Officials faked charges, coerced confessions, and fabricated evidence in routine and expedited fashion. Militia and NKVD troikas worked feverishly to weed out "socially harmful elements." Some cobbled together evidence of alleged conspiracies, sometimes involving hundreds of people. Victims were shot and buried in mass graves. Operational Order No. 00447 was followed by several more aimed at other suspect groups, including Polish nationals, wives of men convicted of counterrevolutionary crimes, and alleged spies from Germany, Romania, Finland, Latvia, and other countries.

Although the Terror was primarily orchestrated by the political police, the criminal justice system played an important supporting role. Technically, the NKVD had no right to conduct arrests on their own authority, so any such arrests had to be approved by procurators. The latter did not dare to raise objections, however, and often supplied backdated or already-signed blank arrest forms upon need. Judges also participated, most spectacularly in the three major show trials held in Moscow in 1936–1938 to try senior party leaders for alleged participation in anti-Soviet conspiracies, but also in dozens of lesser trials held regionally for the punishment of lower-level officials. In fact, a bigger proportion of the Gulag population was sentenced by judicial institutions than by the police. In 1937, the contrast was stark: 69.1 percent sentenced by the courts but only 30.9 percent by various police bodies.[34] Judicial personnel themselves suffered broadly from the Terror. From mid-1937 through the first part of 1938, nearly half of all procurators and judges in the country were fired and arrested—in many cases for failing to facilitate the Terror enthusiastically. Since such personnel often could not be quickly replaced, ad hoc regular police troikas began to try more regular criminal cases.

Following the first Moscow show trial, in August 1936, party organizers in factories read aloud and discussed newspaper articles about the trial.[35] The purpose of such assemblies was apparently to provoke popular anger and channel it against perceived enemies. Factory and office workers used the opportunity to denounce supervisors whom they resented for past slights. Party officials felt obligated to investigate any such allegations, typically anonymous, no matter how absurd they might have seemed. Stalin and other senior leaders were surely worried about popular discontent throughout the country provoked by terrible mistreatment of the peasantry, proliferating accidents on the job, insufficiently numerous and shoddily made consumer goods, and overall poor economic performance. It is therefore plausible that they expected such denunciation campaigns to redirect blame from the regime to other imagined culprits.

In any event, Soviet workplaces soon buzzed with rumors and accusations of "wrecking" and "sabotage." Employees who formerly had close relations often distanced themselves from one another for fear of being tainted by unsavory association. Practically any action could raise suspicion. If someone heard an anti-Stalin joke, to report to the authorities could bring unwanted attention and certainly land the joke-teller in hot water. Not to report, however, was probably more dangerous. Most factories and even many shops within factories produced "wall newspapers," in which unsubstantiated allegations of harm to the Soviet state and economy appeared. Such allegations had to be taken seriously. As of spring 1937, the expression "enemies of the people" became a common element of popular discourse.[36] The Terror turned family members against each other, both to protect themselves and because party rules demanded this. Any party member whose spouse landed in prison was required to denounce and break off all connections with him or her. The Party also required its members to sever ties with anyone excluded from the Party, denounced as an enemy, or closely related to a declared enemy. In general, it seems that more people stood by the Party than by their relatives. Here again, Soviet society was moving toward the traditional, early modern Russian norm of collective guilt and responsibility.

The Terror swallowed up vast numbers of unfortunates. According to official numbers, 1,575,259 people were arrested in 1937–1938. In those two years, at the very least, 681,692 people were executed.[37] Throughout the Terror and indeed, more broadly, in the years 1934–1940, most Gulag inmates and repressed persons were not sentenced for "counterrevolutionary offenses." It is clear, therefore, that the administrative and judicial apparatus was lashing out in all directions, unsystematically, cruelly, in an orgy of repression.

Central officials slowly began to put the brakes on the Terror from spring 1938, and it had wound down by November. Industrial accidents could still result in prosecution, but according to regular criminal law and procedure—not via the political police. Stalin and Molotov issued a secret decree of November 17 ordering an end to mass arrests, the abolition of all troikas as dispensers of criminal justice, and the reestablishment of Procuracy supervision over arrests and investigations. In typical Stalinist fashion, the decree even blamed the NKVD for distorting Soviet law and allowing things to get out of hand. Naturally, therefore, the Terror ended with a purge of high- and mid-level political police officials. Yezhov himself took blame, fell under arrest, and was replaced by a new political police chief, Lavrentii Beria, who purged Yezhov's closest supporters. Beginning in December 1938, the Supreme Court reviewed and reversed tens of thousands of political crime cases, though most such reversals affected trials conducted by transport courts. A very small number (perhaps a few thousand) of convictions imposed by NKVD troikas were overturned, based on their own internal review. That was only a fraction of the nearly 2 million arrests conducted by those bodies.

At the same time, however, Stalin did not feel secure. The Politburo continued to pressure the political police to hunt down and root out enemies. The NKVD therefore worked energetically to uncover plots. In 1939, it arrested tens of thousands of unfortunates, many of them alleged "counterrevolutionaries."[38] In other words, the system of repression remained at a high level of alert, something like a "Stalinist normal." People still ran a serious risk of falling victim to political witch-hunts but at a rate around tenfold lower than the previous two years.

As the criminal justice system recovered from the Terror, the quality of judicial personnel did not easily improve. The level of training remained low. The turnover of investigators, procurators, and judges remained high. In the last years of the decade, the number of law students did increase to nearly 5,000 with 828 graduating in 1940.[39] Still, this was a far from adequate number in so vast a country with so many social, economic, and political tensions and troubles.

[handwritten margin notes: "dual system", "political vs. regular crime", "v. diff from Troika's"]

In part to make up for the personnel shortage, senior judicial officials began to analyze statistics on the prosecution and sentencing of alleged criminals—including sentences resulting in acquittals and appeals—as the basis for the retention and promotion of judicial staff. The latter were bombarded with requests for data. At the local level, moreover, judicial personnel remained dependent on party bosses, who regularly interfered in criminal cases, in which they took a personal interest. In practice, as before, procurators needed to get their permission before prosecuting Communist Party members. Working out the details of how to cooperate with local party officials was a tricky business, since they wielded so much power. In any event, on the eve of the war, the criminal justice system had been restored more or less to its pre-Terror status. A major difference, however, was the weakening of the idea of defense advocates as representatives of the interests of defendants. During the Terror, that tradition was repudiated, and it was difficult to recover in subsequent years.

Criminal justice in the Second World War

At this point, however, Stalin laid a brand-new burden upon the criminal justice system: the criminalization of labor "shirking." A decree of June 26, 1940, specified a punishment of 2–4 months' jail time for quitting an established job without permission, which was typically difficult to obtain. The decree also prescribed 1–6 months of detention and a deduction of up to 25 percent of wages for tardiness of twenty minutes or more. It likewise became a criminal offense for managers to fail to report such violations. The aim of these drastic measures was primarily in preparation for impending war, though government efforts at disciplining the labor force had been ongoing for a decade and continued well after the war. Within a month, the decree had resulted in over 100,000 criminal prosecutions. For Stalin, however, such a statistic revealed judicial laxness. He therefore undertook a campaign against what was called "rotten liberalism" and "petty-bourgeois sentimentality" within the criminal justice system.[40] The result was dramatically harsher punishments for truants, the vast majority now receiving sentences of corrective work for three or more months. Judges also expedited their handling of such cases. As the campaign became a routine feature of criminal justice, however, prosecutions declined and sentences grew more lenient. This was a typical pattern in Soviet criminal justice and indeed throughout society. First, the leadership demanded results and paid close attention to efforts to meet those demands, harshly punishing the failure to do so. Officials therefore feverishly sought to comply. Next, the leadership turned its attention to another "urgent" matter, and the officials relaxed their efforts and often soon returned to an earlier pattern, occasionally stepping up their pace, for example, during periodic inspections.

That same summer, 1940, the Soviet state issued two further decrees to tighten control over industrial production. The first, on July 10, increased the maximum penalty from five to ten years of prison for contributing to shoddy industrial output. In practice, however, proving such cases was difficult. Trial judges often refused to go along with weak prosecution efforts, and many procurators avoided such cases for fear of displeasing local party bosses. The second, which came out on August 10, set a minimum one-year prison term for petty theft from factories. The purpose was to prevent workers from engaging in this activity in order to get fired, so as to move on to a different job. After a spike in prosecutions and convictions during two months of government campaigning on behalf of the decree, the rate of punishment for petty and other forms of theft from factories subsided and remained steady throughout the war. It seems that both judges and factory managers preferred not to crack down. The August edict also provided for harsher sentencing for "hooliganism." Here, prosecutions sharply rose, increasing three or four times in the final months of 1940 as compared to the same months of 1939, with 96.7 percent of convicts receiving prison time as compared to 63.9 percent in the first half of 1940 in the RSFSR.[41] The conviction rate fell just as sharply in 1942 and for the rest of the war, but rose again in the years following. Clearly, judges and procurators had a mind of their own and refused to toe just any official line without intense administrative pressure.

On the eve of the war, a huge number of persons were serving criminal sentences. As of March 1940, there were 53 corrective labor camps of the Gulag system with some 1.3 million inmates. Over 400,000 others were serving time in jails and prisons. Another 315,000 people were being held in 425 "corrective labor colonies," as well as an unspecified number of juveniles in ninety children's homes directed by the NKVD. There were also more than 1.7 million people sentenced in 1940 to noncustodial "corrective labor," mostly at their ordinary places of work, but under some restrictions, such as a prohibition on changing jobs or moving to a new city, and for diminished pay.[42] Finally, some 1 million exiles were still being held in "special settlements."[43] The total custodial population in various correctional institutions, therefore, was around 3 million. Given a population of roughly 173 million, the incarceration rate was around 1,734 per 100,000, or some two and one-half times higher than the current American incarceration rate of 716, the highest in the world today. (In 1940, the US rate was 131.)

Although the mass operations had ceased at the end of 1938, local officials continued to control the population by means of the passport laws and residential restrictions. By mid-1940, people could live only on the basis of special registration rules in 635 cities and districts, as well as in border zones and hundreds of square kilometers around major cities.[44] Among the reasons for maintaining strict residency requirements, in addition to simply controlling the population, were to prevent unauthorized access to militarily and economically sensitive sites, to prevent the overconcentration of population in desirable localities, and to shelter scarce consumer goods from hordes of purchasers. The inability of the consumer sector to provide adequate goods and foodstuffs to ordinary people across the country resulted in extremely long lines, sometimes forming after shops closed in anticipation of the morning and snaking around the block and into courtyards. In the major cities, periodic sweeps of such queues were carried out in order to weed out and expel people without the proper residency permit. A main concern was that many unauthorized people standing in line for scarce goods were profiteers engaging in the crime of speculation.

In August 1939, the USSR and Nazi Germany signed a nonaggression pact with secret protocols calling for the division between them of Eastern European territory. From September, Soviet forces seized the Baltic states and portions of Finland and Romania. In November 1939, the Soviet army went to war with Finland. During the next several months, over 400,000 people were arrested and displaced from these territories to be resettled in remote locations. Tens of thousands were murdered, including some 22,000 Polish officers and other elites.[45]

The Second World War began on Soviet territory with the Nazi German invasion on June 22, 1941. With over 150 divisions, the Nazis rapidly advanced across a 2,000-mile front. Within weeks the Germans had destroyed 1,500 artillery pieces, 2,500 tanks, and 1,200 aircraft. Without air cover, most forward Soviet units could not resist the attack. By year's end, the Nazis had taken 2.4 million prisoners and some 500,000 square miles of Soviet territory containing over 75 million people. Nevertheless, Hitler totally underestimated the Soviet will to fight back. Both soldiers and civilians proved astonishingly brave, resilient, and self-sacrificing. And why not? Their homeland was under siege, and for the first time in twenty years, they faced a real enemy. A fifty-five-hour workweek became the norm, but it seems that relatively few workers complained. Many Soviet citizens on the western and southern borderlands, especially Balts and Ukrainians, initially greeted the Nazis as liberators. Yet the Nazis viewed the entire population as potential slaves and treated the Russians and ethnic minorities cruelly, slaughtering them by tens of thousands. The state appealed to patriotism and community, to love of *rodina* (the motherland), and to pride in *otechestvo* (the fatherland). Stalin addressed the people, not as "comrades" but as "brothers and sisters." Old Russian heroes and stories were brought back into circulation. Tolstoy's *War and Peace* was issued in a print-run of 1 million copies.

The Nazis supposed that the Soviet government would collapse under the strain of war. The economic system was indeed inefficient, and corruption rife. But the centrally controlled administration, with its militaristically minded party leaders, proved highly adaptable and effective in wartime. The government released over 1 million prisoners during the war to send them to the front lines against Germany.[46] The camps did not empty out completely, however, because they were an integral part of the Soviet economy. Military discipline in many key industries, like railways and munitions, meant that laziness on the job could also result in a sentence to a labor camp. Living conditions in the camps were, moreover, especially bad during 1941–1943, when over half of all camp deaths in the 1934–1953 period occurred, largely from malnutrition.[47] Vast cohorts of ethnic minorities, suspected of potential treason or feared for their ability to resist Soviet control, were exiled to concentration camps and special settlements in distant places. These expulsions included 439,000 Volga Germans, over 300,000 other Germans, 182,000 Crimean Tatars, 393,000 Chechens, and 91,000 Ingushs, along with hundreds of thousands of Estonians, Latvians, Lithuanians, Bessarabians, Greeks, Kalmyks, and others.[48] Russians and Ukrainians typically settled in their abandoned villages. These actions sowed bitterness and hatred lasting for decades.

After a grueling battle at Kursk in summer 1943, Soviet troops advanced relentlessly, expelling the Germans from most of their territory by June 1944, and then pressed on through the Baltic region and Eastern Europe. Recent figures indicate that about 27 million Soviet people died, of which perhaps 10 million were soldiers. Roughly 1,700 towns and cities, 70,000 villages, 35,000 plants and factories, and 6 million buildings were either destroyed or severely damaged. Plus, about 25 million people were left homeless. (The USSR also acquired 265,850 square miles of new territory, including the Baltic states, with 23,477,000 more people.) Beginning in July 1946, moreover, the USSR suffered its last major famine. Peaking in the first half of 1947, the calamity took the lives of at least 1 million more people.

Postwar criminal justice under Stalin

The war also had a devastating impact on the judicial system. Many young investigators and judges were sent to fight, and many did not return. Training new personnel proved difficult and slow. A decree of October 5, 1946, demanded a dramatic increase in the training of jurists. The results were impressive: in spring 1949, almost 4,000 lawyers graduated, roughly half from less rigorous correspondence courses. As a result, the proportion of judges and procurators with legal training had doubled or even tripled by 1952.[49] Another way to deal with inadequate personnel working through the growing backlog of cases was the designation of "replacement judges," many of them secretaries and bailiffs without any legal training, to set up parallel courtrooms. Many judges also came up with shortcuts and informal procedures, such as handling batches of cases with similar attributes all at once. It seems also that the police often pressured suspects to give confessions to expedite the hammering together of regular crime cases.

The higher authorities worried about corruption influencing the conduct of governance in general and of criminal justice in particular. A decree of July 15, 1946, directed officials to work harder to root out bribery, by increasing the penalties against those who gave them and those who accepted them. In 1947, therefore, the number of convictions for both types of offender reached 5,600, or three times as many as before the war. Officials throughout the system, however, recognized that the problem was occurring on a grandiose scale; a few thousand convictions could not make much of a difference. The authorities also went after the crime defined as "abuse of office," or any action harming the proper functioning of an official position. Here again, convictions nearly doubled from before the war to 82,000 in 1947, but then tapered off.[50] Once the campaign was over, party officials worked hard to protect their clients, some of whom were friends but all of whom, they would argue, were necessary for the proper functioning of the state apparatus. Most officials seem to have thought that a main benefit of state service was to benefit from it personally.

At the same time, and partly in reaction to such problems, central judicial authorities pressured judges and procurators to improve their performance. Senior officials began, in 1948 and 1949, to emphasize the importance of presenting viable cases to the courts, achieving conviction, and avoiding acquittals, which were now referred to as "unfounded prosecutions" and "unfounded convictions." Senior officials wanted an efficient, predictable, and controlled criminal justice system, but they rejected the rule of law and the separation of powers. Personal, informal, arbitrary governance was how they did business. It is not surprising, therefore, that their subordinates up and down the institutional hierarchies felt the same way, engendering a vicious circle of corruption and arbitrariness.

Following the obvious official trend, judicial personnel throughout the system strived in a variety of ways to construct convincing cases, carry their cases through to completion, avoid cases returned for further investigation, and achieve convictions. Many judges and procurators had to work extremely long hours to achieve the desired results. Efforts were also made to ensure that as few sentences as possible were overturned on appeal. The best way to succeed here was to follow both the law and—most especially— the Party line, for example, avoiding overly lenient sentences when the Party wanted tough sentencing. The higher courts were closely attuned to the shifting Party line and typically based their review decisions on the demands of that line. To avoid decisions being overturned on review or appeal, it certainly made sense for judges to pay close attention to Party trends.

If Stalin strongly influenced the development of criminal law throughout his dominance of the Soviet system, he left his strongest imprint after the war. In fact, no significant change occurred within the system of criminal justice in those years without his direct involvement. The end of the war witnessed an upsurge of theft throughout the country. According to an official reckoning, theft of state property in 1948 alone resulted in a material loss of more than 1.5 billion rubles.[51] Legal experts drafted decrees for dealing with the problem, but Stalin found them overly lenient and he himself prepared replacements, one for personal theft and one for theft of state property. They were issued on June 4, 1947. These acts were draconian, requiring mandatory minimum sentences of 3–5 years of prison for theft of personal property and 6–7 years for theft of state property. Again, during 1947 itself the number of theft prosecutions for both state and personal property increased more than 50 percent over 1946, but then fell below that level in 1948 and subsequent years.[52] Judges, police, and procurators all began to shield offenders—juveniles, factory workers, and women—from the required harsh punishments. Such officials undoubtedly recognized that life was difficult in the postwar USSR, and petty theft was a way for many people to make ends meet. The system also began to turn more of a blind eye to theft by officials. It gradually became a perk of office and was accepted throughout the system as such. Even so, the law could not be completely ignored. Those unfortunates convicted for theft of state property faced lengthy terms of incarceration. In some areas, toward some people, and at some times, the criminal justice system was indulgent and in others draconian. One feature of Soviet criminal justice that remained constant, however, was the underlying principle that the state and its officials were more important than citizens and society.

Another way judicial policy developed under Stalin's influence was through a growing number of secret decrees, for example those implementing the law of August 7, 1932. Such behind-the-scenes legislating grew more frequent during and after the war. One such instance involved decisions adopted by the Presidium of the Supreme Soviet of the USSR in February and June 1948, empowering collective farm assemblies first in Ukraine and then throughout the country to exile to distant localities, for up to eight years, members who failed to work diligently. This right resembled a power peasants had exercised in Russia before the revolution. Indeed, when Khrushchev proposed the idea to Stalin, he apparently sent along a copy of a relevant prerevolutionary statute. Between February 1948 and June 1950, the unpublished law was applied in Ukraine alone to nearly 12,000 "antisocial parasites."[53] Another secret decision, issued by the Presidium of the Supreme Soviet in July 1951, decriminalized labor shirking, which dramatically diminished the number of prosecutions for such activity and radically decreased the caseload of courts throughout the country. Apparently, the leadership wanted to lessen the burden such prosecutions placed upon the judicial system but did not want to broadcast the fact that shirkers could get away scot-free. Such developments contributed to the emergence of an attitude within the population that ordinary people could disregard their responsibilities and act in arbitrary ways just like their political superiors. This attitude was encapsulated in the widespread late Soviet adage: "They pretend to pay us, and we pretend to work."

During the war, it became more difficult to control the population. Large numbers of blank passports entered the public domain, many police were sent to the front lines, and populations moved around more than ever. In order to address this problem, the surveillance network, which had declined in the mid-1930s, expanded to encompass hundreds of thousands of informants. Police troikas no longer functioned after November 1938, but the special committee on exile worked busily, as did the courts.

After the war, mass operations continued against what were perceived as dangerous population groups, though on a lesser scale than during the Terror and the war. (The political police, which carried out these operations, was now called the Ministry of State Security, or MGB.) Between 1946 and 1952, some 678,000 new special settlers were rounded up, mostly in the western and southern borderlands, and deported to distant localities. In 1952, there were a total of 2.75 million special settlers, including 1.8 million national minorities. Those figures were in addition to the Gulag population, which gradually increased from 1947, peaking in 1953 at nearly 2 million.[54] All these Gulag inmates and special settlers stood outside the ordinary criminal justice system and fell under the jurisdiction of special courts operating throughout the country. The Gulag continued to contribute mightily to the economy. Its inmates produced 100 percent of the country's diamonds and platinum, over 90 percent of its gold, more than 70 of its tin, and so on. Also, in 1948, Stalin ordered the creation of special camps for "especially dangerous state criminals." By 1951, ten special camps held some 237,000 prisoners of this designation.[55] Recourse to the death penalty, however, fell back to something like its frequency during the 1920s: around 1,000 executions per year.[56]

The authorities worried less about social disorder. Since the war was over, and the Soviet Union had triumphed, criminality and ordinary social deviance apparently seemed to pose a lesser threat, one no longer potentially manipulated by deadly foreign enemies. In one sign of the sense of confidence the Soviet leaders must have felt, over 500,000 former "kulaks" were released in 1946–1952 from special settlements and returned to the general population.[57] Harsh repression did occur in territories conquered by the USSR during the war, but those developments go beyond the bounds of this study.

In his last years in power, Stalin focused largely on foreign policy and political policing. He still worried about enemies within the Soviet body politic. Several thousand party and state officials fell victim, especially in Leningrad and Soviet Georgia, and were exiled to Kazakhstan and other remote localities. Stalin apparently also deeply feared what he imagined to be Jewish political conspiracies. In early 1953, nine prominent physicians, most of them Jewish, were arrested as part of an alleged "Doctors' Plot" to kill Kremlin officials. Following Stalin's death on March 5, the doctors were all released. In early 1954, the political police were reorganized as the Committee for State Security, or KGB, and subordinated to the Council of Ministers in an arrangement that endured until the collapse of the USSR in 1991. The KGB remained a powerful force, but the almost hysterical search for enemies was over. Political convulsions of either the nature or the scale of the Terror would no longer occur in Russia.

6

The USSR under "Mature Socialism"

After the terrifying experience of a despotic ruler controlling the whole of the state apparatus and wielding unchecked power, the party leadership moved to rule collectively. With Stalin gone, the leadership put forward the concept of "socialist legality," a term Stalin had himself used. Now, it was to serve as a legitimizing factor for the entire system. In terms of criminal justice, the Terror ended, criminal penalties were lightened, the supervisory authority of the Procuracy was strengthened, the independence of the judicial system was enhanced, and mechanisms for popular participation in the administration of justice were instituted or revived.[1] This trend of liberalization was, in turn, undermined and even reversed by tendencies toward official micromanagement, pervasive social control, persistent fear of political dissidence, arbitrary governance, and self-serving administrative interference in the execution of justice. Both currents ran parallel to one another, with liberalization reaching its highest points in the first years after Stalin's death and under Gorbachev, and the tightening of control peaking under Brezhnev and Andropov.

The Khrushchev era

The Party's renewed commitment to legality was embodied first and foremost in the amnesty decree of March 27, 1953, just three weeks after Stalin's death. The system of confinement had remained vast. Some 5.4 million people, out of a total population of 188 million, were deprived of liberty: roughly 2.5 million in 3,500 Gulag camps and colonies, 2.7 million in "special settlements," and 150,000 of the most serious offenders in regular prisons.[2] (In 1950, in the United States, 166,165 people were imprisoned at the state and federal levels.) The amnesty affected persons in all these facilities. It benefited above all inmates with a positive work attitude whose crimes had not greatly threatened the state. Such vulnerable people as the elderly, pregnant women, and children also benefited, as did persons sentenced for some official and economic crimes. Many sentences under five years were halved. The state-controlled press justified the mass release not as evidence of errors of the criminal justice system but rather of its effectiveness at rehabilitating prisoners and preparing them to return to the "path of honest labor." The mass liberation of prisoners testified to the extraordinary faith of the party leadership in the ability of Soviet society to absorb hundreds of thousands and ultimately millions of former convicts. It also marked the end of the Terror. The camps would not empty out completely, nor would they be abolished during the Soviet era. People would still be incarcerated in them merely for political criticism of the political system, the regime, and its officials. But large-scale repression had come to an end.

In addition to the release of millions of prisoners, among whom there were tens of thousands and perhaps hundreds of thousands of hardened criminals, the criminal justice system had grown more lenient in terms of penalties. Even before Stalin's death, the maximum sentence for petty theft of state property was reduced, on January 10, 1953, to six months in prison. Over the following months, the maximum sentence for many administrative and official violations was also lowered.

Many citizens must found it hard to make sense of such rapid changes in criminal justice law and practice. The Kremlin doctors denounced in January, as noted above, were released in April, the charges against them repudiated. Some wondered how a regime that had seemed almost infallible could have made such a terrible error. Others doubted the innocence of the doctors. In July, Beria was denounced as an "enemy of the people" and was accused of impeding the campaign to strengthen legality. (He was tried and executed in December.) A decree of September 1, 1953, announced the abolition of the special committee on exile and required the Procuracy to review all previously implemented sentences of extrajudicial punishment.

It should have been a warning sign that unrest and strikes repeatedly broke out in the Gulag in the years before Stalin's death. Such disorders were massive in spring and summer 1953. (They were crushed with main force, as under Stalin, though most ringleaders were merely beaten.) Almost immediately, many of the released prisoners began wreaking havoc, committing assault, murder, rape, and other crimes, on board trains or at railroad stations on their way home. Throughout the country, in the second and third quarters of the year, criminality shot up, with murders increasing 30.7 percent and rapes 27.5 percent over the previous year.[3] Criminal gangs contributed to the disorder. Rumors of unsafe streets triggered public anxiety. A flood of letters to the editor and to government officials voiced fear of mayhem and demanded a crackdown. One Leningrad citizen appealed to Viacheslav Molotov, a senior party official:

"we mothers ask you, beg you, please make the police more vigilant and keep the people safe."[4]

The regime responded from June 1953 with a press campaign showcasing harsh punishments being meted out to criminal offenders throughout the country. Regular crime reporting—a normal feature before 1917—now emerged in Soviet newspapers. Many such reports represented criminals as outsiders, all but incapable of rehabilitation. Since at the time only anti-Soviet activity (art. 58) carried the death penalty, two notorious violent criminals were given death sentences by emphasizing relatively minor aspects of their crimes, one for killing a policeman and the other for alleged anti-Soviet comments. After a law of April 30, 1954, made aggravated intentional murder a capital offense, press reports often listed execution as the punishment endured by hardened criminals.

A campaign against deviant behavior was undertaken from summer 1954. To some extent foreshadowing the "broken window theory" of crime-fighting in 1980s America, the press warned that drinking or swearing in public was likely to lead to a life of criminality. Members of society were therefore urged to take an active role in calling attention to such transgressions, reporting on them to the authorities. Volunteers (*druzhenniki*) were encouraged to support the work of the police. The Komsomol, the communist youth organization, formed many such brigades to patrol city streets and conduct raids in public places. Throughout these years, however, the government never completely lost sight of the ideal of reeducation, of molding criminals into upright citizens. Guards were urged to treat inmates with respect, though far from all did so.

Further amnesty decrees ensued. In spring 1954, commissions were set up to review sentences for counterrevolutionary crimes imposed by military courts and extrajudicial organs. Petitions requesting rehabilitation poured in from around the country. Between 1954 and 1960, the authorities reviewed the cases of 892,317 people sentenced for counterrevolutionary activity; 715,120 of them were fully rehabilitated. In all, as of September 1958, precisely 4,118,414 prisoners had been released from Gulag camps and colonies.[5] Likewise, special settlers, the majority of whom were deported "enemy nationals," were also gradually released.

Among the ways inmates could exit the Gulag were parole and work credits. The government reinstituted parole, which had been removed from the Soviet criminal justice system in 1939. Henceforth, the regular courts had the right to release prisoners who had served at least two-thirds of their sentence and had demonstrated good behavior and "an honest attitude toward work."[6] This policy aimed to return to the utopian and hopeful roots of the Leninist socialist experiment. It was also in line with reformist developments in Western countries. Similarly, an earlier policy of "work credits" was extended to nearly all inmates. Through conscientious labor, they could earn a reduction of their sentence by up to two-thirds. In practice, many administrators resisted putting productive inmates up for parole, preferring to emphasize work credits. After all, the Gulag retained its economic function. As with other released inmates, parolees received some social services but little supervision. Evidence suggests that the public deplored the leniency toward criminals afforded by the system of parole. Parolees also bore heavy stigmas, making it hard for them to reintegrate into society. The reason for this attitude is likely to have stemmed from bitter feelings widespread in Soviet society about the difficulty of getting by. Such feelings must have turned many people against those who could not manage to follow the rules or who took the easy route of theft and other crimes. Nor was there much love lost on alleged political subversives; most people doubtless feared and resented such troublemakers.

Many former inmates found it hard to find jobs, to reinsert themselves into society. Tight restrictions on residency in dozens of cities, including most major ones, made it even more difficult, since a residency permit was required to obtain work. The number of such "regime" cities plummeted, thanks to a secret order of October 24, 1953, but still hovered around sixty and rose again in subsequent months and years.[7] It was often necessary for convicted political offenders to appeal for formal judicial "rehabilitation" and to obtain a "clean" passport (without an indication of one's criminal past) in order to gain the right to reside in closed cities, to apply to higher education, and to land more desirable jobs, though even full rehabilitation did not ensure success. A report of May 1953 indicated that 30–50 percent of all former prisoners in many regions of the country could find no work. Some were reduced to a nomadic existence, falling in with criminals and other transients. A decree of August 27 prescribed harsh punishments for released Gulag inmates who fell back into criminal activity. Throughout the country, 40,685 were quickly rearrested and returned to the Gulag, 75 percent on charges of hooliganism or theft.[8] It is not surprising that many former prisoners came out angry, hostile to the Soviet system, even favorable toward America and capitalism. Their subculture set them apart. At the same time, their subversive slang, with its "cult of criminality," expressed in song and verse, was attractive to outsiders. Many young people who had never set foot in a camp or a prison began to imitate attitudes and appearances from those realms. The party leadership was not happy. It also had a name for such phenomena: hooliganism.

From 1955, the state-controlled press presented stereotypical images of the hooligan with a cigarette, a bottle, a tattoo, and scruffy hair. A law adopted in 1956 provided for short-term incarceration of "petty hooligans." The law was not part of the movement toward leniency but on the contrary an element of the crackdown on crime. In a climate of rising concern about public safety, police used the law as a tool to attack criminality throughout society. The result was a dramatic increase in both courtroom convictions for serious hooliganism from nearly 127,000 in 1955 to over 207,000 in 1958 and a skyrocketing number of detentions for petty hooliganism to over 1.4 million people annually in 1957 and 1958.[9] The difference in these types of punishment was between one and three years of incarceration for serious hooliganism and three to fifteen days of administrative detention for the petty variant. Judges had to decide cases expeditiously, often a dozen or more per hour. Those found guilty were typically set to work on public clean-up projects, to shame them. It is important to note that this spike in convictions occurred not immediately after the massive release of Gulag inmates began in 1953, but rather as a reaction to increased criminality caused by that release.

Charges of hooliganism and the very concept of the crime were also used more and more for state control over private life such as for protecting women from domestic abuse and inhabitants of the ubiquitous communal apartments from violence and other forms of mistreatment. The authorities received countless complaints about the difficulties of living cheek by jowl with disrespectful people, and the petty hooligan law was used to make life more livable in overcrowded urban spaces by seeking to deter improper speech and insults. Here was also a handy method for removing unpresentable population "elements" on the eve of events in which the authorities wanted to showcase the beauty and orderliness of Moscow, such as the 1957 World Youth Festival.

Along with getting tough on crime, the party leadership also continued to emphasize legality and leniency. Laws in 1955 and 1956 reduced punishments for petty theft of state and public property, legalized abortion, decriminalized leaving one's work without permission, and disallowed administrative exile. In line with these changes was Khrushchev's speech to the Twentieth Party Congress on February 25, 1956. In the speech, Khrushchev spoke of an "unprecedented violation of revolutionary legality." He emphasized the out-of-control political police apparatus and the harm caused to thousands of loyal party members. He did not, however, talk about the terrible injustice to the "kulaks" or the millions of ordinary people swept up in the Terror. To have done so would undoubtedly have undermined the legitimacy of the Party and the regime. He denounced the "cult of personality," by which he meant the autocratic rulership of Stalin. The Party had provided good leadership, it was implied, but Stalin had hijacked the Party. It had suffered at his hands, but now it was on the right track. Many party leaders were uncomfortable with such speaking of the truth, as limited as it in fact was. Were not Stalin and the Party one and the same? How could the Party have made such terrible mistakes? Many ordinary people were just as confused. Who really was to blame?

Part of Khrushchev's criminal justice reform plans involved moving as many prisoners as possible from labor camps to labor colonies. Such colonies typically held under a thousand inmates convicted of lesser crimes and were located close to populated areas. The massive camps, by contrast, often with tens of thousands of prisoners, were usually set up in remote regions and divided into a constellation of sub-camps, hence Solzhenitsyn's metaphor, "archipelago." The camps held criminals convicted for more serious offenses; their terms of confinement were thus much longer. The emphasis in the colonies was supposed to be on correction and rehabilitation, though in practice, the similarities between the two forms of penal institution were great: barracks, barbed wire, watchtowers, armed guards, and mandatory labor. The reform was not entirely successful, because it was easier to accommodate the wild fluctuations in the number of prisoners in the camps than in the colonies, whose detailed rules and regulations specified better living conditions and prohibited overcrowding. Another reason was the refusal of local authorities to agree to the construction of such facilities in their "backyard." In 1957, for example, regional leaders built only 43 of the 276 colonies the plan required them to build.[10] Many colonies that were built in these years, moreover, resembled camps in that they squeezed labor from the inmates.

At the same time, living conditions in the camps themselves dramatically improved, with better rations, more educational and cultural programs, improved medical care, increased opportunities for physical activity, fewer hours of work, and more connections with the outside world. Some of the biggest camps in Siberia and the far north were shut down. Violence, perpetrated by both staff and prisoners, diminished. The number of murders committed in the Gulag declined from 515 in 1954 to 183 in 1958. The overall mortality rate in the Gulag fell from 0.84 percent in 1952 to 0.37 percent in 1957–1959.[11] In the late 1950s, dozens of Western observers were invited to visit a couple of the most presentable places of confinement. The KGB choreographed highly positive experiences, giving impressions abroad of successful reform.[12]

Conditions improved so much that government leaders, criminologists, and the public at large grew suspicious. Many voices were raised, beginning around 1957, in favor of tighter restrictions in places of confinement. Only harsh living conditions, it was argued, could deter crime. A law of late 1958 made many violent criminals ineligible for parole. A torrent of letters to the editor argued that prisoners should not enjoy the experience of incarceration, should not be pampered. A crime wave surging in 1960 did not dispose the public better toward inmates. Official statistics indicated that in the first half of the year, 12.7 percent of the most dangerous crimes had been committed by prisoners released the previous summer.[13] At a Presidium meeting in June 1961, Khrushchev admitted that Stalin had been right about the need to "beat your enemies accurately and without mercy."[14] He did add, though, that such treatment would help facilitate rehabilitation. Rules adopted in April rolled back many of the improvements in living conditions in the camps, but did not return them by any means to the full harshness of the times of Stalin. (Actual conditions depended as before on the personality of individual camp directors.)

Moreover, a series of laws adopted in 1962–1964 moved again in the other direction. Colonies were developed with an even more lenient regime for petty offenders. Better rations were provided for convicts engaged in heavy labor. And well-behaved prisoners could benefit from early release to work in construction projects in the outside world. Public organizations were encouraged to support the work of the camps and colonies. In 1964, the 771 camp subdivisions and colonies in the Russian Republic received support from over 1,300 sponsoring organizations.[15] By this point, however, maintaining order—not reeducation—was the official watchword. Furthermore, a strong emphasis was still placed on the economic contributions of prison labor. An official report of 1963, for example, noted a massive increase in gross output of the camps and colonies from 164 million rubles in 1956 to 462 million in 1963.[16] Convict labor was especially important in economic sectors involving hardship, such as remoteness of location, temperature extremes, and physical danger.

The party leadership had been perpetually concerned about the theft of "socialist property," that is, state property. Such worries spiked again in the late 1950s. A government report of mid-1958 indicated that over 300 million rubles had disappeared from the system of consumer cooperatives "as a result of major, coordinated schemes."[17] Similar thieving, according to the report, occurred in all branches of the economy. Many implicated culprits apparently built themselves summer homes (dachas), purchased automobiles (at a time when almost no ordinary person owned one), and acquired other luxury goods. Such stories were not uncommonly reported in the major newspapers. Many service personnel unlawfully exploited their jobs for personal gain in almost every walk of life, for nearly every conceivable activity, such as finding space in a cemetery to bury a coffin, filling a cavity, securing admission to a prestigious school, and obtaining scarce tickets to the theater or cinema, among many others. Swindlers concocted devilishly clever schemes for earning money. One ring of miscreants gained access to a physical therapy workshop for mentally ill patients and forced them to produce clothing and other goods for black-market sales. Three police officers who took bribes to turn a blind eye to this scheme were sentenced to death.

The fact that the courts imposed capital punishment on swindlers requires some interpretation. The sentences could not have been implemented without high-level approval and probably insistence. Undoubtedly, the leadership understood that corruption permeated the entire system and therefore they believed that truly extreme measures were necessary to combat it. Yet since the system was profoundly inefficient and thus drove people massively to engage in corruption, there was nothing anyone could really do about it. The fact that the state owned practically the entire economy also meant that few individuals took a proprietary interest in its proper functioning, which also promoted fraud. If swindlers were willing to risk death on a daily basis, then dishonest dealing could not be rooted out. In fact, the system was so inefficient, most managers had to deploy fixers—experts in finagling scarce supplies and materials, just to keep their factories running. Such shenanigans were illegal, but without them, the system would have been even less efficient and productive.

In 1959, yet another approach to fighting crime was adopted. Social organizations, like the Komsomol, were encouraged to take wayward people under their wing, to urge them toward a path of redemption. A decree of March 2, entitled "On the Participation of Workers in the Maintenance of Public Order," advocated the creation of voluntary brigades (*druzhiny*) in every factory and farm. Part of the intention was to set up "comrades' courts" within urban collectives—factories, apartment buildings, Komsomol chapters, and schools—(and social courts in villages) with the authority to pass judgment on a wide variety of behaviors, including petty crime, acting out in public, and even objectionable doings in the home. There was no legal prerequisite for the members of the courts, who were popularly elected for a one-year term. By the end of 1963, some 197,000 comrades' courts were hearing over 4 million cases yearly.[18] Many Soviet citizens liked these courts, because they strengthened social control through public humiliation, according to the norms of traditional village life. After all, a high proportion of urban dwellers in the USSR at this time had grown up in the countryside. Many such citizens found it more painful to endure such social pressure than a harsher but more impersonal sentence passed by a court. Even so, crime did not immediately diminish—on the contrary. Official statistics indicate that in the first half of 1960, violent crimes against persons rose 31.2 percent, and theft increased 36 percent, over the previous year in the Russian Socialist Republic.[19]

The authorities responded with tough measures. The Russian Criminal Code of 1960, which entered force on January 1, 1961, prescribed the death penalty for some ordinary crimes, including intentional aggravated murder. Legislation in 1961 and 1962 imposed stiff penalties for many violations, including capital punishment for especially important economic crimes. Many petty criminals, including hooligans and black marketeers, received lengthy sentences. An "anti-parasite law" was adopted in May 1961 in the RSFSR. People's courts were empowered to sentence idlers to coerced labor in far places for up to five years with no right of appeal. (In 1957–1960, similar laws passed in other republics had given that right to local collectives.[20]) Especially targeted were people living from their garden plots in the countryside or from selling goods and services on the side and renting spare apartments in the city. In the Russian Republic alone, some 20,000 persons were exiled as parasites in the first year of the 1961 law, though ten times that number were warned that they were at risk if they did not get a job.[21] Persons sent into exile typically ended up in remote localities. Upon arrival, they were required to register with the authorities in order to receive "socially useful work." Thereafter, they were to remain in at least monthly contact with law enforcement officials.

The "anti-parasite" campaign often targeted youth subcultures. The most famous victim was Joseph Brodsky, a 23-year-old unemployed aspiring Leningrad poet (later a Nobel Prize winner). Such young people typically pursued unconventional lifestyles, made friends with Americans and other foreigners, and rejected the prevailing core values of Soviet society, especially belief in socialism and in working hard in service of the socialist cause. Denounced in the press in November 1963, Brodsky was confined in a mental institution, then secretly put on trial and sentenced to five years' labor on a collective farm in the far north (under international pressure, the sentence was eventually commuted to eighteen months).

The July 1, 1961, law on especially important economic crimes was imposed retroactively on Ian Rokotov and Vladik Faibishenko, the youthful ringleaders of a gang of foreign-currency traders. The KGB conducted the investigation because contacts with foreigners were considered threatening to the state. In conjunction with the investigation and trial, an exhibition of valuables confiscated from the gang was made public. Khrushchev attended the exhibition and supposedly quipped "they need to be shot for this." When the Moscow City Court, in June 1961, sentenced them to fifteen years' deprivation of freedom and the confiscation of all their property, the procurator general of the USSR, apparently having taken Khrushchev's words for law, protested the leniency of the punishment for two of the defendants. A retrial, conducted by the Russian Republic Supreme Court, sentenced the pair to death by shooting and confiscation of all valuables and property without the possibility of appeal. Thousands of letters from ordinary people poured in supporting the decision.[22]

Because of the crackdown on crime, the number of prisoners in corrective labor institutions significantly increased. In other words, the Khrushchev "Thaw" had already started to freeze over. Moreover, whereas people who fell victim to the political terror of 1937 and 1938 could sometimes not only reenter established society but could also enjoy public accolades, ordinary criminal offenders more and more came to be seen by Soviet society as outcasts incapable of rehabilitation.

The fight against "counterrevolutionary" and "anti-Soviet" activity also changed but did not disappear in the Khrushchev era. From 1956 to 1964, the courts issued 5,728 such convictions and prison sentences, nearly 60 percent of them in 1957 and 1958. Imprisonment was gradually less and less resorted to for such cases—in only 341 cases in 1963 and 181 cases in 1964.[23] It is not that "anti-Soviet" activity declined. Subversive leaflets appeared in hundreds and even thousands of copies. Mass protests broke out from time to time throughout the country—over 400 collective protests were reported in samizdat and other unofficial media in 1956–1983.[24] The most dramatic protest took place in 1962 in Novocherkassk, where troops fired on peaceful strikers, killing sixteen and gravely wounding dozens. (Blame for the tragedy was officially placed entirely on the strike leaders, several of whom were executed, thanks to sentences apparently decided in advance.) Another big category of victims of political repression under Khrushchev was religious believers. In 1959–1964, thousands of churches were closed, and thousands of worshippers suffered employment discrimination, social pressure, arrest, exile, and imprisonment. The number of priests was also driven down radically through exile, imprisonment, forced retirement, defrocking, and other methods.

The regime gradually turned to more sophisticated methods of political policing, however, involving a vast network of secret informants, a huge expansion of personnel and resources funneled to the KGB, and "prophylactic" measures. The latter were of two kinds: mass propaganda and social organization, on the one hand, and individual meetings of KGB case officers with persons viewed as unreliable or likely to put attitudes of political discontent into practice. The political leadership came to set great store by this approach, concluding that such meetings were a much more effective way of preventing "political" crime. For every dissident imprisoned in the later Khrushchev years, according to an official reckoning, some 100 were talked to by a KGB operative.[25]

A more sinister method of struggle against "anti-Soviet" activity was apparently first hinted at by Khrushchev in a speech of May 1959 where he blamed mental illness for anticommunist activity. Top officials took the remark as a direct order. Soon dozens and then hundreds of dissidents were locked up as insane. Again, the approach was fairly subtle. A "political" suspect would be arrested and examined by psychiatric experts who would determine the person mentally unfit to stand trial. Such unfortunates often spent several years in special psychiatric hospitals under the jurisdiction of the Interior Ministry, where conditions were often far worse than in the Gulag.[26]

By the time Khrushchev was removed from office in a bloodless coup d'état in October 1964, the reformed Soviet penal system was established as it would essentially remain until the fall of the USSR. The system was smaller and less draconian than Stalin had left it, but it was far bigger than those of other developed countries. Most inmates engaged in forced labor, as they had under Stalin, including in logging, heavy industry, and construction, especially in hard, unskilled labor. But the conditions, while harsher than in developed countries, never returned to the horrors of Stalin's time. And gradually, more inmates engaged in skilled labor, producing hundreds of consumer products from refrigerators to chess pieces. Moreover, many inmates labored under contract, alongside free citizens. Other major changes to society, economics, and politics attempted by Khrushchev—in agriculture, social egalitarianism, censorship, intellectual openness, promoting "socialist legality," and administrative decentralization—were abandoned, but not the reformed penal system. Nor did the new, subtle methods of handling "anti-Soviet" activities go away.

The Brezhnev era

The high party elites, led by Leonid Brezhnev, wanted above all to turn their backs on the incessant reforms and grandiose—often called "harebrained"—schemes of Khrushchev. Stability and order were the watchwords of the new regime. The cultural Thaw was abandoned. Political dissidents suffered repression. Military spending soared. And economic growth gradually slowed from 6 percent per annum in the 1950s to under 2 percent in the late 1970s. People's expectations of continued improvement in their standard of living might have been dashed had not the regime decided to turn a blind eye to all manner of illegal economic activity.

Such was what economist James Millar called the "Little Deal." The Soviet socialist economy was inefficient. Goods and services of all kinds were often or typically scarce or unavailable. Connections, bribes, and official access permitted ordinary people to trick the system, to get things they wanted or needed. People stole, set aside, dissimulated, shared, gave gifts, and traded. Friend and family networks were often the main beneficiaries. Those with skills used state equipment and spare parts to provide needed services on the side. All such activities could have landed one in jail but rarely did, so long as one kept the scale small, did not trade in foreign currency, and did not hire labor. Such parallel economic activity, which included black-market trading and individual agricultural production, kept the inefficient economy far more responsive to consumer demand. At the same time, however, because citizens could not predict what activities would be considered illegal and therefore punishable, it became difficult for them to distinguish between what was lawful and unlawful, which fostered a general disregard for the law and even a contempt for the law. One often had to pay bribes just to avoid prosecution for behaviors that in Western countries would have been considered completely ordinary. It was also common to pay bribes to ensure that proper legal procedure was followed.

Such worries did not typically afflict the political leadership, the so-called *nomenklatura*. Upon coming to power, Brezhnev asserted a policy of "stability of cadres." Whereas Khrushchev had threatened their power and authority with arbitrary administrative changes, the new regime guaranteed their longevity in office and inviolability in authority, barring truly egregious malfeasance. The Little Deal, in other words, applied up and down the political hierarchy and throughout the Soviet system.

Stricter police tactics and harsher treatment of criminals and alleged criminals begun under Khrushchev continued through the Brezhnev era. Police began to be armed with truncheons from summer 1962 after the mass strike in Novocherkassk—and to use them frequently. Similarly, in July 1966, the government adopted laws on fighting crime in general and hooliganism in particular. The emphasis on reeducation and rehabilitation was dropped, but they had been on the way out under Khrushchev. "Especially malicious hooliganism" involving bodily harm was strongly targeted.

In practice, the entire judicial and police systems—including its operations and the selection of its personnel at every level of government—were monitored and controlled by the Administrative Organs Department of the Central Committee of the Communist Party. Such tight supervision was made public in 1965 with the decree "Measures to Improve the Procuracy's Investigative Machinery and the Maintenance of Public Order." Although in principle, the Procuracy was responsible for oversight over the legality of the criminal justice system, it was in fact that the Party bore ultimate responsibility for this task. Nor could the Procuracy exercise supervision over the Party.[27] From the establishment of the Soviet state, prosecution of Communist Party officials had required the approval of their superiors. In an environment of increasing illegality, with the authorities often ignoring the corruption and malfeasance of senior officials, it became all but impossible to bring any of them to account. As under Khrushchev, the "Party line" even expressed in offhand remarks by Brezhnev or other senior party leaders was sometimes taken as legally binding throughout the criminal justice system. A similar process was at work at lower levels of the government apparatus. It was illegal for Communist Party officials to interfere with the criminal justice system, but they did so regularly and with impunity. A popular expression, circulating widely during the late Soviet era, branded this phenomenon "telephone justice" or "telephone law" (*telefonnoe pravo*). State or party officials would communicate their wishes to procurators, judges, and other judicial personnel, often by telephone, and those wishes were typically complied with.

The criminal justice system was in principle guided by strict rules of procedure governing the investigation, prosecution, and trial of alleged criminals. For many ordinary cases, these procedures were adhered to relatively strictly. For cases with some political aspect, or in which senior officials took an interest, the procedures could be quite different. For one thing, the investigation of regular cases was conducted by officials of the Procuracy. The Interior Ministry and the KGB had their own investigators.[28] Also, personal connections in high places mattered. Any case involving a defendant with influential allies in the Party would often proceed according to instructions delivered via the procurator to the judge.

The process was not always smooth. When the son of a well-connected Moldavian composer killed a man in an auto accident in 1962, the driver's father used his clout to secure a lenient sentence for him. A relation of the deceased appealed directly to Khrushchev, however, who publicly denounced the laxity of the judge. The case was reviewed and the offender sentenced to six years' imprisonment. After Khrushchev's ouster two years later, the father complained to Brezhnev. The son's sentence was then reduced to two years, the time already served, and he was released.[29] All systems of criminal justice suffer from some informality and arbitrariness, but the Soviet system was often governed by an almost complete lack of formal principles.

Similarly, public campaigns waged by the party leadership in favor of, for example, harsher punishment would typically be taken into account by judges. Just to be safe, judges might impose a stiffer sentence than demanded by the procurator. At the same time, however, major cases, especially of economic crime, were tricky to adjudicate. Some participants were untouchable because of their party status or because of highly placed patrons. During the Brezhnev era, the number of "untouchables" grew exponentially, as did corruption generally. Such cases also required lengthy and complicated investigation and financial expertise, which was not always available. As a result, big white-collar crime conspiracies could avoid their day of reckoning, though naturally palms had to be greased regularly.

Many factors of the judicial system were stacked against defendants. They had the right to counsel only from the end of the preliminary investigation. In many cases, however, investigators and procurators failed to notify the accused of this right. As a result, defendants were represented by advocates at the pretrial stage in only 14 percent of criminal cases in 1960, though this figure increased steadily, reaching 35 percent in 1972.[30] In order to prevent full involvement of defense advocates at the investigatory stage, investigators often conducted all the preliminary work before officially opening the investigation and then completed the remaining elements within a matter of hours. Also, within the Soviet criminal justice system, the procurator was viewed as an objective party, one primarily seeking the truth. Thus, judges tended to defer to them. The judge and lay assessors all generally presumed guilt, even though in 1978, the Supreme Court affirmed the principle of the presumption of innocence.[31] The defendant sat alone in the dock (often enclosed in a metal cage) at the front of Soviet courtrooms, some distance from the defense advocate. The two were in fact not allowed to communicate except with permission from the judge. In the people's courts—the court of first instance for most criminal cases—the lay assessors, typically lacking knowledge of the law and criminal procedure, deferred almost always to the judge. The accusatory summary, as prepared by the police investigators and signed by the procurator, was typically accepted at face value by the court. The procurator, moreover, typically enjoyed more trust and prestige in the eyes of the court than did the defense advocate. Unless a communist official took an interest in a court proceeding, the judge was the master of the courtroom. Thus, once a decision was reached in the mind of the judge, there was little the defense advocate could do to alter it. Both procurators and defense advocates could appeal a court sentence, the former to request a retrial in the hope of achieving a harsher penalty and the latter in the hope of softening the original sentence. Such proceedings took place in the higher courts without lay assessors and without witnesses. The chances were typically better for a worse outcome than for a better, from the point of view of defendants.

For decades, the Soviet government shied away from publishing comprehensive crime statistics. In fact, the last such statistics had appeared in 1928. Some partial numbers were occasionally released and often they indicated rising crime rates. Such revelations were often accompanied by assurances from senior officials that more resources would be allocated to crime-fighting. Hooliganism was thought to have posed especial problems. According to one set of statistics collected for 1976, the courts handed down 976,090 convictions, roughly one quarter for the vague catchall of "hooliganism." In addition, nearly 1,700,000 minor offenses were punished—879,265 by people's courts and 805,070 by comrades' courts. In all, 2,660,425 convictions were issued.[32] To these numbers, one could add persons tried by "special courts," which functioned in the large number of "closed" cities and territories of the USSR, including classified research campuses and labor camps. If one factors in such alternative courts, it is possible to estimate the total number of cases handled within the broader judicial system in the early 1970s as over 4 million annually.

The incidence of female criminality seems to have fallen roughly within the range witnessed in other developed countries: between 12 and 18 percent. Women committed a very high number of crimes involving theft and embezzlement in the sales–service sector of the economy, where they constituted roughly 75 percent of personnel. The percentage of convictions of women for fraud and deception of consumers in these sectors of the economy comes close to their overall share of employees. As for the types of crimes in which women were found guilty, the largest proportion was theft of personal property (40 percent), followed by theft of state property (18 percent), and various forms of fraud and black marketeering (22 percent). Criminal convictions of men, by contrast, divided into 38 percent for hooliganism, 27 percent for embezzlement, and 18 percent for various forms of violent theft and assault.[33]

Statistics on juvenile crime are harder to come by. Youth offenses appear to have been growing, reaching close to 10 percent of all criminal offenses in the USSR by the mid- to late 1960s. The crimes youths engaged in consisted primarily of theft (over 40 percent), assault with intent to rob (7 percent), and hooliganism (7 percent). Most such criminality was apparently committed by youths between the ages of 15 and 17. Girls accounted for an extremely small fraction of overall youth criminality, hovering around 2 or 3 percent.[34] The vast majority of youth perpetrators were children of blue-collar workers, and most such criminality was urban. Unlike in American cities, however, criminality tended to occur outside city centers, the home to people with the best jobs, most clout, greatest access to consumer goods, and best education and job prospects. Alcohol abuse seems to have been heavily involved with most Soviet youth crime; organized gangs were apparently rare. Institutions of social control were far more elaborate in the USSR than in Western countries. Children participated all but universally in the Pioneer organizations (ages 10–14) and nearly universally in the Komsomol (some 80–90 percent of high school and college students). The militia maintained lists of problem families; procurator offices kept files on problem youth. In both instances, such information was supplied to relevant local authorities when deemed necessary. A host of institutions and procedures aimed at keeping youth offenders out of the regular criminal justice system, including: special courts, special schools, and special colonies. Nevertheless, children under the age of 18 could be incarcerated for up to ten years.

A criminal case in a village outside Moscow probably exemplified both the good and the bad of the Soviet criminal justice system apropos regular crime. In 1965, a 14-year-old girl was raped and murdered. The authorities could not solve the case and therefore closed it. Some local women, including the girl's mother, fired off letter after letter to top officials in Moscow who demanded a resolution. The Central Committee's interest apparently stemmed from the fact that some of the country's most famous writers had vacation homes nearby in Peredelkino and used their clout to draw attention to the case. Connections to the powers that be in the Soviet system were typically king. An investigator sent from the Moscow regional Procuracy seized upon two boys—friends and classmates—of the deceased and detained them without counsel. Under pressure, they confessed to the crimes. At the trial, however, they recanted. Even though the evidence against the boys was weak, the authorities and the local community closed ranks against them, the former to keep up their convictions statistics and the latter to achieve closure, from faith in the Soviet system, and given their tough-on-crime attitude. The Moscow regional court punted the case back to the Procuracy. A second trial was conducted by the Moscow City Court, where a compliant judge was willing to hand down the required verdict of guilty. The centrality of confession to Soviet criminal justice, a holdover from the Stalin (and pre-1864) era, rendered it dependent on unprofessional and arbitrary methods of investigation and fostered simplistic thinking and gullibility. "If they confessed," as a teacher at the school the children had attended asserted, "they must be guilty."[35] The continued interest in the case taken by several Moscow lawyers and other educated elites, nevertheless, turned the tide in the trial by focusing dispassionate, rational thought on the details of the crime and the evidence. Because of their interventions, the case was shunted yet again, in 1969, to the Supreme Court, where the boys were acquitted. Without pressure from those elites, it seems likely that the boys would have served as scapegoats. Even so, external pressure insured that justice was served.

It also occurred that unjust sentences could be overturned without the intervention of intellectuals, typically on procedural grounds. In 1974, for example, a man accused of rape rejected his court-appointed legal counsel because, in his view, she demonstrated both incompetence and lack of support for his case. The trial then proceeded without a defense advocate and resulted in a conviction. Upon review, the Supreme Court pointed out that the court neither offered a replacement defense counsel nor inquired of the defendant if he wished to conduct the defense himself. Consequently, the judgment was vacated.[36]

These cases offer several insights into the Soviet criminal justice system under Brezhnev. It prized confession as the "queen of evidence," even though the Code of Criminal Procedure asserted clearly that confession is not proof of guilt by itself. The "war on crime" prompted many investigators, procurators, and judges to push ambiguous cases through to conviction in order to please senior officials. Political authorities meddled in cases that came to their attention. The best bet for a defendant was to seek protection from powerful operators. Educated elites played a vital role in bringing about justice, when they took an interest in a case. In other words, the system was personalized and often arbitrary but certainly capable of reaching a fair and reasonable outcome. Such was not true regarding political cases.

There were far fewer such cases than under Khrushchev and many fewer than under Stalin. In the years 1966–1980, the courts issued 1,829 convictions in political cases. (During these years, as under Khrushchev, a far bigger emphasis was placed on prophylactic measures, with well over 110,000 such cases in 1967–1974.)[37] But these trials had a far bigger resonance than regular-crime cases, both inside the USSR and abroad and to some extent may be said to have contributed to the fall of Soviet communism. In fact, the turning point for the emergence of the powerful Soviet dissident movement came with the trial of two closeted writers of a socially critical mind-set.

Andrei Sinyavsky and Yuli Daniel, writing under pseudonyms, began arranging to smuggle satirical manuscripts to the West beginning in 1959 and 1961, respectively. In their writings, which were soon published abroad to critical acclaim, they depicted Soviet life with many of its obvious flaws yet avoided direct, sharp criticism. For several years, the KGB worked diligently to trace the authors, piecing together evidence from details of their writing. In 1964, they closed in on them. Ever cautious, the police conducted careful surveillance—using human shadows, bugging devices, and wire-tapping—for several more months. The pair was finally arrested in late 1965 and brought to trial in February 1966. They were accused of violating Article 70 forbidding anti-Soviet agitation and propaganda. The indictment stated that reactionary imperialists abroad, having failed to overthrow the Soviet state by force of arms, did "not shrink from even the most vile means in attempting to compromise socialist society in the eyes of world public opinion and the Soviet people. Toward these ends the propaganda centers of the imperialist states actively employed the anti-Soviet defamatory writings of certain renegades whom the West passes off as 'true' representatives of Soviet literature."[38] From the beginning of their regime, it was a common method of the Soviet authorities to blame foreign enemies for any popular discontent, as if Soviet life was completely beyond reproach.

During the trial, the procurator emphasized the moral degradation of the accused. Most people in the courtroom expressed contempt, indignation, and hostility toward them. The prosecution did not need to demonstrate their guilt, but rather the defendants had to prove that they had not intended to harm the Soviet system, to oppugn Marxism-Leninism or to discredit the party leadership. They tried to prove their innocence, arguing that they used literary devices, engaged in psychological analysis, loved their country dearly, and would not dream of harming it in any way. Yet it was no use. The entire system was against them: the procurator, the public accusers, the public at large, and the media. Sinyavsky was given seven years in a labor camp, and Daniel, five years.

The institution of "public accuser" was intended to involve ordinary people in the judicial process, to bring it closer to the people. Anyone could assume this role. The only requirement was to denounce the accused. The Soviet public got involved with criminal justice in other ways as well. Voluntarily providing information about criminal activity was one such method. In the USSR, it was perfectly legal to build a house on property one had legal possession of or to remodel an existing house. It was extremely difficult to acquire the necessary tools and materials legally, however, though not impossible. High officials built themselves magnificent summer homes, often with diverted materials and labor, typically behind tall fences in remote areas, and nearly always with impunity. Ordinary people ran up against popular envy and the building code, which stipulated that homes should not exceed 650 square feet of living space (not counting kitchens, bathrooms, closets, and hallways). One could get away with exceeding this figure so long as a disgruntled neighbor did not alert the authorities, which apparently happened all too often. Once the inspectors descended, the procurator and the courts would get involved. The result was usually the confiscation of the offending structure. Such broad social involvement continued its course also in the comrades' courts, which multiplied steadily throughout the Brezhnev years, numbering 300,000 in 1983, together handling some half million cases yearly.[39]

The death penalty was resorted to far less in the years after Stalin's death, though the numbers were still quite high under Brezhnev and his immediate successors. Between 1962 and 1990, roughly 21,000 people were executed by firing squad. Nearly all of these death sentences were imposed for various ordinary crimes, including murder and theft of state property. (To put this statistic into perspective, the total number of executions in the United States from 1700 until 2015 was roughly 15,760.) The incidence of capital punishment gradually diminished in the Soviet Union over these years from a yearly average of 500–1,000 in the 1960s to a few hundred in the 1970s, though the number and range of capital crimes remained extensive, from treason and sabotage to stealing state property on a large scale and rape under certain circumstances.[40]

While capital punishment was gradually imposed less frequently, over the course of the Brezhnev era the inmate population of the Gulag steadily expanded, reaching 1,071,497 adult prisoners in 1979, for an incarceration rate of 406.7 prisoners per 100,000 population. In these same years, however, more and more convicted criminals were released to finish part of their sentence by working for reduced pay in economic enterprises—820,659 people in all from 1968 to 1973, for an average of nearly 137,000 annually or 27 percent of all prisoners.[41] In other words, the system remained strongly controlling but also committed to making criminals productive members of society.

The state-controlled media were permitted to criticize the failings of individual officials—for example, among the police, Procuracy, and judiciary—but not the system as a whole and not a given class of officials. Thus, in the 1960s and 1970s, one could not find any image in the Soviet press of the police, Procuracy, and judiciary as a whole other than as helpful, tireless, efficient, and dedicated to upholding truth and justice.

In reality, the militia remained or grew ever more corrupt, involved with organized crime, and constantly paid off to turn a blind eye to both petty and major criminal activity. They also wielded great arbitrary power. By law, they could hold suspects for nine months without filing charges against them, and this interval could be extended almost indefinitely by order of the Presidium of the Supreme Soviet. The militia could ask for a citizen's internal passport at any time. Legally, they had no right to enter a residence without a search warrant, but in practice, they did so on a regular basis, as did members of the voluntary police assistance brigades. The passport and residency restrictions were powerful tools, which the police systematically used to control the population: for example, following periodic sweeps of the major cities, they were supposed to remove all persons without proof of residency status. Young men of crime-prone age, moreover, rarely received permission to live in the major urban centers, especially Moscow and Leningrad. All such tools, as well as arbitrary power and a willingness to bend the rules, enabled the militia in 1980 to "clear" (make an arrest or identify a suspect in) 90 percent of reported crimes, a very high proportion.[42]

Many ordinary people, and not only the poor and ethnic and racial minorities, as is often the case in Western countries, preferred to avoid any dealings with the militia. True, society was expected to back the efforts of the police by participating in voluntary support brigades, and hundreds of thousands took part. Moreover, thousands of Komsomol brigades helped maintain order among young people. (Of course, never more than a small fraction of the total population of over 240 million people participated in such organized assistance to the police.) In addition to the police and voluntary brigades, well over 1 million people served in paid positions as inspectors or guards posted at the entrance of every official building, on every floor of every hotel, and in many other institutions. Their job was to watch out for unauthorized personnel and improper and potentially criminal activity. Soviet society, in other words, was tightly controlled.

As corruption and illegal activities spread throughout Soviet society, the flourishing prison and camp subculture began to seep out into ordinary life, influencing literature and music. The most popular singer-songwriter of the 1960s and 1970s, Vladimir Vysotsky, laced his lyrics with camp and prison slang, for example. While something of the prison ethos gained a wide following, especially among the youth, networks of organized crime reached further into official institutions and organizations. In fact, it reached right to the very top of the system (see below). A key reason for the pervasiveness of white-collar and official crime was the disregard in which the leadership held the law.

Although the USSR had a complex political system, with parallel lines of authority in a hierarchy of party and state institutions, all governed by clearly defined legal jurisdictions and obligations, as well as a sophisticated criminal justice system, the number of trained jurists was comparatively small. In 1978, there were 127,000 jurists in the Soviet Union.[43] In the United States, by contrast, in that year, there were 464,851 lawyers (well before the dramatic expansion of the American legal profession in the later twentieth century). That was roughly four times more legal professionals, despite a population 14 percent smaller. Acquiring a legal education was one thing. It was possible to do it by correspondence course. Joining the Bar as an advocate, especially in Moscow, the summit of the legal profession, was quite another. Even in the late 1980s, the Moscow Bar Association limited the number of new candidates each year to the astonishingly low number of twenty.[44] Furthermore, Soviet jurists felt greater loyalty to the institutions they served—such as the Procuracy, the KGB, the Ministry of Interior, or the Ministry of Justice—rather than to the broader legal profession.

A further sign of the low esteem in which the law was held in Soviet society was the fact that the proportion of women jurists was far higher than in Western societies. There was great opportunity for advancement for women in Soviet society, but the glass ceiling was quite low. Any profession or status that was prestigious had a small proportion of women. For example, the proportion of women party members rose from only one-fifth in 1957 to one-quarter in 1981. The proportion of women jurists, by contrast, increased from 32 percent in 1959 to over 50 percent in 1976 (including one-third of all judges), while in roughly the same years, the feminization of the highly prestigious law profession in the United States went from 3.4 to only 10.4 percent. Moreover, most Soviet women jurists worked in lower-level positions. In general, the legal profession in the USSR was far less prestigious than in Western countries. Partly, this was due to the lack of independence and relative powerlessness of legal practitioners within the political structures of the country. The relatively low prestige was also made obvious by the shabby premises throughout the judicial system, even for the highest courts.

Rather than the entire system functioning according to the law, which only trained lawyers can advise their clients how best to follow, in the USSR informal patterns of behavior and decision-making were prevalent. Throughout the economy, in fact, it was typically necessary to engage in barter deals, employ devious procurement agents, set up elaborate circumventions of established rules and laws, and devise other under-the-counter mechanisms for fulfilling official plans within a hostile environment for managers and entrepreneurs. It seems that the environment was even more hostile to whistleblowers who might have denounced the pervasive corruption and illegal wheeling and dealing.[45]

An exception to this rule seems to have been the prosecution or removal from office of senior officials for political purposes. An example of such machinations enabled Eduard Shevardnadze to take the place of the notoriously corrupt first secretary of the Georgian Communist Party, Vasilii Mzhavanadze, in 1972. Shevardnadze seized his chance during a dinner party when he noticed that Mzhavanadze's wife was wearing a giant diamond ring, which had appeared on a wanted list put out by Interpol. Shevardnadze immediately informed his patron in Moscow, Yuri Andropov, the head of the KGB, who persuaded Brezhnev to dismiss the corrupt official and appoint in his stead Shevardnadze. It is interesting to note that Mzhavanadze was not prosecuted, nor was his wife. She was good friends with Victoria Brezhnev, the First Lady, who was able to shield her from prosecution.[46]

Andropov parlayed his law-and-order campaign into a means of strengthening his political position and that of his institutional and client bases. As Brezhnev grew more feeble, he could not resist this push. In July 1978, the status of the KGB was raised to that of a full-fledged state committee. In August 1979, the Central Committee adopted a resolution "On Improving Work to Safeguard Law and Order and Intensifying the Struggle against Law Violation." The resolution specifically mentioned cracking down on alcohol abuse, juvenile delinquency, official crime, and parasitism, among others. Over the next four years, convictions of senior officials for corruption of various kinds increased by 44 percent, according to one reckoning.[47] The campaign was strengthened in November 1981 by the Central Committee, which urged a crackdown on material extravagance displayed by senior officials.

Many such prosecutions targeted clients of Brezhnev's political cronies; that is to say, networks of corruption required high-level protection. As Andropov and aligned officials sought to break up such networks, the threads of malfeasance inevitably led up the hierarchy to some of the senior-most officials in the country, in fact right up to the Central Committee. Such powerful figures could not be prosecuted, but they could be transferred to less exalted positions. One such example was Nikolai Shchelokov. Brezhnev's decades-long client had been made interior minister of the USSR soon after Brezhnev came to power, despite having no experience of any kind in policing. A supremely corrupt official, he apparently diverted vast resources to his own family network, including imported cars, consumer electronics, and furs. In fact, he set up an entire closed-access store purveying scarce consumer goods for the exclusive use of his close relations and clients. After falling from grace, he was removed from the Central Committee, stripped of his military rank, and appointed police chief for a construction site in Siberia. Rather than face these humiliations, he committed suicide. The campaign also reached into Brezhnev's immediate family and relation network. In February 1982, his daughter Galina was brought in for questioning about her potential connection to a big illegal-diamond-exporting ring.

After Brezhnev died in November, Andropov took his place as general secretary of the Communist Party. In that position, he carried forward his anticorruption campaign. Effective January 1, 1983, major revisions to the Criminal Code of the Russian Republic went into effect, with an emphasis on crimes against public and personal property. The prescribed punishments for dozens of crimes were stiffened. It became easier to prosecute people for "parasitism." Discipline and penalties for misbehavior were strengthened in the corrective labor camps. Over the following months, punishments for "anti-Soviet" and unauthorized religious activities were made harsher. In the spring, police carried out vigorous sweeps of retail stores, beauty salons, and bathhouses in the middle of the day in order to nab and prosecute the vast number of workers absent from their places of employment for shopping or leisure. The intensified legal prosecution of misdeeds, which were frequently engendered or at least multiplied by systemic inefficiencies and restraints or even prohibitions on initiative and entrepreneurship, bespoke a misunderstanding by senior officials of the nature of the political and economic system. Corruption and everyday criminality were pervasive not because of laxness but because of extreme social micromanagement and the criminalization of ordinary economic activity.

The crackdown struck officials and not only citizens. In 1983, some 161,000 Interior Ministry personnel were fired from all levels of the hierarchy throughout the country.[48] Without high-level protection, many more corrupt officials were prosecuted or fell from grace. In Moscow, the most exclusive closed grocery store was Gastronom No. 1, nicknamed Eliseev's, after its prerevolutionary owner. Yuri Sokolov, the store's director for years, had provided the Moscow party elite with access to luxury foods unavailable to ordinary citizens and pocketed vast wealth himself. He was arrested in fall 1983 and executed the following year.[49] Many other formerly untouchable elites fell into Andropov's nets during his sixteen months in office. Yet when corruption, fraud, trading on the side, black marketeering, and other shady activities were a way of life for ambitious Soviet citizens starving for opportunities to show initiative, no campaign imaginable was likely to succeed at stamping them out.

After Andropov died in February 1984 and was replaced by the Brezhnev crony, Konstantin Chernenko, the crackdown on corruption—including the purge and replacement of law enforcement agents and officials— was slackened. Its intensity continued only in such peripheral areas as Uzbekistan, where 1,056 employees in the retail and medical sectors were fired and indicted.[50] Official corruption, which scarcely diminished, persisted. An aggravating factor making it hard to root out corruption in high places was the extent to which nearly the entire population—as much as 83 percent, according to one sociological study—obtained goods, and especially foodstuffs, from within the "shadow economy."[51] At the same time, political dissidents continued to face stiff repression. For example, Andrei Sakharov who had been banished to the Volga River city of Gorky in 1980 was still being held there under house arrest when, in 1984, his wife, Yelena Bonner, was tried, convicted, and sentenced to five years of internal exile for defamation of the USSR. Many others suffered similar fates. Political hospitalizations in mental institutions were still carried out, though at an apparently diminished rate.[52] Finally, the government pursued a hard line on crime-fighting, with particular attention to juvenile crime and petty criminality.

Gorbachev and the fall of Soviet communism

The death of Chernenko and his replacement in March 1985 by Andropov's more vigorous, reform-minded protégé, Mikhail Gorbachev, ushered in an era of dramatic reform involving efforts at economic restructuring (*perestroika*), gradually more open media (*glasnost*), and broadened political participation (*demokratizatsiia*). Together these changes shook the Soviet system to its foundations and resulted in a half-decade in its utter collapse.

Gorbachev's first instinct in his effort to tackle economic and social problems—like that of his deceased patron Andropov—was to focus on personal misbehavior of citizens rather than systemic defects. Alcohol consumption and abuse had increased steadily in the post-Stalin years. Between 1960 and 1979, alcohol sales had nearly quadrupled. By the early 1980s, Soviet citizens were consuming nearly twice as much alcohol as Americans (fourteen liters of pure alcohol compared to eight). According to official statistics, 50 percent of all persons convicted for criminal activity were inebriated at the time of their offense in the late Soviet era.[53] Andropov had commenced a campaign to reduce alcohol consumption, but Gorbachev launched something like a war against it. In May 1985, shortly after he became General Secretary, the Politburo and the Central Committee issued a series of resolutions entitled "Measures to Overcome Drunkenness and Alcoholism." Distilleries and breweries were shut down and vineyards were uprooted. Restrictions on permitted hours and locations of alcohol sales were tightened. The price of liquor increased by 50 percent over the next year and a half. Penalties for drunkenness in public places and on the job and for private alcohol production rose dramatically. More funding was allocated for leisure and cultural activities and for the treatment of alcoholism. The campaign produced results. From 1984 to 1988, alcohol sales dropped by over 50 percent.[54] (Homebrewing and the use of often dangerous alcohol substitutes, by contrast, increased.)

Gorbachev also returned to Andropov's policies intended to fight against shirking on the job and official corruption throughout the system. It was only under Gorbachev, in fall 1988, for example, that Brezhnev's son-in-law, Yuri Churbanov, was finally put on trial as a front man for a massive embezzlement scheme involving millions of rubles and hundreds of officials in Uzbekistan. The conspiracy involved phantom deliveries of cotton to

Russian industry and the siphoning off of five or six million rubles annually. Churbanov apparently received bribes of at least 400,000 rubles. He landed in jail, even though according to an astute legal journalist, the accusations against him were not proven in court. Even so, most people in the courtroom called for his execution. The Supreme Court of the USSR sentenced him to twelve years and loss of all property, military rank, and government awards.[55]

Gradually, because economic indices stubbornly refused to improve, Gorbachev developed a program to reform the Soviet system from top to bottom. Yet surprisingly little change in the criminal justice system came about, despite some earnest efforts. In fall 1986, for example, senior officials proposed giving suspects the right to legal counsel during the pretrial phase, and specifically during the criminal investigation. A law of 1970 had given procurators the authority to allow access to counsel during such proceedings. Even when they permitted such access, however, criminal investigators typically hammered together their cases before the official investigation actually began, rendering such a right entirely meaningless. In July 1988, the Nineteenth Party Conference decided in favor of the involvement of defense advocates during the preliminary stage of criminal proceedings, but it did not determine at what point such access should be granted. Nor was it clear who would pay for the relevant additional legal fees, which made most legal advocates weary of taking on the extra work. In November 1989, the Supreme Soviet granted both suspects and accused the right to counsel "at the moment of detention, arrest, or indictment."[56] A law of April 1990 guaranteed government payment for legal assistance to indigent suspects, but it was still unclear who would pay the fees in other instances. Nor, outside the major cities, were there enough advocates to provide such services to all suspects. In practice, it seems that few advocates went out of their way to participate at an earlier stage in the criminal proceedings. Likewise, persons under arrest did not jump at the opportunity to request legal counsel. For one thing, there was nothing like the U.S. *Miranda* provision. Moreover, Soviet law neither granted defense advocates access to case files until the end of the preliminary investigation nor permitted them to question witnesses and collect evidence except under the supervision of judicial investigators. So, although procedural rules had improved theoretically, in practice not much changed.

Reformers in the Gorbachev era sought to tackle many other aspects of criminal justice with mixed results. One effort concerned pretrial detention. As noted above, for decades after the death of Stalin, police and investigators could still detain suspects without formally filing charges for months and even years. Such abuse gradually declined from the early 1980s but still continued. In the Gorbachev era, politicians and legal experts pushed for laws limiting such detentions to serious criminal cases, disallowing the Supreme Soviet to extend pretrial detention indefinitely, and requiring procurators to seek judicial approval before imposing pretrial detention.

These proposals failed to garner enough support to become law before the fall of the USSR.

Allies of Gorbachev similarly pushed for a diminished resort to harsh criminal penalties. Custodial punishments continued a downward trajectory from previous years, declining from 52.9 percent of all convictions in 1983 to 33.7 percent in 1987.[57] The consignment of criminals to labor colonies also gradually diminished, with the population of such colonies more than halving in the four years preceding May 1990. Yet the remaining colonies and other correctional institutions were scattered typically far from major urban areas. Thus, most inmates were still sent thousands of kilometers from home, such that their punishment remained quite severe, given the absence in most cases of family members and friends nearby. While some reformers hoped to abolish the death penalty outright, public opinion favored its retention. Still, its application against persons convicted of gross economic malfeasance had ceased in practice by fall 1988. The number of capital offenses also declined to sixteen listed in the Criminal Code of the RSFSR, five related to crimes against persons and the rest to crimes against the state.[58] Here too, despite all the reformist exertions, the state retained a far higher status from the point of view of criminal law than did the individual.

Other reforms targeted so-called political and economic crimes. Already in 1987, the courts had ceased pursuing such prosecutions. Despite efforts by some hardliners to retain political crime laws on the books, in April 1989 the first session of the newly created Congress of People's Deputies repealed the remaining relevant statutes. Reformers and the government also took steps to decriminalize such activities as trading in foreign currency, engaging in shady deals in order to fulfill state-imposed economic plans, selling goods for foreign currency, and similar "economic crimes." In practice, most of the laws rendering such activities criminal offenses remained on the books but were enforced less and less. Here, significant progress was made, because dismantling the complex legal apparatus aiming at total control of political and economic life was fairly easy to effect.

Achieving reform in criminal justice was complicated by two factors. First, violent crime rose significantly in 1987–1989. Higher crime stemmed in part from more lenient policing, caused in part by massive press revelations of police brutality, abuse, and bribe-taking in 1986–1988. Thousands of police were investigated and convicted or dismissed for such malfeasance. The police managed to "clear" a diminishing proportion of reported crimes—50 percent in 1988 and only 36 percent in 1989.[59] Of the alleged offenders arrested in those years, over one-third had to be released in compliance with the campaign to enforce procedural norms.

Second, glasnost made it possible for the first time in Soviet history for journalists to report openly and truthfully about criminality (in addition to a host of other problems, which the state-controlled media had so carefully concealed). Suddenly, Soviet citizens were flooded with information about murder, mayhem, organized crime, and Mafia-like criminal structures as facts of life all around them. In reality, such phenomena had existed for decades. Organized crime had flourished throughout the Brezhnev era, but one could only know of it from rumors. Moreover, with the expansion of unregulated economic activity and entrepreneurship, young go-getters were making money and flaunting it. They were also hiring private security details, often directly from the militia and the KGB. Ordinary citizens complained bitterly that the police were doing too little to protect them from the rising tide of crime. The politicians were listening, and further major reforms of criminal justice were not attempted. In January 1990, a permanent committee on combating crime was created within the Supreme Soviet. In June, the Supreme Soviet authorized police wiretaps in pursuit of any serious crime for up to six months with the approval of either a procurator or a judge. Yet crime continued to surge, and as always the powerful and well-connected, but now also the rich, seemed to get the lion's share of protection.

Efforts were also made to raise the status of the judiciary in general and of judges in particular. Commentators lamented the shabby premises in which justice was conducted in the USSR.[60] Unfavorable comparisons were unavoidable between courthouses, even of the highest court in the land, the USSR Supreme Court, and buildings housing other state institutions. A constitutional amendment of December 1988, for example, doubled the term in office of judges from five to ten years. Also in 1988, a law on the status of judges required higher legal education and the passing of a qualifying examination for all judges. They were also, henceforth, to wear robes. Living quarters were to be provided by local authorities. Even when that was possible, however, and in reality it often was not, such accommodations naturally rendered judges dependent on local officials. Unfortunately, the dependence of judicial officials on the executive branch was a deeply rooted feature of Russian and Soviet criminal justice and difficult to undermine. Inculcating respect for the law and legal authorities would require major efforts, after seven decades of neglect. A law of November 1989 prescribed penalties for exhibiting disrespect for the court or court personnel. Other laws adopted in 1989 and 1990 expanded the jurisdiction of judges to include a wide variety of official government activities.

In practice, judges did begin to assert themselves, if rather tentatively. In 1989, for example, courts throughout the USSR rendered some 5,000 acquittals, a number roughly double the figure from five years before. For a country as large as the USSR, this was a comparatively small number. Indeed, given the strong pressure to drive down the acquittal rate beginning in the late 1940s, it remained extremely low—around 1 percent.[61] Even so, in a country where acquittals had been seen as evidence of incompetence within the criminal justice system, it seems this was a step forward toward judicial independence. Some judges allowed cases against senior officials to go forward, while others protected citizens from unlawful government harassment, though such cases were admittedly rare. In practice, the Ministry of Justice, the Procuracy, and the Communist Party all continued to exert powerful influence over the courts.

In January 1989, the Presidium of the Supreme Soviet issued a decree rehabilitating "all citizens" repressed by extrajudicial process in the Stalin era. By June, nearly 2 million people had benefited from this determination. Then in August, Gorbachev issued a decree restoring full rights to all persons who suffered political repression from the 1920s to the 1950s (though not from the Khrushchev era onward).[62] Both public activists and some officials urged a reconsideration of sentences issued against dissidents in the post-Stalin era, but such acts of restitution did not become possible until the post-Soviet era.

In August 1991, hardliners within the government attempted to pull off a coup d'état against Gorbachev. Lacking adequate support within the military and facing strong popular leadership from Boris Yeltsin, the conspirators failed and were placed under arrest. Tensions between Yeltsin as president of the Russian Republic and Gorbachev as president of the Soviet Union came to a head at the end of the year when the USSR was dissolved into its fifteen constituent republics. Henceforth, far more dramatic reform of criminal justice would become possible.

7

Criminal Justice since the Collapse of Communism

During the reign of communism in Russia, the judiciary could not be independent, law could not stand above political leaders, individuals could not be sure of the protection of the law, and in general, the criminal justice system remained politicized. In the late Gorbachev years, serious—but ultimately fruitless—efforts were made to rectify these flaws. Influential personages could still intervene in criminal justice, individuals could be prosecuted for acts that were either not illegal or at least not clearly defined as illegal, and judges could not always adjudicate according to the letter of the law. The question was: Could Russia emerge from the collapse of communism with such procedural guarantees and judicial institutions as to render justice predictable, impartial, reasonable, and relatively consistent?

The era of Boris Yeltsin

Yeltsin and his closest advisors had a radical conception of judicial reform aimed at creating a law-governed state. Instead of seeking to implement this program directly through government institutions, however, they created a separate agency, the State-Legal Administration. Critics denounced it as a parallel structure just like the Communist Party. Such a bureaucratic circumvention, not unlike His Majesty's Own Private Chancellery of Nicholas I in the early nineteenth century, bespoke a distrust of state institutions and government officials. It also signified a preference for irregular administrative procedures. Since the essence of what needed to be squeezed out of the existing institutions was arbitrariness and informality, this was probably not the best approach.

The institution that opposed Yeltsin's judicial reforms with the greatest vehemence was the Procuracy. In Soviet times, that institution was seen as the system's primary guarantor of legality and justice. The reformers aimed to strip away its broad supervisory authority, leaving only the prosecutorial function. Leading procurators fought back, warning of increased criminality, a weakening of the state, and a concomitant undermining of all "power institutions," like the FSB (formerly the KGB) and Interior Ministry. Officials even claimed for the Procuracy a uniquely Russian evolution and essence, even though the original model for the institution was adopted from Sweden by Peter the Great. The main goal for the defenders of the Procuracy was to maintain administrative control over the judicial system and to impede the emergence of an independent judiciary.

After the attempted coup of August 1991 by communist hardliners, Yeltsin seized control of Communist Party property and transferred some buildings and office equipment to the judicial system. After all, in the Soviet era, courthouses were often among the least impressive and most dilapidated of official buildings. Most courts had no photocopy machines or even typewriters, much less computers. Funding for the judiciary also sharply increased. Judges were banned from joining the Communist or any other party. Thus, they no longer had to heed party resolutions or interference.

Legal reformers achieved significant modifications to the criminal law. The distinction between stealing private and state property was eliminated, a major departure from Soviet jurisprudence, when protecting the state was deemed the highest goal of criminal justice. Engaging in "speculation," or buying and selling goods for a profit, was decriminalized, fostering the further emergence of an autonomous private economic sector. The use of the criminal justice system to supply labor to state-owned industries was abolished. The death penalty was no longer to be imposed against "state criminals," but only against aggravated murderers, rapists, and terrorists. Laws were adopted specifically to tackle organized crime, for example, legislation targeting extortion. Thanks to an amendment of the Criminal Code adopted in June 1993, homosexual acts among consenting adults no longer constituted a criminal offense.

The judicial institutions and structure underwent change as well. A significant new departure was the adoption on June 26, 1992, of the Law on the Status of Judges. Most important, it decreed the appointment of judges for life (following a three-year probationary term) and the increased authority of professional institutions for the supervision of judges' qualifications and discipline in office, called qualification collegia and created originally in 1989. These bodies, instituted at the regional and national levels, were henceforth to be comprised solely of judges with full authority to oversee the disciplining and removal of judges. Together, these changes contributed toward the emerging independence of the judiciary.

Following a standoff with Russia's parliament, still called the Supreme Soviet, including an artillery barrage against the parliament building in

October 1993, a new Constitution was approved by referendum. It established a bicameral legislature, the Federal Assembly, comprised of the State Duma and the Federation Council. The presidency gained enormous power. Both the president and many government agencies, including all ministries, were endowed with legislative authority to issue a wide variety of binding executive orders. At the top of the judicial hierarchy stood three supreme courts: the Supreme Court (first established in 1923), the Constitutional Court, and the High Arbitrazh Court for commercial disputes (which was folded into the Supreme Court in 2014). (See Figure 7.1) The latter two courts were first instituted by Yeltsin in July 1991. The Constitution reinforced the independence of the judiciary previously set out in the law on the Status of Judges, adding personal immunity. Henceforth, a judge could face criminal charges only on the basis of federal law. The Constitution guaranteed extensive rights and protections of individuals, including the presumption of innocence, the exclusion of evidence gathered illegally, and the right to remain silent, to trial by jury, and to defense counsel from the moment of detention. It also forbade ex post facto laws, torture, double jeopardy, and forced confession. Restrictions on travel were also lifted. The Constitution retained capital punishment but only "as an exceptional penalty for especially grave crimes

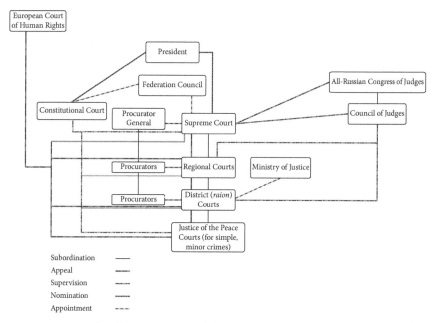

FIGURE 7.1 *Judicial organization of the Russian Federation from 1991 to the present. "Telephone justice" continued to function at the higher levels of criminal justice, but the courts enjoyed more independence than in the Soviet era. The Constitutional Court reviews cases alleging unconstitutional application of the law.*

against life."[1] Persons tried in such cases had the right to a jury trial. Unlike in Soviet times, a person could not be executed for economic or political crimes or for rape.

Despite the clear victories of the reformers, the system resisted judicial liberalization. It was hard if not impossible to decree respect for the law, fair treatment of suspects, the independence of judges, the presumption of innocence, and other elements of Western law, especially when such principles had been alien to Soviet tradition and practice for seven decades. Several factors pushed back against the reforms. Enacting them cost a lot of money, yet the Russian economy and the state budget were in free fall throughout the 1990s. The personnel responsible for implementing the reforms were the same as before 1991, at least until the older generation began to retire. Some laws and the Constitution itself retained key principles of the old system. Thus, for example, the Procuracy's supreme, government-wide supervisory role was preserved. Moreover, Soviet law sometimes remained in force. According to post-1991 law, only the courts had the power to authorize arrests and detention. Yet in practice procurators continued to authorize arrests and detention, as it were by inertia. Even a decision of the Constitutional Court, rendering such actions unconstitutional, was of no avail, because the Soviet-era Code of Criminal Procedure, which had not been superseded, "in effect trumped the Constitution for the better part of a decade," according to Eugene Huskey.[2]

Many other elements of the old Soviet criminal justice system persisted. Judges continued to participate in the questioning of witnesses and to call for additional evidence, instead of acting as impartial adjudicators. They also often interrupted participants in trial and permitted prejudicial outbursts from the courtroom. As previously, the courts (now called district or regional and not people's courts) were presided over by a professional judge and two people's assessors, that is, lay judges who had to be at least 25 years of age. The long-standing Soviet proclivity to avoid acquittals, moreover, continued throughout the Yeltsin era. In most instances, when a case brought before the court proved weak, instead of acquitting, judges typically sent the case back to law enforcement officials for a "supplementary investigation," just as in the Soviet era. The main reason for taking this approach was to avoid embarrassing law enforcement investigators. Of course, this provided no incentive for them to hammer together the best possible case. Moreover, with investigators and procurators expected to achieve conviction in nearly every case they took on, it is not surprising that they felt compelled to pressure judges to convict.

Likewise, despite the theoretical independence of the judiciary, institutional compulsion remained, taking many other forms. The president and his administration had shown generosity toward judges and often awaited reciprocal consideration. Senior officials had their pet cases and expected to influence their outcome. The system had a penchant toward efficiency expressed in high conviction rates. Caseloads were heavy, so judges and other judicial personnel could rarely devote adequate time to deliberation. Police officials conducted nearly all preliminary investigations (the proportion handled by investigators of the Ministry of the Interior rose from 70 in the 1970s to 89.2 in 1999).[3] As during the pre-1864 reform and Soviet eras, police and administrative officials were thus in a strong position to influence the judicial process by constructing tendentious case files. Most judges worked conscientiously but often found it difficult to avoid questionable decisions and unpleasant compromises.

The legal and judicial reforms, furthermore, unfolded against the backdrop of a major rise in crime. The reported crime rate increased by 32.2 percent in 1990, by 18 percent in 1991, and by 30 percent in 1992. In the first half of 1993, crimes involving the use of weapons increased more than 300 percent. The homicide rate in Russia reached 33 per 100,000 persons in 1994, or 47,000 homicide victims—almost four times the US rate. As the economy grew more vibrant, moreover, property crimes also increased strongly. Whereas in 1978, violent crimes constituted 50 percent of all criminality, in 1998, the proportion had plunged to 23 percent. This was a more typical balance for a developed country: property crimes are ordinarily scarce only in societies with comparatively little private wealth. The total crime rate in Russia increased steadily from 1,404.3 per 100,000 population in 1989 to 2,482.2 in 1999. (Surprisingly, the juvenile crime rate, having surged from 8.68 percent of all offenses in 1986 to 17.2 percent in 1990, gradually declined to 9.6 percent in 1999.) Drawing on crime victimization surveys, however, scholars have concluded that Russian citizens dramatically underreported criminality throughout the 1990s—by as much as 70 percent.[4] In other words, the already alarming crime statistics concealed an even worse everyday experience of criminality. The growth in Russia's prison population almost exactly tracked the increase in recorded crime, with recorded crime rising by 37 percent in the years 1991–2001 and the number of people in prison increasing by 36 percent to 979,285 inmates, or 667 per 100,000 population.[5] That was more than 60 percent higher than the rate in 1979.

Organized crime and criminal syndicates also proliferated. By 1993, there were an estimated 3,000 organized criminal gangs,[6] wreaking havoc in the major cities, extorting "protection money" from most businesses, recruiting children for their operations, corrupting officials to disregard their activities, intimidating potential witnesses and judicial personnel, and in general helping to undermine the efforts to inculcate a respect for the law. Ironically, but not surprisingly, a large proportion of the bosses of organized crime structures emerged from governance roles in the Communist Party and the Komsomol. After all, in the Soviet era, there was essentially no other source of leadership recruits. The crime wave was accompanied by a surge of vandalism, graffiti, antisocial conduct, and ubiquitous petty theft. Car owners had to remove their windshield wipers when parking outdoors, for example. Predictably, public attitudes toward crime and criminals hardened.

A major innovation occurred in December 1993 when, as noted above, the Constitution brought trial by jury back to Russian criminal justice after a hiatus of seventy-five years. Started as a pilot program, partly because of inadequate financial resources, jury trials were allowed only for the gravest crimes (for which the maximum sentence was ten years' incarceration or capital punishment). Defendants in such cases could choose either a jury trial or a regular court proceeding. The program was implemented in Moscow and five other regional cities during the first year (and four more in 1995). In the first such case, heard in Saratov on the Volga River, two brothers, who had killed three people, were found guilty of "excessive use of force in self-defense" and sentenced to twelve and eighteen months, respectively. Commentators at the time suggested that in a regular court they would have been found guilty of murder and quite possibly given the death penalty. Most procurators opposed the new institution, believing it to contribute to an overly lenient treatment of defendants. It seems that the major procedural difference consisted in jurors upholding a higher standard of evidence than did the regular courts. Defense advocates, by contrast, generally supported the experiment as liable to level the playing field and create a more adversarial system of justice. By law, jurors were to be selected at random from voter lists, but in practice they were sometimes recruited on the recommendation of local businesses and government institutions.[7] Many local officials remained dissatisfied with jury trials, so they were not soon extended beyond the original nine localities and were in fact scaled back for want of funding in some of these.

What was ultimately distinctive about a jury trial, especially in the post-Soviet context, is that jurors acted independently from the judge and therefore independently from the state. Since jurors did not have access to the summary of accusations (unlike the professional and lay judges), it was necessary for the procurator and the advocate to argue the case to them. In other words, it brought to life adversarial judicial procedure. It also made necessary for the first time the preparation of an accurate and detailed record of court proceedings.

The most sensational trial in the early years of the Yeltsin era saw the Communist Party itself in the dock. Communists and ex-Communists battled, in the second half of 1992, over the nature of the Soviet system, its crimes, the complicity and guilt of party leaders in these crimes, and kindred matters.[8] It was a problematic issue because fully incriminating the party might have undermined the legitimacy of the emerging political order. After all, Yeltsin and all the Democrats had been loyal Communists. The Constitutional Court reached a compromise decision. It judged that the Communist Party of the Soviet Union had been neither a political party nor a voluntary association, but rather the state itself. Yet the court did not condemn it as an agent of totalitarian and dictatorial rule. Since the CPSU had already been disbanded, the new government was within its right to seize its property. At the same time, however, the party could rebuild itself, thus making for significant political continuity across the 1991 divide. Unlike after the Second World War, there was no Nuremberg-like trial, no equivalent of denazification, and no official repudiation of the past. The essential authoritarian nature of political power and governance carried over into the post-Soviet era.

A series of moderate reforms was undertaken beginning in 1996, partly in order to fulfill obligations relating to human rights and the judiciary imposed on Russia at the time of its joining the Council of Europe, an organization dedicated to promoting human rights, the rule of law, and democracy. Extra funding was allocated for the operation of the courts. The office of court bailiff was created both to provide security in courthouses, a necessity given the violent activity of organized crime, and to ensure the implementation of court judgments, including the proper collection of fines and debts. The salary and benefits of judges were increased, not only to provide them with a decent standard of living but also to ensure their material independence. In 1998, judicial departments were created to supervise the work and oversee the budgets of the courts, taking that authority away from the Ministry of Justice, which previously had not been above diverting funds for other purposes. The judicial departments answered ultimately to the Council of Judges and therefore reinforced judicial autonomy.

One requirement for joining the Council of Europe was for Russia to abolish the death penalty. Yeltsin suspended capital punishment, but not before fifty more executions had taken place in 1996. Without a parliament-adopted moratorium, the courts continued to issue death sentences—106 in 1997 and 116 in 1998, all of which the president commuted to life imprisonment.[9] Further efforts at abolition miscarried in the Duma in 1999 and 2001. Meanwhile, the Constitutional Court suspended both death sentences and executions in 1999 on the grounds that jury trials, as required for capital cases by the Constitution, were still available in only nine out of ninety-nine regions.

The first post-Soviet Criminal Code of the Russian Federation was adopted in 1996. It prohibited the use of capital punishment for women, minors, and men over 65 at the time of sentencing and permitted the president to commute any death sentence to imprisonment for twenty-five years or for life. It criminalized many acts liable to infringe upon personal rights and civil liberties. Among these were the coercive harvesting of human organs, unjustifiably committing a person to a mental institution, infecting a person with HIV, and violating a person's right to keep private information out of the public domain. The code also added many new environment- and computer-related crimes. The crime of obstructing the administration of justice was a new formulation of an old offense. In practice, it was rarely prosecuted. In the years 2000–2003, obstruction of the administration of justice resulted in convictions only twenty-two times,[10] though such obstruction remained a routine occurrence in the Russian judicial system. The situation was similar with the offense of infecting a person knowingly with HIV. It was rarely prosecuted. Quite likely, therefore, in both cases the Russian government was bowing to international pressure to act, rather than pursuing an offense the domestic authorities were particularly worried about. Over the next two decades, hundreds of new crimes were added to the books, such as failing to pay wages, employing slave labor, and engaging in human trafficking.

Many new criminal offenses added to the books made it hard to do business in Russia, by creating obscure and complicated rules and regulations, some of them contradictory. Whatever the reasons for such ambiguity in the law—inadvertence or intentionality—entrepreneurs could rarely get by without paying bribes to government officials. The police in fact routinely filed charges against businesspeople with the express intention of dropping the charges in exchange for bribes. As during the Soviet era, corruption remained pervasive. In fact, in 1997, Yeltsin himself denounced corruption as "Russia's most serious problem."[11]

In order to divert some of the growing judicial caseload away from the regular courts, in December 1998 the institution of justices of the peace was instituted throughout the Russian Federation. One justice of the peace was to be appointed for every 15–30 thousand people. Over time, these judges brought justice much closer to the population and were expected to take on some 50 percent of criminal cases, 80 percent of civil cases, and all cases concerning administrative offenses.[12] In practice, the institution functioned well and certainly made the justice system more responsive to the needs of ordinary people in instances of relatively minor disputes and offenses. It was one of the success stories of the Yeltsin reforms.[13]

The rule of Vladimir Putin

In 1999, Vladimir Putin was named prime minister, and a few months later acting president, as Yeltsin's designated successor. In an election held in March 2000, Putin was elected on the first round of voting and went on to serve two terms in office. As a trained lawyer—the third to govern Russia along with Lenin and Gorbachev—he recognized the importance of law. Putin's intended approach was to recentralize control over the criminal justice system. He proposed to establish a "dictatorship of law,"[14] by which he meant a system in which statutory law would stand above and trump executive orders issued throughout the bureaucracy. Unlike Yeltsin or even Gorbachev, Putin personally pushed for and orchestrated judicial reform and even drafted some parts of relevant legislation himself. His main goal was to build up the prestige of the state, so he devoted concentrated effort to weakening regional and local authorities and strengthening his own power. A favorable legal infrastructure was important to him as well, to promote economic development. If businesses had to contend with intrusive and rent-seeking government agencies and could not count on fair adjudication in the courts, he reasoned, economic growth would continue to suffer. Thanks to a more favorable business environment, but especially dramatic increases in the price of oil and natural gas, the country's biggest exports, the size of the Russian economy nearly doubled during Putin's time in office.

Beginning in December 2001, Putin signed into law several major changes to the criminal justice system. Among the most important changes was the adoption of a new Code of Criminal Procedure. The new code, which replaced statute law dating to 1960, emphasized not "rooting out crime" but "the defense of the rights and lawful interests ... of victims ... and the protection of any person from illegal and ungrounded accusations, convictions, and limitations of freedoms."[15] For the first time, the burden of proof was at least theoretically placed upon the prosecution. In fact, the role of the court was to "create the conditions necessary for the parties to perform their procedural duties and to exercise the rights granted to them."[16] Judges were therefore expected to find guilt based upon evidence, and if evidence was lacking, then guilt was not possible to prove.

Many judges found this difficult to square with their conception of adjudication. During Soviet times, the judge simply made sure that the summary of accusations adequately reflected the evidence as presented by witnesses and the accused. Under the new system, a representative of the police or the Procuracy had to attend the trial and defend the summary of accusations. Defense advocates also typically needed to attend and ideally to contest that summary. The new arrangement was expected to prod judges toward a more neutral stance. Oral evidence and disputation now became central to the proceedings. Hearsay evidence was excluded, nor could testimony given during the pretrial phase be admitted in court. All these features taken together moved Russian criminal justice toward an adversarial system, but some inquisitorial features endured. Most important, the police remained almost exclusively in charge of the pretrial investigation, and of course one cannot view the police as neutral participants in the judicial process.

A modest form of plea-bargaining—"special procedure court hearings"—was introduced by the 2001 Code of Criminal Procedure for crimes whose maximum possible punishment was three years' incarceration (ten years', starting in July 2003). The accused had to confess to the crime and no trial would take place, but the penalty could not exceed two-thirds of the maximum statutory sentence. A combination of other mitigating circumstances often resulted in an even lower ultimate penalty. In 2003, this procedure was requested in roughly 20,000 cases, most of them involving trade in illegal drugs. Gradually, more and more defendants chose this procedural option: 63.9 percent in 2010. Ironically, it naturally resulted in a drastic decline in the adversarial form of jurisprudence, since defense advocates were very little involved. In fact, in 2013 only 8 percent of accused had their cases taken to court. The other 92 percent were handled through either plea agreement or reconciliation (typically with restitution of some kind).[17] This procedure, thus, pushed the Russian criminal justice system back toward Soviet practice when judges meted out justice based on the case file alone with little input from defense advocates. Judges undoubtedly liked this approach, since it was familiar and also lightened their caseloads. It is not clear, however, that it was fairer for defendants.

The Soviet-era Committees on Juvenile Affairs, which were intended to handle criminal cases involving minors, had fallen into disuse at the end of the 1990s. As of mid-2001, more than 17,000 children were serving prison sentences in 64 special education colonies, and many more were being held in pretrial detention.[18] The conditions in many such institutions, however, were far from satisfactory. Putin's criminal justice reforms defined partial criminal responsibility as commencing at age 14 and full criminal responsibility as commencing at age 16. Minors had to be tried in the regular courts, given the absence of juvenile courts in Russia. Some protections were nevertheless available to them. Defense counsel was required from the moment an accusation had been presented. A teacher could be present as well, at the request of the investigator, procurator, or defense advocate. Beginning in 2002, juvenile offenders had to be informed of their right to counsel. In the early 2000s, however, inadequate funding for alternative noncustodial penalties made it difficult to avoid incarcerating juveniles.

Most of the new rules governing arrest and detention favored the accused but not consistently. Pretrial detention required a court order, as did search, seizure, and wiretapping. Only a procurator could open a case, though a suspect could be detained in most cases for up to five days without an accusation being registered. Once a suspect was detained, access to a legal advocate had to be granted within twenty-four hours. The defense had to be given access to the accused at will. The results of any questioning without the presence of defense advocates, including of witnesses and experts, were inadmissible in court. Advocates now had the right to some documents related to the case, though as before they gained access to the entire file only at the conclusion of the investigation. The defense could request the admission of new evidence at the trial, but the judge did not have to grant such requests. As a result, the defense was still at a disadvantage, as it had been during the Soviet era.

Other reforms narrowed judges' immunity from prosecution. Criminal charges or administrative sanctions could be imposed by the procurator general with the approval of a panel of three Supreme Court judges and the consent of the High Qualification Collegium of Judges. In 2002, public representatives and one representative of the president were added to both the central and the provincial-level collegia, because of allegations of judges systematically shielding corrupt judges from prosecution. The principal worry about judicial malfeasance was judges potentially taking bribes aimed at influencing their decisions. In the years 2000–2002, however, only four judges in the entire country were charged with receiving bribes.[19] Given the deeply rooted practice of official corruption in Russia, it seems likely that vastly more judges had been guilty of this offense. In practice, also, disciplinary measures could be imposed on judges at the discretion of the chairperson of the given court, rendering judges dependent on a single individual rather than an institution with checks and balances. All federal judges were to be appointed by the president with input from regional officials, court chairman, and the security police, which had to provide a background check whose methods were not transparent and whose conclusions could not be contested. In other words, the FSB exercised a veto over any judicial nomination.

Increased funding and support for advocates, the courts, and judges materially improved the experience of participating in the justice system but also increased state control. A law of May 2002 required advocates to join a single Advocates' Chamber with branches throughout the country and to provide some legal services to the economically disadvantaged in exchange for modest payments from the state, along with access to some of the perquisites of state employees. Among these were subsidized office space, apartment location services, reduced tax rates, and advantageous pension-fund options. Financial support for the courts also dramatically rose in 2002–2006. Courthouses were repaired and provided with computers. The number of justices of the peace more than doubled from roughly 2,000 in 2001 to some 5,000 in 2004. (By 2013, justice of the peace courts adjudicated 41.6 percent of all first-instance criminal cases.)[20] Several thousand additional judicial clerks and judges, most of them women, were recruited. More judicial personnel meant a reduced caseload for each. Higher salaries for judges made it—at least theoretically—easier for them to resist the temptation to accept bribes from interested parties. Yet they remained dependent on their judicial superiors and other government officials. Higher court judges, the qualification collegia, and the regional chapters of the Union of Judges also exerted supervisory, vertical control over judges.[21] Russia had traditionally had a highly personalized political life, with reliance on connections, patron–client dependencies, allegiance to one's profession via personal bonds, and a high value placed on friendships. It is not surprising that the Russian criminal justice system often continued to function according to personalized and informal rules, dependencies, values, and customs.

Jury trials were by far the most adversarial; they also continued to result in the highest number of acquittals. In the 1990s, the overall acquittal rate was on average 0.4 percent. Partly since the option of "supplementary investigation" had been declared unconstitutional in 1999, the acquittal rate climbed to 0.8 percent in 2003, still an extremely low rate by European and world standards. (The typical rate in European countries in the late 1900s was 3–5 percent.) By contrast, 15 percent of the 479 jury trials conducted in 2003 in the Russian Federation resulted in acquittals. Jurors typically imagined the worst of law enforcement, for example, suspecting confessions to have been coerced. They also tended to listen carefully to both advocates and procurators. The latter aggressively appealed most verdicts, but some 60 percent were upheld, resulting in a still astronomical (by Russian standards) acquittal rate of 9 percent.[22] Of course, 479 jury trials for the entire country in one year was a tiny fraction of the totality of criminal cases. Moreover, as noted above, more and more cases were settled by "special procedure court hearings" and thus avoided judicial adversarialism altogether.

The tragic events in Beslan, North Ossetia, in the North Caucasus region, in September 2004, where Islamist terrorists seized control of a school and took over 1,000 hostages, had a powerful impact on political developments. On the third day of the crisis, Russian special forces stormed the building. Nearly 400 people died, roughly half of them children. Following the massacre, Putin went on television and asserted: "We have allowed corruption to affect the judiciary and law enforcement systems."[23] Here, Putin was echoing public perceptions of widespread judicial corruption. He was probably bending this sentiment toward a pretext.

Following the tragedy, Putin gradually recentralized administrative and political power. Already, he had asserted control over or shut down all independent national television channels, established dominance in both houses of parliament, restored state hegemony over the energy industry, and neutralized uncooperative business tycoons. He had also ended the right of governors to take part in the deliberations in the Federation Council, or upper chamber of parliament, and had appointed seven presidential envoys to oversee the work of governors. Henceforth, by a law of December 2004, the president would appoint all eighty-nine regional governors to create a "single chain of command."

The government used systematic measures to undermine and shut down independent media outlets. Police conducted raids of editorial offices looking for violations of the law. The use of pirated software, in a country where most available software was pirated, provided an easy opening for prosecution. A 2002 law "On Combating Extremist Activity" (amended in 2007) permitted police to prosecute or intimidate journalists and public activists for such vague crimes as "arousing social, racial, national, or religious discord."[24] Government officials routinely brought charges of libel against media figures. They could be made to pay hefty fines or spend up to five years in jail if convicted, which was not unusual, since the judicial system was stacked against them. Journalists and editors frequently suffered intimidation, for example in the form of extralegal raids and disruptive confiscation of documentation and computers conducted by the FSB.

Access to jury trials was modestly restricted, after they became available in 2006 in all districts of the country, save in war-torn Chechnya. The right to a jury trial for state crimes like treason, armed uprising, and terrorism, permitted in 2003, was disallowed beginning in 2008. In 2013, kidnapping and sexual offenses were put under the jurisdiction of district courts, which did not offer jury trials. Obviously, such restrictions enhanced government control, diminished adversarialism, and undermined judicial independence. One might assume that the restrictions were superfluous, since the number of jury trials remained minuscule—juries reached only

555 verdicts in 2009, out of over 1 million completed criminal cases.[25] It seems likely, however, that the principle of central executive control trumped considerations of common sense.

Indeed, for cases in which senior officials took an interest, improper administrative meddling was almost unavoidable. An obvious example were the 2004 charges and trial against Mikhail Khodorkovsky, then Russia's richest man and the founder of Yukos Oil. The charges of fraud and tax evasion may or may not have been justified, but the guilty verdict was apparently a foregone conclusion. (Khodorkovsky was sentenced to prison and stripped of his property.) Similarly, also in 2004, vague charges of inciting ethnic hatred were brought against the organizers of an art exhibition following criticism by the Russian Orthodox church and a resolution adopted by parliament demanding prosecution. The case against the defendants was so weak that the judge sent it back to the prosecution for further work. Critics in general pointed to suspicious instances of judges reaching verdicts about complex cases within minutes, sometimes after receiving a cell phone call. In other words, "telephone law" continued to function whenever government officials took an interest in particular cases. Surveys and research conducted in 2007 and 2010 corroborated that most members of the public continued to believe that such illegal outside influencing of the criminal justice system was widespread. Judicial professionals and other experts held similar opinions.[26]

Even behind apparently completely legitimate criminal cases, improper official machinations sometimes played out, especially when a lot of money was at stake. Such was case of the Three Whales (*Tri Kita*) furniture superstore. Behind lawful furniture sales, investigators uncovered massive operations of oil smuggling, arms trafficking, money laundering, underpayment of customs duties, bribery of officials, and law enforcement turning a blind eye to these machinations right up to the top of the administrative pyramid.[27] In fact, when an Interior Ministry investigator brought charges in 2000, he himself was indicted for abuse of office, and the case was dropped against the Three Whales. (The investigator was found not guilty by the Moscow City Court, but the Supreme Court demanded a retrial, and in 2003, he was given a two-year sentence of probation.) Over the next several years, the illegal operations continued, and several highly placed officials were dismissed, moved to other positions, or indicted. In 2003, a key witness and a journalist following the case both died under mysterious circumstances, and a participant in the conspiracy was seriously injured when bullets tore into his automobile. Behind the scenes, high-level officials battled for turf control. In 2006, the case was reopened with Putin becoming personally involved. Another high-level power struggle ensued, allegedly with Putin clients settling scores with remaining Yeltsin supporters.

The nature of criminal threats to commercial activity also shifted during the first Putin administration. Previously, businesspeople had the most to fear from criminal gangs and organized crime. Business owners frequently made deals with such criminals, paying them "protection money" or contracting from them security services. Entrepreneurs often risked violence against their person. High-profile instances of such danger persisted, but physical threats were no longer as pervasive as in the 1990s. The number of businesspeople murdered in the Central Federal District of the Russian Federation, for example, plummeted from 217 in 1997 to 33 in 2005. Thus, hiring private security firms became a far less prominent feature of doing business in Russia. Businesspeople also gradually developed a trust in the legal system, bringing an increasing number of suits to court, including against state agencies. In a growing number of cases, such plaintiffs were successful—70 percent of the time in the late 2000s in cases contesting tax levies. Such changes were accompanied by a dramatic growth in the number of advocates from 26,300 in 1996 to 63,740 in 2010.[28] Clearly, businesspeople were hiring more lawyers to help them navigate—not to avoid—the legal system. Under Putin, nonviolent attacks on business continued, but now they typically came from government officials, acting on their own or on behalf of criminal organizations. Such operations might involve official inspections of various kinds, the imposition of fines, the collection of obscure payments, or the takeover of entire businesses. At the same time, many businesspeople themselves hired government officials to protect them from competition, to pressure delinquent debtors, to settle business disputes, or to facilitate corporate takeovers.

Despite ongoing official shady dealings, efforts toward reforming and improving the judicial system continued during Putin's second term in office (2004–2008). One focus was improving transparency, by making court decisions available on the Internet, which encouraged judges to set out their reasoning more carefully, and establishing the post of Press Secretary of the court. In part, thanks to Putin's reforms, the adjudication of criminal cases was made admirably efficient. In 2006, 97.1 percent of all criminal cases were completed in less than three months—faster than those in Western countries.[29]

Even so, public perception of the courts remained abysmal. A survey conducted in 2007 by the highly respected Levada Center found that only 6 percent of 1,600 randomly selected adults professed a belief that court decisions was guided solely with reference to the law. By contrast, 54.8 percent considered bribery an important influencing factor (or 68.8 percent of those who had a personal experience of the judicial system).[30]

Nor was public perception of the police better than it had been in Soviet times. According to official statistics, Russia crime rates fell markedly during the early Putin years. Yet, it seems, the decline was largely due to massive underreporting by mistrustful citizens (according to a 2007 study, only about one-quarter of all crimes were reported to police) and to the police's failure to process reports on as many as 11 million crimes each year.[31] It was assumed that in most such cases, clearing the crimes would be difficult and therefore would count against the police officers in question. Better, they apparently thought, to sweep them under the carpet.

The collapse of communism, with the shrinking of the social safety net, made it harder for many women to make ends meet. Some turned to sex work, which became more acceptable in society. Lawmakers and government officials began to express major concern about the trafficking of women in 1997. In 2000, the Organization for Security and Co-operation in Europe estimated that in the previous five years, over one-half million women had been trafficked from the former Soviet Union into sex slavery in fifty countries across the globe. Although many police officers systematically extorted "protection" money from prostitutes and pimps, they also cracked down on the crime of "organizing prostitution" beginning in 2003. In that year, the number of such cases was 356 in 2003; it jumped to 1,831 in 2007. Unfortunately, the problem of human trafficking in the Russian Federation remained acute. The number of Russian women trafficked abroad has been estimated at between 10,000 and 60,000 each year through 2006. (As late as 2013, the Global Slavery Index placed Russia in the top ten of worst offenders worldwide.)[32]

In May 2008, Dmitry Medvedev became president of the Russian Federation, replacing Putin, who now served as his prime minister. "We must eliminate the practice of unjust decisions based on the telephone or money," the former law professor asserted on the eve of his election, and "we must humanize the administration of justice, promote extrajudicial dispute resolution, and compensate citizens for unjust decisions and red tape in court." The root of the problem, he argued, was a sort of legal nihilism in Russia. "No other European country," he lamented, "can boast of such a level of disregard for law."[33] Medvedev called for the reform of Russia's criminal justice system, which he denounced as overly harsh and inefficient.

He first targeted the police. In 2009, a series of scandals involving police brutality, murders, rapes, and random shootings shocked the public in Russia. One case that reverberated throughout the world was the death in police custody (after nearly a year in detention, accused but not brought to trial) of Sergei Magnitsky, a corporate lawyer and auditor who uncovered evidence of an illegal government takeover of a major foreign-owned investment firm, Hermitage Capital Management. An investigation discovered Magnitsky had been beaten and denied necessary medical treatment. The reforms Medvedev pushed through in 2009 included a code of police behavior and increased training. An April 2010 ban on pretrial detention for persons suspected of having committed business-related crimes prompted a huge decline in prosecutions—for example, a 65 percent drop in cases for illegal entrepreneurship. Apparently, law enforcement officers were less inclined to prosecute when they had no opportunity to extort money for releasing suspects from custody. Further reform came in February 2011. The police force itself was no longer to be called *militsiia* but rather *politsiia*, just like before 1917. The size of the force was cut by 20 percent, and those who remained had a significant salary boost, in large part to wean them away from graft. Gaining public confidence would, however, be a herculean task. Distrust of the police remained a hallmark of the service. Opinion polls conducted between 2004 and 2011 indicated consistently that 30–35 percent of citizens—even when in mortal danger—would rather avoid contacting the police.[34]

Medvedev's administration also worked to reform the judiciary. In October 2010, the government published a plan for recasting the entire penal system within ten years. A key intention was to abolish correctional colonies, with their emphasis on collective living and obligatory labor, and to replace them with Western-style penitentiaries. In March 2011, a package of reforms was adopted by the Duma. It included an increase in noncustodial punishments—such as community service and "corrective work" fulfilled at one's place of employment—and a prohibition on sentencing to prison any first offender for crimes entailing a maximum of three years' incarceration. A series of reforms in 2010–2012 made it harder to remove judges except for serious violations of the law.[35] Unfortunately, judges typically remained beholden to their superiors for promotions and perks and therefore did not become significantly more independent. Medvedev had wanted much more sweeping changes, yet powerful officials throughout the bureaucracy managed to stymie them.

In a wide-ranging study based upon court records, survey material, and detailed interviews conducted during Medvedev's presidency with legal professionals and participants in the criminal justice system, Alena Ledeneva has argued for the existence of a network-based governance system.[36] The judiciary in this interpretation is staffed by many dedicated professionals who almost inevitably must come to terms with political pressure from powerful authorities, pressures that come in the form of both carrots and sticks. In most cases, judges, investigators, and procurators simply know what is or is likely to be expected of them. In fact, judges are often appointed based on their willingness to play by informal rules of decision-making. Furthermore, the complexity of the official, formal rules makes it difficult to avoid breaking them from time to time. Such noncompliance can then be used against actors at all levels of society to ensure acquiescence in informal demands. This interpretation of a "dualistic" criminal justice system, in which persons accused of ordinary criminal offenses can hope for a reasonably fair trial, so long as no powerful political actor takes an interest in the proceedings, is similar to the one also defended by two of the most authoritative and prolific scholars in the field, Kathryn Hendley and Peter Solomon.

Further proof that the Russian authorities were both moving forward with efforts at reform and unable to radically improve the system is provided by Russia's participation in relevant European conventions and institutions. Given Russia's membership in the Council of Europe, for example, its citizens have the right to bring perceived violations of basic rights before the European Court of Human Rights (ECHR). In 2009, they brought 14,000 civil cases to that court. As a result, every year, Russia was found in violation hundreds of times. The largest number of such cases concerned procedural violations in the Russian courts. The fact that the Russian government continued to subject itself to such critical outside scrutiny, and to comply with the ECHR at least partially in all instances,[37] suggests a desire to continue to try to align Russian criminal justice with European best practices. The ability of Russian citizens to hold their government to account by appealing to an objective arbiter probably increased their confidence in the potential for fair treatment in Russia.

Of course, anticipated fairness and impartiality in the criminal justice system did not apply to high-profile political cases, and presumably most people understood that fact. Indeed, in December 2010, Mikhail Khodorkovsky was again found guilty of tax fraud and other crimes, but this time it was revealed via YouTube that the presiding judge of the Moscow City Court had signed a decision prepared in advance by other officials. When the case was taken to cassation review, the sentence was merely reduced from 14 to 13 years' incarceration.[38] In other words, even the most glaring evidence of malfeasance and impropriety could not make a difference when powerful officials had set their face against a given defendant.

When Vladimir Putin returned to the presidency in May 2012 (again naming Medvedev prime minister), he presided over a further tightening and harshening of the criminal justice system. For example, the plans to replace labor colonies with modern prisons were scrapped in June. Massive anti-Putin demonstrations in late 2011 and early 2012 had not prevented his election, but undoubtedly worried him and led to a crackdown. Perhaps especially troubling to him was the anti-Putin and anti-church performance staged inside Moscow's Cathedral of Christ the Savior, not far from the Kremlin, in February 2012 by the punk rock group Pussy Riot. Three of the group's members were arrested and held without bail through their trial in July and August. Two of them were found guilty of "hooliganism motivated by religious hatred" and were sentenced to two years in a labor camp. In the words of the verdict, "Swear words that were uttered in the Cathedral were blasphemy against God and were unambiguously perceived as a manifestation of religious hatred and enmity."[39] These words encapsulated well the symbiotic relationship of power established by authorities of church and state in Russia under Putin.

Putin also began signing laws restricting civil rights. In June 2012, fines for unauthorized assemblies were raised from a maximum of 5,000 to 300,000 rubles for participants and 600,000 rubles for organizers. In July, slander against officials was recriminalized, and Russian NGOs receiving foreign funds were legally compelled to advertise themselves as "foreign agents," a requirement tantamount to admitting treason. Refusing to register could result in hefty fines and prison sentences of up to two years for an organization's leader. In November, the crime of treason was expanded at the request of the FSB to include "providing financial, technical, advisory, or other assistance to a foreign state or international organization ...

directed at harming Russia's security."[40] Harming Russia's security, in Putin's mind, apparently included bringing world attention to human rights violations and abuses by law enforcement. The government also worked to restrict other forms of expression. In June 2013, the Russian parliament, by a vote of 436 to zero with one abstention, passed a bill banning "the distribution or expression of information that portrayed 'nontraditional' sexual relationships in a positive light," ostensibly to protect children. Putin quickly signed it into law.[41] The totality of this legislation did not return Russia to anything like the total social control of the Soviet era, but certainly moved it further away from the principles and practices of modern, liberal, open societies.

In July 2013, a ruling of the Constitutional Court made it easier for a judge to return cases to the Procuracy at the start of a trial so that more evidence could be gathered, permitting a ratcheting of the indictment to a more serious crime, similar to the old Soviet practice of supplementary investigation. The decision was presented as unifying judicial and investigatory procedure, in contradiction to the earlier move toward adversarial justice.[42] There had also been a push from late 2012 to require procurators, defense advocates, and judges all to seek "objective truth," which was a central feature of Soviet criminal justice and a key plank of its inquisitorial judicial system, where judges were considered a member of the prosecution team. To a large extent and for many judges, such an attitude was never abandoned in the post-Soviet era.

One of the two members of Pussy Riot, Nadezhda Tolokonnikova, was exiled to Penal Colony No. 14—infamous for its harsh conditions—in the Republic of Mordovia, around 300 miles southeast of Moscow. Forced to work 16–17 hours a day sewing police uniforms, harassed and humiliated by other inmates, she was often punished for infractions. Punishments included forced standing without permission to use the bathroom, sewing naked, and deprivation of access to the showers. (Other inmates were beaten regularly.) In many ways, her treatment was reminiscent of the Stalinist Gulag: incarceration far from home, habitation in barracks, compulsory labor, inmate housekeeping tasks, mutual responsibility of prisoners, militaristic administration, and a pervasive use of informants. When Tolokonnikova filed an official complaint about these unbearable and inhumane conditions, the other prisoners were made to suffer. On September 23, 2013, she went on a hunger strike "until they start treating us like humans."[43] After a prison transfer, she was amnestied in December 2013, apparently in connection with Russia's hosting of the Winter Olympics in Sochi in February 2014.

During the games, the pro-Western and anti-corruption Euromaidan movement came to a head in Ukraine. The pro-Moscow president, Viktor Yanukovych, and other senior officials fled the country in late February. Amid the political crisis, Russia commenced efforts to take control of the Crimean Peninsula. On March 18, the territory was annexed by the Russian Federation. Pro-Russian separatists in eastern Ukraine clashed with government forces beginning in April. The Russian military supported the separatists—both covertly and overtly—and a bloody conflict dragged on. Western countries responded by imposing sanctions against Russia. The sanctions, combined with the falling price of oil, depressed the Russian economy, its GNP plummeting from $2.23 trillion in 2013 to $1.33 trillion in 2015—a 40 percent drop.

On March 1, 2014, a professor of history at the Moscow State Institute of International Relations, Andrei Zubov, published an article in which he likened the Russian annexation of the Crimea to the Nazi annexation of the Sudetenland in 1938 and 1939. Both operations, he noted, were officially justified by pointing, respectively, to the large number of Russian or German speakers in the area. A week after Putin, speaking in parliament on March 18, denounced a "disparate bunch of national traitors," Zubov was fired from his position for the "commission of an immoral act incompatible with the continuation of work." Two months later, in May, the "rehabilitation of Nazism" was made a crime. It seems the purpose was to keep people from making such comparisons. In December, Vladimir Luzgin, a small-town blogger, was charged under the law for posting the assertion: "The communists and Germany jointly invaded Poland, sparking off the Second World War." In July 2016, the Perm District Court convicted Luzgin and fined him 200,000 rubles. In September, the Supreme Court of the Russian Federation let the sentence stand.[44] Given the fact that the USSR in September 1939 in conjunction with Nazi Germany invaded Poland, the conviction and the upholding of the conviction demonstrate that, in the final years of Putin's third term as president (the presidential term increased to six years in 2008), one could be punished for telling an obvious truth. Even appeals to the ECHR in Strasbourg were no longer a surefire way to achieve redress. For several years, senior politicians and the chairman of the Constitutional Court himself, Valery Zorkin, had begun to question the right of a judicial institution in Europe to preempt Russian law. When relations with Europe began to sour because of events in the Crimea and eastern Ukraine, it was not completely surprising that the court should challenge that right on constitutional grounds. In July 2015, the Constitutional Court, emphasizing the primacy of the Russian Constitution, asserted the right of Russian state institutions to disregard a judgment of the Strasbourg Court that violated "principles and norms of the Constitution." Then, in December 2015, Putin signed legislation authorizing the Constitutional Court to reject any ruling of the ECHR as unconstitutional. In April 2016, the court in fact vacated such a ruling (guaranteeing convicted prisoners' right to vote) on these grounds.[45]

Transparency International in 2016 ranked Russia 131 out of 176 in its Corruption Perception Index, along with Iran, Kazakhstan, and Nepal, that is, below Mexico, Honduras, and Laos, which were ranked at 123 (Denmark and New Zealand were tied for first place, as the least corrupt).[46] Despite some fluctuation, Russia remained stuck toward the bottom of the list from its first ranking in 1996. Perception is not, of course, reality, but given the evidence presented in this chapter, it seems that the perceptions relied upon to compile the index faithfully reflect post-Soviet Russian reality. The rule of law has not put down deep roots. The government is relatively unresponsive, often poorly functioning, distrusted by ordinary people, and regularly unable to provide impartial, predictable, and consistent justice.

The criminal justice system was typically stacked most heavily against defendants when government officials, especially the powerful, had a stake. Such stakes could involve ideological and cultural norms. For example, in late January 2017, the Duma easily passed a bill decriminalizing domestic battery for first-time offenders, so long as it does not result in major injuries. Although official statistics indicate that many serious injuries occur within the household, most lawmakers supported the measure as a means, they argued, to reinforce the traditional family. The criminal justice system, thus, grew more lenient toward domestic batterers but less fair toward their victims. The system also remains stacked against political opponents of the regime. In February 2017, the district court in Kirov, 500 miles northeast of Moscow, found Aleksei Navalny guilty of fraud. Navalny, who spearheaded the mass anti-Putin demonstrations in Moscow in 2011–2013, had intended to run for president in 2018—and would have been the most credible opposition candidate. The conviction, however, made him ineligible to run. One of Navalny's signature themes is investigating and denouncing official corruption. A mere three weeks after his conviction, Navalny went public with a major report alleging that Prime Minister Medvedev had amassed an empire of sprawling mansions, yachts, and other valuable property through a complex web of bribes and diverted state funds.[47] It seems reasonable to suppose that the conviction was meant to preemptively undermine the credibility of Navalny, a widely respected and trusted public figure. Ultimately, in other words, the reforms of Yeltsin, Putin, and Medvedev failed to give Russia an independent and rule-governed criminal justice system in exceptional cases.

What was the situation in ordinary cases? Here, the record is better, but still mixed—far from fair and procedurally consistent. Law enforcement personnel, senior managers in business, government officials, entrepreneurs, and white-collar workers, while making up 7 percent of all defendants, accounted for 49 percent of all acquittals in Russia in 2011. (In 2014, the acquittal rate had fallen to 0.1 percent.)[48] Such persons enjoy the highest level of due process available in Russian criminal justice. By contrast, the acquittal rate was much lower for common laborers, students, and "marginal" people. The latter were practically never acquitted. Persons in categories that were frequently acquitted presumably also rarely faced charges for their criminal activity. The reasons for these discrepancies were structural, inherent in the Russian criminal justice system. Beginning in the late Stalin era, personnel working in criminal justice—police, investigators, procurators, and judges—began to be strictly evaluated based on statistical data relating to performance, such as number and type of cases handled, clearance rate, and convictions. As discussed in Chapter 5, acquittals came to be seen as a black mark on the record of such officials. Therefore, they strived above all to achieve convictions, which required police and procurators to avoid difficult and ambiguous cases, for judges to send problematic cases back to the procurator for further work, and for judges and procurators to close ranks against defendants. These or similar strategies remain operative in Putin's Russia.

A recent, well-regarded study thoroughly analyzes this process. The relevant personnel in criminal justice work both individually and together to receive the highest performance evaluations. Criminal detectives and investigators avoid pursuing cases involving suspects able to enlist the support of influential people. Thus, an ordinary police officer may have a better status in the system than a wealthy entrepreneur and may therefore be more likely to evade prosecution. Cases are rarely opened for instances of burglary and other hard-to-solve crimes, such as domestic battery, because the victims often prove uncooperative. Serious crimes are preferred, since officials receive more points for carrying them to conviction. But not all violent crimes are pursued. Since the Russian police achieve a whopping 90 percent formal clearance rate for such crimes, they obviously rarely register violent crimes they do not expect to clear. "The ideal case for law enforcement to process," according to Ella Paneyakh, "involves a relatively serious crime, with a 'deserving' victim or without a victim at all, and with a stigmatized, socially marginalized defendant."[49]

Police and investigators often resort to pressure and intimidation to extract evidence, nor do they shun fabricating evidence and other underhanded methods of strengthening their cases. As a result, over 90 percent of cases taken to court include a confession by the defendant. The Procuracy, as the Russian watchdog of legality, should shine a light on procedural improprieties, but its procurators also stand to gain from successful convictions and to lose from "failed cases." In fact, all personnel in Russian criminal justice work out compromises and means of collaboration to achieve statistical success in what the professionals call "the processing chain."[50] At the same time, they also all look out for themselves. Investigators, for example, avoid cases where police detectives have not uncovered a suspected perpetrator. Moreover, since the performance statistics of all criminal justice personnel are compared against the average, it is next to impossible for any given individual to avoid the questionable practices deployed by the majority. Such factors lead to what Peter Solomon has called "accusatorial bias."

Thus, entering the criminal justice system in today's Russia with enemies in high places will almost never end well. A criminal trial for a member of the elite, so long as the person harmed lacks powerful friends, might well unfold according to high standards of judicial procedure. The experience of an average person is more likely—but not inevitably—to take a bad turn. People from the lowest ranks of society are even less likely to get a fair shake.

Conclusion

Historical overview

The evolution of criminal justice in Russia from early modern times to the present has exhibited dramatic change and striking continuity. Three hundred years ago, Russia was not so very different in this area from its neighbors to the West. Nowhere did effective police forces solve crimes. Punishments were harsh and often violent, with public beheadings and bodily mutilation common. Judicial torture was a mainstay of criminal investigation. Flogging and execution were the chief penalties for serious offenses.

Criminal law emerged in Russia and Europe in a similar manner, though with a time lag in Russia. Inquisitorial procedure dominated for many centuries and only gradually and quite late gave way to adversarial procedure with two parties making their case before an impartial judge. Official law slowly replaced customary law, that is, traditional norms. Detailed legal codes were compiled. In some areas, the lag was especially great. Legal experts in Russia began to grapple with questions of judicial philosophy many centuries after their Central and Western European counterparts. For example, the widely circulated and repeatedly published Germanic *Sachsenspiegel* (early 1200s) affirmed that "God is Law itself; therefore, justice is dear to Him." Such a conception of the law as an emanation from the divine and therefore higher and more authoritative than monarchs could not have been formulated in an official law book at any point during the Imperial (much less Soviet) period, though some scholars (under European influence) began to articulate such ideas in the late 1700s. Innovation and reform occurred in Russia but nearly always from the top down and only rarely, unlike in Europe, from political and intellectual movements promoted by powerful nongovernment elites.

Criminal justice reform in the eighteenth century was dramatic and far-reaching. Peter the Great worked feverishly from 1696 to 1725 to impose in Russia administrative, economic, cultural, military, legal, and judicial institutions and practices borrowed directly from Europe. He created a central judicial agency, the College of Justice; a central executive organ, the Senate, which became the highest court of appeal; a system of judicial oversight, the Procuracy; and a uniform hierarchy of courts. He also adopted some harsher forms of punishment from Europe, such as public executions and running the gauntlet for military officers. All of these reforms survived Peter's demise, except the uniform system of courts.

Moreover, his reforming impulse continued. At mid-century, Peter's daughter Elizabeth suspended capital punishment. She also authorized rural communities and landlords to dispose of "undesirables" using administrative exile, a policy that would continue well into the twentieth century under various guises. Building on Peter's framework, Catherine the Great, at the end of the century, erected a new and more durable hierarchy of courts. They were not, however, governed by a principle of equality before the law: separate courts functioned for each social estate (nobility, town dwellers, and peasantry). Catherine also restricted the use of judicial torture, banned the application to minors of harsh forms of corporal punishment, and invested landowning and urban elites with civil rights for the first time in Russian history. Her conscience courts afforded to certain categories of alleged offenders legal protections that were advanced for the time, including something like habeas corpus. Nevertheless, in practice, administrative officials wielded great power over the judicial system, and no independence of the courts was achieved. The French Revolution, moreover, provoked a crackdown on independent thought and harsher treatment for "political crimes."

Following the death of Catherine II, her son Paul rolled back some of her reforms and attempted a recentralization of the government apparatus. He remained on the throne for only five years, however, and his son Alexander intended a radical liberalization of both government in general and the judiciary in particular. Alexander's autocratic proclivities, combined with the Napoleonic Wars, prevented most of the program from being fulfilled. True, Peter's administrative colleges were replaced by somewhat more centralized ministries, including a Ministry of Justice. Judicial torture was officially abolished, along with some of the more heinous forms of penal bodily mutilation, like nostril slitting.

It fell to Alexander's younger brother Nicholas, who came to the throne in 1825 amid a rebellion of officers, to complete the codification of Russian law for the first time since 1649. The resultant Digest of Laws (1832) systematized and made somewhat more lenient criminal law. The Penal Code of 1845 abolished the harshest instrument of corporal punishment, the knout, but also prescribed extremely harsh punishments, including the death penalty, for mere intentions of harming the ruler. Legal training expanded and matured in these years, setting the stage for further judicial reform. On the eve of the Crimean War (1853–1856), the criminal justice system was still dominated by administrative officials but was beginning to show signs of greater efficiency and fairness. Even so, contemporaries lamented lengthy delays, backlogs of cases, police interference, accusatorial bias, and the lack of participation of defense advocates at any stage of the judicial process.

A humiliating loss in the Crimean War put the new emperor, Alexander II, under pressure to carry out dramatic reforms. He emancipated 20 million serfs in 1861 and in 1864 created institutions of local self-government in the countryside, called zemstvos, and established an independent judiciary, institutionally his most important and sweeping innovation, because it created for the first time in Russian history a separation of governmental powers. The new judicial system had a uniform hierarchy of courts, required jury trials for serious crimes, instituted an independent Bar, and imposed adversarial procedure with the right to defense counsel during the trial but not during the criminal investigation. The defect of accusatorial bias was greatly undermined by the introduction of jury trials, since for the first time procurators and defense advocates had to argue their sides of the case directly and orally before ordinary people who typically lacked the institutional tendency to defer to the procurator. Political terrorism, which commenced with an attempt on the life of the emperor himself in 1866 and continued through to his assassination in 1881, drove the government to remove "political crime" from the purview of the ordinary judicial system and to transfer it to military courts, special high courts, and administrative officials invested with broad punitive authority.

The reign of Alexander III witnessed repeated attempts by high officials to roll back the earlier reforms. In a few instances, they were successful, such as the abolition in most places of justices of the peace as first- instance adjudicators and their replacement by administrative officials called land captains under the control of the Ministry of the Interior. Nevertheless, the basic structure and norms of the judicial reform remained in place, and judicial and legal reform continued in the reign of Alexander and of this son Nicholas. The 1903 Criminal Code, which was only partially implemented, moved Russia much closer to Europe in terms of how crimes were to be defined and punished. Even the Revolution of 1905–1907, which saw terrible violence by both revolutionaries and government officials, did not fully derail the movement toward reform. Laws of 1906 established basic civil rights, a law of 1909 instituted a system of parole, and both capital punishment and administrative exile were deployed less and less frequently on the eve of the First World War. As in all the belligerent countries, administrative power was dramatically enhanced during the war. Popular discontent increased, because of grueling hardships, until mass demonstrations and troop mutinies in early 1917 caused the fall of the monarchy. The Provisional Government dismantled the entire police apparatus, abolished the concept of "political crime," put an end to the death penalty but restored it at the front lines in July, eliminated administrative exile, and freed thousands of political prisoners.

The Bolsheviks came to power in late 1917 with a vision of reform even more radical than that of their immediate predecessors, the liberal and socialist leaders of the Provisional Government. They immediately abolished the entire judicial system, reestablished a unified administration without balance of power, restored capital punishment as a punishment for civilians, and proclaimed a faith in "revolutionary consciousness" where judges were to be guided by class and ideological insights. At the same time, many early Soviet criminologists took inspiration from Western legal reformers, who emphasized the importance of environmental factors in triggering criminality. The regime also decriminalized such behaviors as abortion and homosexual acts between consenting adults, which were made legal only much later in Western countries.

During the Civil War, which soon broke out, however, the Bolshevik leaders relied increasingly on extrajudicial punishments and a political police apparatus to maintain order and to reinforce their authority. Having secured victory in 1920, they attempted to rein in arbitrary officials and to curtail extrajudicial punishment. Popular unrest and rebellion in 1921 and 1922 convinced the leadership to abandon such initiatives. Fear of political disorder ensured the continued centrality of the political police to Soviet governance. Thus, even more so than before 1917, a highly dualistic judicial system emerged, where political opponents faced harsh repression and few legal guarantees, while ordinary criminals could count on at least some procedural protections.

In 1921, the government instituted the New Economic Policy, which decriminalized ordinary commercial activity, a move incompatible with the official interpretation of Marxism and therefore anathema to many party leaders and activists. Debates throughout the 1920s raged about how to treat the peasantry, viewed as the only potential source of major investment for undertaking the industrialization required by the Bolshevik conception of "building socialism." An uneasy peace between the city and the countryside, between the Bolsheviks and the peasantry, continued so long as Lenin lived. His death in 1924 opened the way toward a recommencement of civil war policies and a dramatic hardening of both criminal justice and political repression.

Stalin outmaneuvered his rivals by pretending to be a team player and a champion of Lenin's peasant policy. Then in 1928 and 1929, he pushed through callous measures on the confiscation of grain, the collectivization of agriculture, and the exile to distant localities of millions of peasants who refused to submit to strict government control. The criminal justice system took a direct part in the repression, but the political police were an even more central actor. In fact, the OGPU's service as the primary force driving collectivization transformed a relatively marginal agency into a mainstay of the Soviet political system, which it remained (under various acronyms) until the collapse of communism in 1991. Its centrality was reinforced throughout the 1930s by a series of political crises culminating in the Great

Terror in 1937 and 1938, when nearly 700,000 people were executed without due process.

Judicial personnel suffered in the late 1930s as much as any other professional category, which made institutional stability and professionalization difficult to achieve. Moreover, many crimes were politicized, such as labor shirking and stealing government property, which entailed heavy penalties. Labor camps and settlements swelled to hold over 4 million people. The inmates suffered deprivation throughout this era but especially during the Second World War. After the war, the government pressured police investigators and judicial personnel to demonstrate effective performance as evidenced by such statistics as conviction and acquittal rates. Acquittals were viewed from 1948 to 1949 as an unacceptable stain on the record of procurators and judges. Also, after the war, collective farms acquired the authority to recommend the administrative exile of undesirable members (an authority enjoyed by peasant communities before 1917). Police operations targeting alleged political dissidents continued, though on a lesser scale. When Stalin died in 1953, he had been promoting a campaign against Kremlin doctors, most of them Jewish, which likely would have escalated into an anti-Semitic bloodbath.

Stalin's death in 1953 marked the end of state terror in Russia. Under Khrushchev's leadership, millions of inmates were liberated from the camps and settlements, and many were rehabilitated. A wave of crime plagued the country almost immediately, however, and reached a crest in the middle and later 1950s. The public expressed outrage and the government adopted laws to fight criminality—in particular "hooliganism." Society was encouraged to support law enforcement, and millions joined volunteer police brigades. Millions more took part in comrades' courts or served as voluntary public accusers in regular courts of law. Performance evaluation of law enforcement and judicial personnel continued and formed the basis for success in these professions. The criminal justice system in ordinary cases, when no influential person took an interest, could be fairly impartial and straightforward, though an accusatorial or prosecutorial bias persisted. Procurators remained the most influential figures throughout the investigatory and judicial processes. Political dissidence, while far more tolerated than under Stalin, could still result in harsh penalties, including unwarranted psychiatric institutionalization.

All these features of criminal justice and political repression continued during Brezhnev, with one difference. The government began to turn a blind eye to illegal moneymaking ventures, such as plying official trades on the side with state-owned tools and materials and even black marketeering, so long as they remained on a small scale and did not involve foreigners. At the same time, government officials and employees felt free to exploit their offices and connections for personal gain. Corruption spread insidiously throughout the system. The economic inefficiency, lack of civil rights, political monopoly of the Communist Party elites, and a host of other troubles contributed to a decline in perceived legitimacy of the system, especially when Gorbachev relaxed the formerly stringent censorship controls. His efforts to reform criminal justice made some progress, such as striking from the books most "political crimes" and giving criminal suspects the right to legal counsel from the start of their investigation by law enforcement. But the political system collapsed before major changes could be implemented or become deeply rooted.

Both dramatic change and stubborn continuity have characterized Russia's criminal justice since the collapse of the Soviet Union in 1991. Boris Yeltsin adopted a series of reforms aiming at increasing lay participation, enshrining in law the presumption of innocence, instituting lifetime appointments for judges and other means of securing judicial independence, and moving firmly from inquisitorial to adversarial judicial procedure. Yet the 1990s also saw a drastic increase in criminality, both individual and organized. Criminal gangs threatened political, economic, and administrative actors so much that guards had to be introduced into courthouses, and businesspeople hired thousands of private security forces.

After coming to power in the year 2000, Vladimir Putin further pursued judicial reform, providing better salaries to judges, increasing funding for the courts, adopting a law on plea-bargaining, and expanding the availability of jury trials. At the same time, however, strong accusatorial bias persisted in the system. Judges never really became independent of the administration. Juries, which acquitted a substantial proportion of defendants (roughly 15 percent), decided only a tiny fraction of criminal cases. Powerful government figures sometimes exerted pressure throughout the judicial process. Corruption remained rife. In high-profile cases, sentences were often decided in advance. Dmitry Medvedev, during his term as president in 2008–2012, also gave a show of desiring sweeping criminal justice and police reform, and some progress was made. But the fundamentals of the system did not greatly change. When antigovernment protests broke out in late 2011, Putin in his third term in office (2012–2018) increased political repression and government control over independent social actors and media outlets. It seemed that much of the reforms had been in vain and that the autocratic principle in Russia had endured.

Key themes

Several themes emerge from the story of Russian criminal justice over the past 300 years. They concern Russia's relationship toward Europe and the West, the status of law in Russian society, the attitudes of Russians toward the courts, judicial and legal dualism, what one may call the autocratic principle in Russia, and long-term continuities. These themes will be discussed in turn.

The extraordinary material, technological, military, and cultural success of Europe was obvious for anyone with eyes to see in the early modern era. Peter the Great, who traveled in Europe for eighteen months soon after becoming sole ruler of Russia in 1796, implemented his wide-ranging administrative and judicial reforms almost entirely with reference to Central and Western European models and practice. Catherine the Great was a European who prided herself on a close acquaintance with the latest European thought on government and the law. She too carried out reforms in these areas with a constant orientation toward existing models in the West. Her conscience courts, for example, are thought to have been modeled directly on the English equity courts, though the German lands had the most concrete influence in her reign. Throughout the nineteenth century, the expanding cohort of highly trained legal experts in the Russian bureaucracy rarely drafted a proposal without first scouring European sources for ideas and precedents. Jury trials were instituted in 1864 only after careful consultation of European jurists and their learned works. During this era, the dominant influence was French and English. It bears emphasizing that throughout the Imperial era, Russia's elites engaged in creative adaptation rather than mere imitation of foreign models.

The Bolsheviks came to power also imbued with a Western progressive doctrine, this one aimed not at tweaking the existing order but rather at obliterating it. Even so, they too pursued some of the latest criminological ideas and were in close contact with European activists and intellectuals through the 1920s. Under Stalin, such contacts ceased, but the judicial system in principle still owed much to "bourgeois" legal thinkers. The main "bourgeois" civil rights like freedom of speech and conscience were enshrined in the Constitution of 1936 (and of 1977), although in practice such rights were enjoyed by no one in Soviet society. Even if the political system was autocratic and arbitrary, and powerful officials could work their will on citizens, the party leadership recognized the implicit desirability and even superiority of the legal norms of the capitalist West, at least for propagandistic purposes. After communism fell in 1991, the floodgates of Western ideas again poured in. Under Vladimir Putin, a deep respect for Western values was at least paid lip service to, though less and less in the later years of his third term as president.

The status of the law in Russia has followed a somewhat analogous trajectory. Peter the Great constantly trumpeted the importance of law. He regularly asserted himself to be its servant. Didactic statements were added to many of his decrees on the law and criminal justice. All of his successors down to 1917 affirmed their respect for the law, though especially in conjunction with the demand that the law be respected by their loyal subjects. The communist leaders who held power from 1917 until 1991 also repeatedly asserted law's importance with phrases like "revolutionary legality" and "socialist legality." And, of course, Vladimir Putin intended to establish a "dictatorship of the law."

Of course, all such formulations are oxymorons. There can be no revolutionary legality any more than a bourgeois or a conservative legality.

Legality means respect for the law, a willingness to follow the law, and it does not matter whether one is a revolutionary or reactionary. There can be laws with a socialist or a conservative content, but once they are laws they should be binding on all. By "dictatorship of the law," Putin presumably meant such a legal regime, but legality is the polar opposite of dictatorship, so his formulation was unhelpful. Ultimately, modern societies need the rule of law, where every person, including the most powerful, views the law as necessary for the smooth functioning of public and private life. Predictable, impartial, impersonal, and consistent law is one of the great achievements of modern Western societies. Peter the Great recognized that adopting principles and institutions from European governance would help Russia strengthen its state, mobilize greater resources, and grow more powerful. He wanted a *pravovoe gosudarstvo* (*Rechtsstaat* or regime of law) and called himself the first servant of the state. He also professed devotion to society's welfare and larger interests. But, in practice, he could not imagine the law as higher than himself, and therefore he could not advocate the rule of law. Nor was Russian society well disposed toward such a development, since government officials and landed elites were accustomed to ruling arbitrarily in their jurisdictions. Despite repeated affirmations of the importance of law by subsequent Russian monarchs, not one was willing to rule under the law.

True, Alexander II created an independent judiciary, but it is clear that he did not realize that this political departure entailed placing himself under the law and making the judiciary immune from his influence and authority. Alexander III craved to place the judiciary anew under the monarchical power, though he discovered that the entire higher bureaucracy functioned somewhat autonomously, especially when it was divided against itself, as was the case when senior officials were tasked with rolling back the judicial reform. Meanwhile, Russia continued on its path toward the rule of law and constitutional governance. The legislature created in 1906 earnestly crafted bills on the inviolability of the person and on limiting the arbitrary power of government officials by a system of administrative justice. Although the latter project became law in December 1916, it was swept away by the revolution.

The Bolsheviks and their successors at the helm of the Soviet Union were even less disposed to placing themselves under the law than their Imperial predecessors had been. A judicial system with at least the outward appearance of procedural norms and adherence to legality emerged and continued to function, but nearly any criminal case could become politicized if a powerful official felt a personal stake in it. The inevitable result was over seventy years of inculcating lawlessness into three generations of Russians. Thus, it was not surprising that Putin and Medvedev found it difficult to root out such deeply entrenched arbitrary power-wielding, disregard for the law, deference to authority, and the mentality of "gaming" the system to one's own personal benefit.

Richard Wortman chose the phrase "a legal consciousness" in his second book "to make clear that it is not necessarily the only legal consciousness in Russian history, or one that was generally shared." In the long run, he continued, "it encountered formidable and eventually insuperable obstacles, and its rise appears more as a glorious but tragic episode than as a central trend of Russian history." It was a "consciousness" rather than a "mentality," because it was an intellectual construct, not a spontaneous belief system emerging organically from society.[1] Leaving aside the question of whether a consciousness or a mentality (or indeed an ideology or a Weltanschauung) arises more organically, it seems that a commitment to legality remained a minority position throughout these 300 years in Russia. Such a commitment was strong among many educated elites and was probably growing among the broader population in the final decades of Imperial Russia. The same can likely be said of today's Russia, though of no other periods, and even in these two peaks of respect for legality, the strongest tendency was and still is toward arbitrariness.

Marc Raeff has perceptively addressed this matter, pointing to tensions and even contradictions in the history of Russian law and justice. "The people recognizes the existence of justice (*pravda*)," he wrote, "but it does not respect the law (*zakon*) and is deprived of rights (*prava*). As for the intelligentsia, its members believe in legality (*zakonnost'*) but do not have a legal consciousness (*pravosoznanie*)."[2] It is undoubted that human beings have an innate sense of fairness and justice. In the societies they build, they ground their institutions and customs upon such principles. Law gradually develops in all societies as an abstract form of custom and mores. In modern societies, where communities are more populous and impersonal, and, above all, where commercial relations become central to private life and individuals expect to participate in government and avoid arbitrary treatment by officials, the law has gradually become supreme. In modern Western societies and non-Western societies that have adopted Western legal principles and institutions, most people respect the law, enjoy rights, and have a deep appreciation of legality. In such societies, political figures and administrative officials are usually held to account and consider themselves under the law. The Corruption Perception Index, as discussed in Chapter 7, is a handy yardstick in this regard. The top twenty societies with the least perceived corruption in 2016 were all Western, Westernized (such as Japan), or ruled long term by Western colonial powers (for example, Singapore and Hong Kong). Many of Russia's elites in its two high points of legality desired—at least intellectually—their country's transition to the rule of law. Unfortunately, that transition for any society in which arbitrary power is deeply entrenched among leaders and ordinary people is hard to achieve.

That entrenchment resulted in a self-perpetuating tendency pervasive in Russian culture to seek to influence the law rather than appeal to it. Marianna Muravyeva points to "the famous Russian saying—'Everyone has his own law' (*U kazhdogo svoia pravda*)" as a way to capture the essence of this attitude.[3] Most Russians in most epochs went to court not so much hoping for the best but fearing the worst. Blind justice, in this conception, could not be counted on but had to be wrestled into submission by whatever means one disposed of. True, people in all societies seek to influence legal outcomes, for example in Western societies by hiring the best lawyer one can afford. This tendency seems to have been much stronger, however, in Russia.

How is one to understand, therefore, the abundant historical scholarship showing that Russians have relied assiduously on the courts to resolve their disputes and to seek justice? "As in Europe," Nancy Shields Kollmann has written in regard to the early modern era, "governance united formalized law and institutions with flexible practice and popular concepts of justice. On the ground, European 'rationalizing' states look less rational and Muscovy's proclaimed 'autocracy' looks less autocratic."[4] Of the pre-1864 reform era, Sergei Antonov argues that the Russian legal system "retained enough integrity to occasionally punish a corrupt official and to rescue a wrongfully accused serf, and even before the reform of 1864 fulfilled— however imperfectly—its ideological, as well as its practical functions."[5] For the post-reform period, Jane Burbank argues that peasants encountered in the township courts, to which they flocked after the turn of the century, "due process—efficient, regulated, effective, and recorded justice."[6] As to Russia today, Kathryn Hendley reaches a similar conclusion. "Russians routinely negotiate solutions to their problems with others in the shadow of the law or, when informal efforts prove futile, take their problems to the courts and have them resolved in accordance with the law."[7]

It is telling that these scholars are referring primarily to civil litigation and not criminal law. In the past 300 years in Russia (though not during the Soviet era when civil law was all but missing from the judicial system), litigants could hope to find some satisfaction in their disputes with one another. Perhaps this was primarily by the sort of means Muravyeva considers a central feature of Russian justice: individually tailored outcomes dependent on various forms of manipulation, pressure, and influence. Scholarship demonstrating the confidence of defendants entering the criminal justice system in Russia in the likelihood of their receiving fair treatment, for most time periods, is nonexistent. It is also telling that while peasants would willingly and frequently bring economic disputes to the township courts in the 1890s, when an offense was grave enough to be self-evidently heinous in the minds of nearly all peasants, like horse stealing, they typically preferred dealing with the crime themselves, through vigilante justice (*samosud*).[8]

Nevertheless, the guarantees of due process—in regular criminal cases— were greatest in the post-reform era, from 1864 to 1917. A fair trial in those years was not inevitable, but it was more likely than in any others. The judicial reform of 1864 was a major step toward the rule of law, however imperfectly implemented. Therefore, the Bolshevik dismantling of the independent judiciary marked an unfortunate deviation away from that vital principle of modern, developed societies. One can argue that the criminal justice system in the late Imperial era protected property and personal rights at a standard not greatly different from what citizens could expect in the major Western countries, while protecting civil and political rights to a much lesser degree. After 1917, by contrast, certain civil rights—for example, of women, ethnic minorities, and homosexuals, but not of religious believers—were better protected than before 1917. Overall, however, restraints on administrative power and freedom from arbitrary treatment by government officials were fairly weak throughout both eras. Significant protections were enjoyed by economic and social elites in the late Imperial period and by party elites during much of the Soviet era.

Such conflicting tendencies between institutions and informal practices, between official law and popular norms ("customary law"), and between ordinary or "everyday" criminal procedure and special variants deployed in emergency circumstances are what Hendley helpfully construes as evidence of the dualistic nature of the Russian criminal justice system. High-profile victims of often politicized legal retribution—from the musketeers under Peter to Mikhail Khodorkovsky under Putin—must be distinguished, she argues, from the more humane and predictable treatment of ordinary defendants and litigants.

There is no doubt that throughout the era arcing from the dawn of the Russian Empire to the present, ordinary people on a daily basis have fared far better at the hands of administrative officials, procurators, and judges than have persons accused of political crimes and of actions offensive to people in high places. Judicial and legal dualism was real, despite the thread of accusatorial bias in criminal cases running through Russia's history of criminal justice.[9] Yet even in the decades following the Judicial Reform of 1864, when Russians enjoyed real guarantees of due process in criminal justice, all police and gendarmes wielded daunting arbitrary power. Thanks to the Security Law of 1881, they could detain for up to seven days anyone, in any locality, suspected of merely planning a political crime or of belonging to an illegal organization. They could also arrange that person's exile to distant places for up to five years without any due process or right of appeal.[10] Those rules were in force in ordinary times; police officials wielded even more arbitrary power under the two states of emergency defined by the Security Law. A key feature of the mentality of most government officials in late Imperial Russia was the belief that order could not adequately be maintained without recourse to special rules and measures outside the normal system of law. It is true that the "emergency" rules were less draconian than those they replaced. In other words, the Russian government was attempting to limit unconstrained administrative power. Indeed, one can argue that the very adoption of the Security Law showed that Russia was on a path toward more limited government, toward constitutionalism.

It was an important moment of transition in Russian history. "The Russian Empire was far from being lawless in 1913," according to Wayne Dowler, "but the laws were not yet fully independent of will. The Judicial

Statute of 1864 had created the basis for a comprehensive legal system and the rule of law. It challenged the state's assumption that law served administrative goal, and fostered instead a legal culture based on the notion of individual rights that vied with state rights."[11]

At the same time, there is no denying what seems to have been an ingrained and deeply rooted tendency toward wielding arbitrary power, of resisting checks and balances, of preferring informal legal rules and practices, of ascribing a higher value to state and official interests than to private and personal interests, and toward personalized rule in Russia during the past 300 years. Scholars have given this tendency various labels—such as "patrimonial" (Richard Pipes) and "autocratic" (Richard Wortman).[12] Quibbling over semantics aside, the meaning and import are the same. Even the Bolsheviks' vaunted "revolutionary consciousness," by which ordinary people acting as judges were expected to reach just decisions through the power of something like Hegel's world spirit, simply opened the back door to the reemergence of this traditional tendency toward unity of political power, a government of men rather than laws, and personal influence by persons with power on the process of criminal justice. Even after the Bolsheviks reinforced their justice system with codes of procedure, appeals for respect of the law, and an official veneration of "socialist legality," informality continued to reign, breeding uncertainty, partiality, dependence on the powerful, and pervasive corruption.

Of course, no criminal justice system in the world is perfect. In all, some categories of people enjoy preferential treatment, be it because of their social or economic status, political standing, gender, race, ethnicity, or other factors. To say, however, that no system is perfectly fair is not to deny immense differences in performance, in approaching the ideal from country to country.

In fact, the persistence of such features in Russian criminal justice as arbitrariness, informal rules, personalized decision-making, and treating mere threats to state authority as graver offenses than bodily harm to private individuals makes one wonder about the resistance to change of the underlying political culture. Such an idea was famously propounded by Richard Pipes in *Russia under the Old Regime*. More recently, the idea has been reformulated in the term "transcontinuities," meaning "elements ... which survive revolutionary alterations and always re-emerge."[13] It is hard to come away from a careful study of the history of criminal justice in Russia without a healthy appreciation for transcontinuities. William E. Butler, a leading scholar in the field, concludes that "Russia has inherited its burdens of the past, both Imperial and Soviet—autocracy, intolerance, russification, bureaucratism, backwardness, absence of modern legal tradition."[14] It seems unlikely Russia had to remain a prisoner of its political culture. The dramatic reforms brought about by many of its rulers and leaders suggest that multiple paths were possible. Yet the historical record shows that the actual path followed was one mostly of continuity.

NOTES

Preface

1. See Richard Hellie, "Migration in Early Modern Russia, 1480s–1780s," in *Coerced and Free Migration: Global Perspectives*, ed. David Eltis (Stanford: Stanford University Press, 2002), 292–323 [here: 293].
2. See Cyril Bryner, "The Issue of Capital Punishment in the Reign of Elizabeth Petrovna," *The Russian Review* 49, no. 4 (October 1990): 389–416.
3. See Roger Hood and Carolyn Hoyle, *The Death Penalty: A Worldwide Perspective*, 5th ed. (Oxford: Oxford University Press, 2015), 11–13.
4. See William E. Butler, "Russian Legal History: The Pre-revolutionary Heritage," in *Russia and the Law of Nations in Historical Perspective: Collected Essays* (London: Wildy, Simmonds & Hill Pub., 2009), 3–23 [here: 21].
5. See Aaron B. Retish, "Breaking Free from the Prison Walls: Penal Reforms and Prison Life in Revolutionary Russia," *Historical Research* 90, no. 247 (February 2017): 134–50.
6. See William E. Butler, "Russia, Legal Traditions of the World, and Legal Change," in *Russia and the Law of Nations in Historical Perspective*, 170–76 [here: 175].

Introduction

1. As quoted from Maria Dobozy, trans. and ed., *The Saxon Mirror: A Sachsenspiegel of the Fourteenth Century* (Philadelphia: University of Pennsylvania Press, 1999), 67.
2. See William E. Butler, "Russian Legal History," 5.
3. See Boris N. Mironov, with Ben Eklof, *A Social History of Imperial Russia, 1700–1917*, 2 vols (Boulder, CO: Westview Press, 2000), 2:231–48.
4. See George B. Weickhardt, "The Modernization of Law in 17th-Century Muscovy," in *Modernizing Muscovy: Reform and Social Change in Seventeenth-Century Russia*, ed. Jarmo Kotilaine and Marshall Poe (London: RoutledgeCurzon, 2004), 76–92.
5. For a translation of the *Ulozhenie*, see Richard Hellie, ed., *The Muscovite Law Code (Ulozhenie) of 1649*, Part 1: Text and Translation (Irvine, CA: Charles Schlaks, 1998).
6. Quoted from Hellie, ed., *The Muscovite Law Code*, 23.
7. See Hans J. Torke, "Crime and Punishment in the Pre-Petrine Civil Service: The Problem of Control," in *Imperial Russia, 1700–1917: State, Society, Opposition: Essays in Honor of Marc Raeff*, ed. Ezra Mendelsohn and Marshall S. Shatz (DeKalb: Northern Illinois University Press, 1988), 7–21.
8. See Butler, "Russia, Legal Traditions of the World, and Legal Change," 174.

9   See Richard Hellie, "Early Modern Russian Law: The Ulozhenie of 1649," *Russian History* 15, nos. 2–4 (1988): 155–79 [here: 160].

10   See Alan Wood, "Sex and Violence in Siberia: Aspects of the Tsarist Exile System," in *Siberia: Two Historical Perspectives*, ed. John Massey Stewart and Alan Wood (London: The Great Britain-USSR Association and The School of Slavonic and East European Studies, 1984), 23–42 [here: 24].

11   Statistic from Andrew A. Gentes, *Exile to Siberia, 1590–1822* (Basingstoke, UK: Palgrave Macmillan, 2008), 37.

12   See Alan Wood, "Administrative Exile and the Criminals' Commune in Siberia," in *Land Commune and Peasant Community in Russia: Communal Forms in Imperial and Early Soviet Society*, ed. Roger Bartlett (New York: St. Martin's Press, 1990), 395–414 [here: 397].

13   See Mironov, *A Social History of Imperial Russia*, 2:307–12.

14   See Jerome Blum, "The Internal Structure and Polity of the European Village Community from the Fifteenth to the Nineteenth Century," *The Journal of Modern History* 43 (December 1971): 541–76 [here: 546–47].

Chapter 1

1   Statistics in Lindsey Hughes, *Russia in the Age of Peter the Great* (New Haven, CT, and London: Yale University Press, 1998), 454.

2   The best general survey of Russian criminal justice from earliest times to 1917 is Mironov, *A Social History of Imperial Russia*, 2:223–365.

3   See John P. LeDonne, "The Evolution of the Governor's Office, 1727–1764," *Canadian-American Slavic Studies* 12, no. 1 (Spring 1978): 86–115.

4   See Claes Peterson, *Peter the Great's Administrative and Judicial Reforms: Swedish Antecedents and the Process of Reception* (Stockholm: Juridska Fakulteten, 1979), 84–94.

5   As quoted in John Keep, "No Gauntlet for Gentlemen: Officers' Privileges in Russian Military Law, 1716–1855," *Cahiers du monde russe et soviétique* 34, nos. 1–2 (January–June 1993): 171–92 [here: 173].

6   See William E. Butler, "On the Formation of a Russian Legal Consciousness: The Zertsalo," in *Russia and the Law of Nations in Historical Perspective*, 91–101 [here: 91–92].

7   Statistics from Isabel de Madariaga, *Russia in the Age of Catherine the Great* (New Haven, CT: Yale University Press, 1981), 602n1.

8   See Marianna Muravyeva, "Russian Early Modern Criminal Procedure and Culture of Appeal," *Review of Central and East European Law* 38 (2013): 295–316 [here: 304–5].

9   See N. N. Efremova, *Sudoustroistvo Rossii v XVIII—pervoi polovine XI vv. Istoriko-pravovoe issledovanie* (Moscow: Nauka, 1993), 42–43.

10   See Nancy Shields Kollmann, *Crime and Punishment in Early Modern Russia* (Cambridge: Cambridge University Press, 2012), 411–13.

11   See Mironov, *A Social History of Imperial Russia*, 2:248.

12   See Marc Raeff, "Russia's Autocracy and Paradoxes of Modernization," in *Political Ideas and Institutions in Imperial Russia* (Boulder, CO: Westview Press, 1994), 116–40; Marc Raeff, *The Well-Ordered Police State: Social and Institutional Change through Law in the Germanies and Russia, 1600–1800* (New Haven, CT: Yale University Press, 1983).

13 Hughes, *Russia in the Age of Peter the Great*, 295.

14 Marc Raeff, "Codification et droit en Russie impériale: Quelques remarques comparatives," *Cahiers du monde russe et soviétique* 20, no. 1 (1979): 5–13.

15 See Efremova, *Sudoustroistvo Rossii*, 43.

16 See Gentes, *Exile to Siberia, 1590–1822*, 97–108.

17 See Roger Bartlett, "Serfdom and State Power in Imperial Russia," *European History Quarterly* 33 (2003): 29–64.

18 Statistics in John P. LeDonne, *Ruling Russia: Politics and Administration in the Age of Absolutism, 1762–1796* (Princeton, NJ: Princeton University Press, 1984), 189.

19 Statistics in Cyril Bryner, "The Issue of Capital Punishment in the Reign of Elizabeth Petrovna," *The Russian Review* 49, no. 4 (October 1990): 389–416 [here: 394–95].

20 See Jonathan Daly, "Russian Punishments in the European Mirror," in *Russia in the European Context, 1789–1914: A Member of the Family*, ed. Susan McCaffray and Michael Melancon (New York: Palgrave Macmillan, 2005), 161–88 [here: 161].

21 See Isabel de Madariaga, "Catherine II and the Serfs: A Reconsideration of Some Problems," *The Slavonic and East European Review* 52, no. 126 (January 1974): 34–62.

22 Gentes, *Exile to Siberia, 1590–1822*, 108 (laws), 123 (statistics).

23 See Thomas Esper, "Hired Labor and the Metallurgical Industry of the Urals during the Late Serf Period," *Jahrbücher für Geschichte Osteuropas* 29 (1980): 62–70.

24 See Isabel de Madariaga, "Penal Policy in the Age of Catherine II," in *Politics and Culture in the Eighteenth Century: Collected Essays by Isabel de Madariaga* (London and New York: Longman, 1998), 97–123.

25 See A. Lentin, "Beccaria, Shcherbatov, and the Question of Capital Punishment," *Canadian Slavonic Papers* 24, no. 2 (June 1982): 128–37.

26 See John P. LeDonne, "The Judicial Reform of 1775 in Central Russia," *Jahrbücher für Geschichte Osteuropas* 21, no. 1 (1973): 29–45 [here: 36].

27 See Madariaga, *Russia in the Age of Catherine the Great*, 557.

28 See Madariaga, "Penal Policy in the Age of Catherine II," 109.

29 Quoted and cited in Simon Dixon, *Catherine the Great* (London: Profile Books, 2001), 131.

30 Statistics in S. Frederick Starr, *Decentralization and Self-Government in Russia, 1830–1870* (Princeton, NJ: Princeton University Press, 1972), 48.

31 Statistic in Robert E. Jones, *Provincial Development in Russia: Catherine II and Jacob Sievers* (New Brunswick, NJ: Rutgers University Press, 1984), 13.

32 Statistic in LeDonne, "The Judicial Reform of 1775 in Central Russia," 31.

33 Quotations from Janet M. Hartley, "Catherine's Conscience Court: An English Equity Court?" in *Russia and the West in the Eighteenth Century*, ed. A. G. Cross (Newtonville, MA: Oriental Research Partners, 1983): 306–18.

34 Andrew A. Gentes, "Katorga: Penal Labor and Tsarist Siberia," in *The Siberian Saga: A History of Russia's Wild East*, ed. Eva-Maria Stolberg (Frankfurt am Main: Peter Lang, 2005), 73–85 [here: 77].

35 See Madariaga, "Penal Policy in the Age of Catherine II," 109.

36 See John P. LeDonne, "The *Guberniia* Procuracy during the Reign of Catherine II, 1764–1796," *Cahiers du monde russe* 36, no. 3 (July–September 1995): 221–48.

37 See Marianna Muravyeva "'Till Death Us Do Part': Spousal Homicide in Early Modern Russia," *The History of the Family* 18, no. 3 (2013): 306–30 [here: 312–14, 318, 322–23].

38 Statistic in Janet Hartley, "Bribery and Justice in the Provinces in the Reign of Catherine II," in *Bribery and Blat in Russia: Negotiating Reciprocity from the Middle Ages to the 1990s*, ed. Stephen Lovell, Alena Ledeneva, and Andrei Rogachevskii (New York: St. Martin's Press, 2000), 48–64 [here: 59].

39 Quoted from Muravyeva, "Russian Early Modern Criminal Procedure and Culture of Appeal," 316.

40 See M. N. Gernet, *Istoriia tsarskoi tiur'my*, 5 vols., 3rd ed. (Moscow: Gos. izd. iuridicheskoi literatury, 1961–1963), 1:228–29.

41 See Gentes, *Exile to Siberia, 1590–1822*, 123.

Chapter 2

1 See Sergei M. Kazantsev, "Judicial Reform of 1864 and the Procuracy," in *Reforming Justice in Russia, 1864–1996: Power, Culture, and the Limits of Legal Order*, ed. Peter H. Solomon, Jr. (Armonk, NY, and London: M.E. Sharpe, 1997), 44–60 [here: 50].

2 On court organization in this period, see Efremova, *Sudoustroistvo Rossii*, 148–52.

3 Quotation in Janet M. Hartley, *Alexander I* (London and New York: Longman, 1994), 31.

4 See Abby M. Schrader, *Languages of the Lash: Corporal Punishment and Identity in Imperial Russia* (DeKalb: Northern Illinois University Press, 2002), 197n38.

5 Nancy Park, "Imperial Chinese Justice and the Law of Torture," *Late Imperial China* 29, no. 2 (December 2008): 37–67 (quotation: 57).

6 See John P. LeDonne, *Absolutism and Ruling Class: The Formation of the Russian Political Order, 1700–1825* (New York and Oxford: Oxford University Press, 1991), 126.

7 John Gooding, "The Liberalism of Michael Speransky," *The Slavonic and East European Review* 64, no. 3 (July 1986): 401–24 [here: 423].

8 See Keep, "No Gauntlet for Gentlemen," 179.

9 V. A. C. Gatrell, *The Hanging Tree: Execution and the English People, 1770–1868* (New York: Oxford University Press, 1994).

10 See Angus McLaren, *The Trials of Masculinity: Policing Sexual Boundaries, 1870–1930* (Chicago and London: The University of Chicago Press, 1997), 13–16.

11 See R. S. Alexander, *Europe's Uncertain Path, 1814–1914: State Formation and Civil Society* (Chichester, UK: Wiley-Blackwell, 2012), 18.

12 Barry Hollingsworth, "John Venning and Prison Reform in Russia, 1819–1830," *The Slavonic and East European Review* 48, no. 113 (October 1970): 537–56.

13 See Marc Raeff, *Siberia and the Reforms of 1822* (Seattle: University of Washington Press, 1956).

14 Andrew Gentes, *Exile, Murder, and Madness in Siberia, 1823–61* (Basingstoke, UK: Palgrave Macmillan, 2010), 46.

15 Gernet, *Istoriia tsarskoi tiur'my*, 1:231.

16 See Andew A. Gentes, "'Completely Useless': Exiling the Disabled to Tsarist Siberia," *Sibirica* 10, no. 2 (2011): 26–49 [here: 35].

17 Statistics in Richard Stites, *The Four Horsemen: Riding to Liberty in Post-Napoleonic Europe* (Oxford and New York: Oxford University Press, 2014), 318–19.

18 See Sidney Monas, *The Third Section: Police and Society under Nicholas I* (Cambridge, MA: Harvard University Press, 1961).

19 Sergei Antonov, *Bankrupts and Usurers of Imperial Russia: Debt, Property, and the Law in the Age of Dostoevsky and Tolstoy* (Cambridge, MA and London: Harvard University Press, 2016), 22–23, 41–45 [quotation: 41].

20 See Alexander Moutchnik, "Soziale und wirtschaftliche Grundzüge der Kartoffelaufstände von 1834 und von 1841–1843 in Russland," in *Volksaufstände in Rußland: Von der Zeit der Wirren bis zur "Grünen Revolution" gegen die Sowjetherrschaft*, ed. Heinz-Dietrich Löwe (Wiesbaden: Harrassowitz Verlag, 2006), 427–51.

21 See Keep, "No Gauntlet for Gentlemen," 180.

22 John P. LeDonne, "Civilians under Military Justice during the Reign of Nicholas I," *Canadian-American Slavic Studies* 8, no. 2 (Summer 1973): 171–87.

23 See Norval Morris and David J. Rothman, eds., *The Oxford History of the Prison: The Practice of Punishment in Western Society* (New York and Oxford: Oxford University Press, 1998), Chaps. 4–7.

24 Gentes, *Exile, Murder, and Madness in Siberia*, 66, 181.

25 Gentes, *Exile, Murder, and Madness in Siberia*, 48.

26 Manuel Eisner, "Long-Term Historical Trends in Violent Crime," *Crime and Justice* 30 (2003): 83–142 [here: 99].

27 See W. Bruce Lincoln, *In the Vanguard of Reform: Russia's Enlightened Bureaucrats, 1825–1861* (DeKalb: Northern Illinois University Press, 1982), 72–74.

28 See Susan K. Morrissey, *Suicide and the Body Politic in Imperial Russia* (New York: Cambridge University Press, 2006), 96–99 [quotation: 99].

29 Statistics in Daly, "Russian Punishments in the European Mirror," 163.

30 Mironov, *A Social History of Imperial Russia*, 2:258.

31 Gentes, "Completely Useless," 35.

32 Quoted from O. I. Chistiakov, ed., *Zakonodatel'stvo pervoi poloviny XIX veka*, vol. 6 of *Rossiiskoe zakonodatel'stvo X–XX vekov* (Moscow: Iuridicheskaia literatura, 1988), 233.

33 Richard Pipes, *Russia under the Old Regime* (New York: Charles Scribner's Sons, 1974), 293, 295.

34 Statistics in this paragraph from Mironov, *A Social History of Imperial Russia*, 2:299–301.

35 Antonov, *Bankrupts and Usurers of Imperial Russia*, 262–75.

36 See Sergei Antonov and Katherine Pickering Antonova, "The Maiden and the Wolf: Law, Gender, and Sexual Violence in Imperial Russia," *Slavic Review* 77, no. 1 (Spring 2018).

Chapter 3

1 Wood, "Administrative Exile and the Criminals' Commune in Siberia," 398–99.

2 Statistics in Mironov, *A Social History of Imperial Russia*, 2:257.

3 See Cathy Frierson, "Crime and Punishment in the Russian Village: Rural Concepts of Criminality at the End of the Nineteenth Century," *Slavic Review* 46, no. 1 (1987): 55–69.

4 See N. S. Tagantsev, *Russkoe ugolovnoe pravo: Letktsii: Chast' obshchaia*, 2 vols. (Moscow: Nauka, 1994), 2:112–13.

5 Gentes, *Exile, Murder, and Madness in Siberia*, 47.

6   Stephen G. Wheatcroft, "The Crisis of the Late Tsarist Penal System," in *Challenging Traditional Views of Russian History*, ed. Stephen G. Wheatcroft (Basingstoke, UK, Palgrave Macmillan, 2002), 27–54 [here: 35].

7   Andrew A. Gentes, "The Institution of Russia's Sakhalin Policy, from 1868 to 1875," *Journal of Asian History* 36, no. 1 (2002): 1–31.

8   Bruce F. Adams, *The Politics of Punishment: Prison Reform in Russia, 1863–1917* (DeKalb: Northern Illinois University Press, 1996).

9   See Samuel Kucherov, *Courts, Lawyers, and Trials under the Last Three Tsars* (New York: Praeger, 1953).

10   See John W. Atwell, Jr., "The Russian Jury," *Slavonic and East European Review* 53 (January 1975): 44–61.

11   See Jörg Baberowski, *Autokratie und Justiz: Zum Verhältnis von Rechsstaatlichkeit und Rückständigkeit im ausgehenden Zarenreich, 1864–1914* (Frankfort am Main: Vittorio Klostermann, 1996).

12   See Louise McReynolds, *Murder Most Russian: True Crime and Punishment in Late Imperial Russia* (Ithaca, NY, and London: Cornell University Press, 2013), 4.

13   See S. A. Zavrazhin, "Juvenile Courts in the Russian Empire," *Russian Education and Society* 38, no. 2 (1996): 67–74.

14   Eugene Huskey, "The Politics of the Soviet Criminal Process: Expanding the Right to Counsel in Pretrial Proceedings," *American Journal of Comparative Law* 34, no. 1 (Winter 1986): 93–112 [here: 97].

15   See Eric Lohr, *Russian Citizenship, From Empire to Soviet Union* (Cambridge, MA, and London: Harvard University Press, 2012).

16   On the extending of the judicial reform throughout the empire, see Baberowski, *Autokratie und Justiz*, Chap. 5 [statistic: 389].

17   Christine D. Worobec, "Horse Thieves and Peasant Justice in Post-Emancipation Russia," *Journal of Social History* 21 (Winter 1987): 281–93.

18   See William C. Fuller, Jr., "Civilians in Russian Military Courts, 1881–1904," *The Russian Review* 41, no. 3 (July 1982): 288–305.

19   Statistics in McReynolds, *Murder Most Russian*, 20.

20   Statistics from Mironov, *A Social History of Imperial Russia*, 2:346–47.

21   See Sandra Dahlke, "Old Russia in the Dock: The Trial against Mother Superior Mitrofaniia before the Moscow District Court (1874)," *Cahiers du monde russe* 53, no. 1 (2012): 95–120.

22   See Sergei Antonov, "Russian Capitalism on Trial: The Case of the Jacks of Hearts," *Law and History Review* 36, no. 1 (February 1918).

23   Statistic in Ana Siljak, *Angel of Vengeance: The "Girl Assassin," the Governor of St. Petersburg, and Russia's Revolutionary World* (New York: St. Martin's Press, 2008), 126.

24   See Jonathan W. Daly, "On the Significance of Emergency Legislation in Late Imperial Russia," *Slavic Review* 54 (Fall 1995): 602–29 [here: 605–6].

25   Statistics in Jonathan Daly, *Autocracy under Siege: Security Police and Opposition in Russia, 1866–1905* (DeKalb: Northern Illinois University Press, 1998), 22.

26   See Baberowski, *Autokratie und Justiz*, 669–79.

27   Statistics in Daly, *Autocracy under Siege*, 35.

28   Statistics from Daly, *Autocracy under Siege*, 47.

29   Mironov, *A Social History of Imperial Russia*, 2:306.

30   See Jane Burbank, *Russian Peasants Go to Court: Legal Culture in the Countryside* (Bloomington: Indiana University Press, 2004).

31 See Theodore Taranovski, "The Aborted Counter-Reform: Murav́ev Commission and the Judicial Statutes of 1864," *Jahrbücher für Geschichte Osteuropas* 29, no. 2 (1981): 161–84.

32 Statistics in Daly, "On the Significance of Emergency Legislation in Late Imperial Russia," 617.

33 Statistics in Tagantsev, *Russkoe ugolovnoe pravo*, 2:180–81.

34 Mironov, *A Social History of Imperial Russia*, 2:259.

35 Statistics in Mironov, *A Social History of Imperial Russia*, 2:247.

36 Statistic from John Bushnell, *Mutiny amid Repression: Russian Soldiers in the Revolution of 1905–1906* (Bloomington: Indiana University Press, 1985), 52.

37 See, for example, George Gilbert, *The Radical Right in Late Imperial Russia: Dreams of a True Fatherland?* (London and New York: Routledge, 2016), 118, 123–26.

38 Statistics in Maureen Perrie, "The Russian Peasant Movement of 1905–1907: Its Social Composition and Revolutionary Significance," *Past & Present* 57 (November 1972): 123–55 (nearly 4,000: 126n10); Daly, "On the Significance of Emergency Legislation in Late Imperial Russia," 622 (dozens); M. I. Leonov, *Partiia sotsialistov-revoliutsionerov v 1905–1907 gg.* (Moscow: Rosspen, 1997), 129 (hundreds).

39 Statistics from Wheatcroft, "The Crisis of the Late Tsarist Penal System," 48–49.

40 Statistics from S. S. Ostroumov, "Repressii tsarskogo pravitel'stva protiv revoliutsionnogo dvizheniia v Rossii v period imperializma: Ugolovno-statistichekoe issledovanie," *Vestnik moskovskogo universiteta*, Series 8: Pravo, no. 3 (1976): 35–41 [here: 40].

41 Statistics from Ostroumov, "Repressii tsarskogo pravitel'stva," 36.

42 Statistics in Daly, "Russian Punishments in the European Mirror," 167.

43 Mironov, *A Social History of Imperial Russia*, 2:335, 345.

44 See Neil Weissman, "Rural Crime in Tsarist Russia: The Question of Hooliganism, 1905–1914," *Slavic Review* 37 (June 1978): 228–40.

45 Eric Lohr, *Nationalizing the Russian Empire: The Campaign against Enemy Aliens during World War I* (Cambridge, MA: Harvard University Press, 2003), 122–44, 150–52.

46 See Tsuyoshi Hasegawa, "Crime and Police in Revolutionary Petrograd, March 1917–March 1918: Social History of the Russian Revolution Revisited," *Acta Slavica Iaponica* 13 (1995): 1–41.

47 See E. A. Pravilova, "Organizatsiia sistemy administrativnoi iustitsii v Rossii: Pravovye reformy Vremennogo pravitel'stva," in *Rossiia v XIX–XX: Sbornik statei k 70-letiiu so dnia rozhdeniia Rafaila Sholomovich Ganelina*, ed. A. A. Fursenko (St. Petersburg: Dmitrii Bulanin, 1998), 226–30.

48 Jonathan W. Daly, *The Watchful State: Security Police and Opposition in Russia, 1906–1917* (DeKalb: Northern Illinois University Press, 2004), 209–14.

Chapter 4

1 As quoted and analyzed in Neil Harding, *Lenin's Political Thought: Theory and Practice in the Democratic and Socialist Revolutions* (Chicago: Haymarket Books, 2009), 135.

2 See Samuel Kucherov, *The Organs of Soviet Administration of Justice: Their History and Operation* (Leiden: E. J. Brill, 1970), 21–35.

3 See William E. Butler, *The Russia Legal Practitioner* (The Hague: Eleven International Publishing, 2011), 41.

4   V. I. Musaev, *Prestupnost' v Petrograde v 1917–1921 gg. i bor'ba s nei* (St. Petersburg: Dmitrii Bulanin, 2001), 119.

5   E. M. Balashov, "Novoe obshchestvo—'Novyi chelovek,'" in *Petrograd na perelome epokh: Gorod i ego zhiteli v gody revoliutsii i grazhdanskoi voiny*, ed. V. A. Shishkin, et al. (St. Peterburg: Dmitrii Bulanin, 2000), 272–73.

6   See S. V. Iarov, *Krest'ianin kak politik: Krest'ianstvo severo-zapada Rossii v 1918–1919 gg.: Politicheskoe myshlenie i massovyi protest* (St. Petersburg: Dmitrii Bulanin, 1999), 88–89.

7   Iarov, *Krest'ianin kak politik.*

8   See D. B. Pavlov, "Tribunal'nyi etap sovetskoi sudebnoi sistemy, 1917–1922 gg.," *Voprosy istorii*, no. 6 (2007): 3–16.

9   Matthew Rendle, "Revolutionary Tribunals and the Origins of Terror in Early Soviet Russia," *Historical Research* 84, no. 226 (November 2011): 693–721 [here: 696].

10   Adele Lindenmeyr, "The First Soviet Political Trial: Countess Sofia Panina before the Petrograd Revolutionary Tribunal," *The Russian Review* 60, no. 4 (October 2001): 505–25.

11   See George Leggett, *The Cheka: Lenin's Political Police* (Oxford: Clarendon Press, 1981).

12   Statistics in S. V. Leonov, *Rozhdenie sovetskoi imperii: Gosudarstvo i ideologiia, 1917–1922 gg.* (Moscow: Dialog-MGU, 1997), 147.

13   Matthew Rendle, "Mercy amid Terror? The Role of Amnesties during Russia's Civil War," *The Slavonic and East European Review* 92, no. 3 (July 2014): 449–78.

14   See for example Severov, "Golodovka levykh sots.-rev. v Butyrskoi tiur'me," in *Kreml' za reshchetkoi: Podpol'naia Rossiia*, ed. M. A. Spiridonova and A. A. Izmailovich (Berlin: Izd. "Skify," 1922), 70–82.

15   See Donald J. Raleigh, *Experiencing Russia's Civil War: Politics, Society, and Revolutionary Culture in Saratov, 1917–1922* (Princeton, NJ: Princeton University Press, 2002), 58.

16   A. L. Litvin, *Krasnyi i belyi terror v Rossii, 1918–1922 gg.* (Kazan: Tatarskoe gazetno-zhurnal'noe izd., 1995), 54–55.

17   See Golfo Alexopoulos, *Stalin's Outcasts: Aliens, Citizens, and the Soviet State, 1926–1936* (Ithaca, NY, and London: Cornell University Press, 2003).

18   See Richard Pipes, "Lenin's Gulag," *International Journal of Political Science and Development* 2, no. 6 (June 2014): 140–46.

19   Quotations and estimate from B. N. Kolodizh, "Iul'skoe 1918 goda antibol'shevistskoe vosstanie v Iaroslavle: Politiko-istoricheskoe osmyslenie," in *Iaroslavskoe vosstanie, iiul' 1918*, ed. V. Zh. Tsvetkov, et al. (Moscow: Posev, 1998), 19–27 [here: 21–22].

20   As quoted in the Cheka weekly, *Ezhenedel'nik chrezvychainykh komissii po bor'be s kontr-revolutsiei i spekulatsiei*, no. 1 (September 22, 1918): 8–9.

21   See G. A. Gavrilov, "Rol' chekistov v stanovlenii Sovetskoi vlasti na territorii Viatskoi gubernii v 1918 godu," in *Iz istorii Viatskikh spetssluzhb (pervaia polovina XIX–vtoraia polovina XX v.v.)*, ed. V. E. Musikhin (Kirov: Triada-S, 1997), 53–62 [here: 58–59].

22   Statistic in Litvin, *Krasnyi i belyi terror*, 84n26.

23   As quoted in Michael Melancon, "Revolutionary Culture in the Early Soviet Republic: Communist Executive Committees versus the Cheka, Fall 1918," *Jahrbücher für Geschichte Osteuropas* 57, no. 1 (2009): 1–22 [here: 15].

24   Murray Frame, "State Expansion and the Criminal Investigation Militia during the Russian Civil War," *History* 98 (July 2013): 406–27 [here: 417].

25   Statistics in Litvin, *Krasnyi i belyi terror*, 39.

26 S. K. Tsvigun, et al., eds., *V. I. Lenin i VChK: Sbornik dokumentov, 1917–1922 gg.* (Moscow: Izd. Politicheskoi literatury, 1975), 151–52, 163, 218–19.

27 Litvin, *Krasnyi i belyi terror*, 39, 66.

28 Statistic in M. Jacobson and M. B. Smirnov, "Sistema mest zakliucheniia v RSFSR i SSSR, 1917–1930," in *Sistema ispravitel'no-trudovykh lagerei v SSSR, 1923–1960: Spravochnik*, ed. M. B. Smirnov (Moscow: Zvenie, 1998), 10–24 [here: 12].

29 Musaev, *Prestupnost' v Petrograde*, 98.

30 Portnov and Slavin, *Stanovlenie pravosudiia Sovetskoi Rossii*, 119.

31 Stephen Velychenko, *State Building in Revolutionary Ukraine: A Comparative Study of Governments and Bureaucrats, 1917–1922* (Toronto, Buffalo, NY, and London: University of Toronto Press, 2011), 162.

32 Statistics in Litvin, *Krasnyi i belyi terror*, 76.

33 See Aaron B. Retish, "Controlling Revolution: Understandings of Violence through the Rural Soviet Courts, 1917–1923," *Europe-Asia Studies* 65 (November 2013): 1789–1806 [here: 1801–03].

34 Statistics in Litvin, *Krasnyi i belyi terror*, 38.

35 Portnov and Slavin, *Stanovlenie pravosudiia Sovetskoi Rossii*, 122.

36 V. P. Naumov and A. A. Kosakovskii, eds., "Kronshtadtskaia tragediia 1921 goda," *Voprosy istorii*, no. 4 (1994): 3–21 [here: 10–11].

37 V. I. Shishkin, ed., *Sibirskaia Vandeia*, 2 vols. (Moscow: Mezhdunarodnyi fond "Demokratiia," 2001), 2:213, 282.

38 Litvin, *Krasnyi i belyi terror*, 276–77n157; Nicholas Werth, "A State against Its People: Violence, Repression, and Terror in the Soviet Union," in *The Black Book of Communism: Crimes, Terror, Repression*, ed. Stéphane Courtois, et al.; trans. Mark Kramer and Jonathan Murphy (Cambridge, MA: Harvard University Press, 1999), 109.

39 Stuart Finkel, *On the Ideological Front: The Russian Intelligentsia and the Making of the Public Sphere* (New Haven, CT: Yale University Press, 2007), 17–19.

40 Quoted from O. B. Mozokhin, "Vnesudebnye polnomochiia VChK," in *Istoricheskie chteniia na Liubianke, 1998 god: Rossiiskie spetsluzhby na perelome epokh: Konets XIX veka-1922 god*, ed. A. A. Zdanovich, M. N. Petrov, and V. N. Khaustov (Moscow: Velikii Novgorod, 1999), 75–83 [here: 81].

41 V. N. Khaustov, V. P. Naumov, and N. S. Plotnikov, eds. *Lubianka: Stalin i VChK-GPU-OGPU-NKVD, ianvar' 1922–dekabr' 1936* (Moscow: Materik, 2003), 40–63.

42 Portnov and Slavin, *Stanovlenie pravosudiia Sovetskoi Rossii*, 134.

43 A. A. Kosakovskii, "Bol'sheviki utverzhdaiut gosudarstvennuiu vlast'," in *Drama rossiiskoi istorii: Bol'sheviki i revoliutsiia*, ed. O. V. Volobuev, et al. (Moscow: Novyi khronograf, 2002), 345–426 [here: 385].

44 Mark Jansen, "The Bar during the First Years of the Soviet Regime: N. K. Murav'ev," *Revolutionary Russia*, no. 2 (1990): 211–23 [here: 214–17].

45 Jacobson and Smirnov, "Sistema mest zakliucheniia v RSFSR i SSSR," 13.

46 Statistic in Litvin, *Krasnyi i belyi terror*, 98n143.

47 Paul Hagenloh, *Stalin's Police: Public Order and Mass Repression in the USSR, 1926–1941* (Baltimore: The John Hopkins University Press, 2009), 41, 349n80.

48 Louise Shelley, "Female Criminality in the 1920s: A Consequence of Inadvertent and Deliberate Change," *Russian History* 9, nos. 2/3 (1982): 265–84.

49 A. A. Piontkovskii, "Kontr-revoliutsionnye prestupleniia v Ugolovnom Kodekse R.S.F.S.R.," *Sovetskoe pravo*, no. 1(7) (1924): 7–40 [here: 14].

50 Statistics in T. V. Tsarevskaia, "Prestuplenie i nakazanie: Paradoksy 20-x godov," in *Revoliutsiia i chelovek: Byt, nravy, povedenie, moral'*, ed. P. V. Volobuev, et al. (Moscow: Institut rossiiskoi istorii RAN, 1997), 214.

51 Statistics from Stephen G. Wheatcroft, "The Great Terror in Historical Perspective: The Records of the Statistical Department of the Investigative Organs of OGPU/ NKVD," in *The Anatomy of Terror: Political Violence under Stalin*, ed. James Harris (Oxford and New York: Oxford University Press, 2013), 287–305 [here: 304].

52 See Aaron B. Retish, "Breaking Free from the Prison Walls: Penal Reforms and Prison Life in Revolutionary Russia," *Historical Research* 90, no. 247 (February 2017): 134–50.

53 Peter H. Solomon, Jr., *Soviet Criminal Justice under Stalin* (Cambridge: Cambridge University Press, 1996), 43.

54 Portnov and Slavin, *Stanovlenie pravosudiia Sovetskoi Rossii*, 137–38; D. L. Golinkov, *Krushenie antisovetskogo podpol'ia v SSSR*, 2 vols. (Moscow: Izd. Politicheskoi literatury, 1978), 2:165–66.

55 Statistic quoted in A. V. Kvashonkin, et al., eds., *Bol'shevistskoe rukovodstvo: Perepiska, 1912–1927: Sbornik dokumentov* (Moscow: Rosspen, 1996), 303.

56 Litvin, *Krasnyi i belyi terror*, 304; Peter H. Solomon, Jr., "Soviet Penal Policy, 1917–1934: A Reinterpretation," *Slavic Review* 39, no. 2 (June 1980): 195–217 [here: 202].

Chapter 5

1 Statistics in Solomon, *Soviet Criminal Justice*, 51.

2 Peter H. Solomon, Jr., "Criminalization and Decriminalization in Soviet Criminal Policy, 1917–1941," *Law & Society Review* 16, no. 1 (1981–1982): 9–44.

3 This story draws on my *Hammer, Sickle, and Soil: The Soviet Drive to Collectivize Agriculture* (Stanford, CA: Hoover Institution Press, 2017).

4 Statistic from Peter H. Solomon, Jr., "Criminal Justice and the Industrial Front," in *Social Dimensions of Soviet Industrialization*, ed. William G. Rosenberg and Lewis H. Siegelbaum (Bloomington and Indianapolis: Indiana University Press, 1993), 227.

5 Sheila Fitzpatrick, "The Great Departure: Rural–Urban Migration in the Soviet Union, 1929–1933," in *Social Dimensions of Soviet Industrialization*, ed. Rosenberg and Siegelbaum, 15–40 [here: 18].

6 Statistics in N. A. Ivnitskii, *Repressivnaia politika sovetskoi vlasti v derevne, 1928–1933* (Moscow: Institut rossiiskoi istorii RAN, 2000), 61, 70.

7 Statistic in Solomon, *Soviet Criminal Justice*, 133.

8 Statistics in V. N. Zemskov, "Spetsposelentsy: Po dokumentam NKVD—MVD SSSR," *Sotsiologicheskie issledovaniia*, no. 11 (1990): 3–17 [here: 3].

9 Statistics and comparison in Roberta T. Manning, "The Rise and Fall of the Extraordinary Measures, January-June, 1928: Towards a Reassessment of the Onset of the Stalin Revolution," *The Carl Beck Papers in Russian and East European Studies*, no. 1504 (January 2001): 1, 33.

10 Statistics in N. A. Ivnitskii, *Golod 1932–1933 godov v SSSR: Ukraina, Kazakhstan, Povolzh'e, Tsentral'no-Chernozemnaia oblast', Zapadnaia Sibir', Ural* (Moscow: Sobranie, 2009), 223.

11 See Solomon, "Criminal Justice and the Industrial Front," 223–47.

12 "Food Scarcity in Russia," *The Times* (December 6, 1932): 13 (ration tickets);
    Al'bert Baiburin, "Vvedenie pasportnoi sistemy v SSSR," in *Status dokumenta:
    Okonchatel'naia bumazhka ili otchuzhdennoe svidetel'stvo?* ed. I. M. Kaspe (Moscow:
    NLO, 2012), 75–102 (filter out); Jörg Baberowski , "Stalinismus 'von oben':
    Kulakendeportationen in der Sowjetunion 1929–1933," *Jahrbücher für Geschichte
    Osteuropas* 46 (1998): 572–95 (statistics: 585).

13 See Robert Conquest, *The Harvest of Sorrow: Soviet Collectivization and the Terror-
    Famine* (New York: Oxford University Press, 1986), 257.

14 V. B. Zhiromskaia, "Golod 1932–1933 gg.: Liudskie poteri," in *Golod v SSSR:
    Dokumenty*, 3 vols., ed. V. V. Kondrashin, et al. (Moscow: Mezhdunarodnyi fond
    "Demokratiia," 2011–2013), 3:649–718 [here: 653].

15 See David R. Shearer, *Policing Stalin's Socialism: Repression and Social Order in the
    Soviet Union, 1924–1953* (New Haven, CT: Yale University Press, 2009).

16 Statistics from Hagenloh, *Stalin's Police*, 204.

17 Statistics from Hagenloh, *Stalin's Police*, 38.

18 See Louise I. Shelley, *Policing Soviet Society: The Evolution of State Control* (New York:
    Routledge, 1996), 30–33.

19 Statistics from Shearer, *Policing Stalin's Socialism*, 90 (assistants), 135–36 (informants).

20 See Z. I. Peregudova, *Politicheskii sysk Rossii, 1880–1917* (Moscow: Rosspen, 2000),
    234–38. .

21 Statistic from Hagenloh, Stalin's Police, 86.

22 Statistics from Shearer, *Policing Stalin's Socialism*, 85, 87.

23 Solomon, "Soviet Penal Policy, 1917–1934," 214–15.

24 Statistics from Solomon, *Soviet Criminal Justice*, 224.

25 See I. E. Zelenin, "'Revoliutsiia sverkhu': Zavershenie i tragicheskie posledstviia,"
    Voprosy istorii, no. 10 (1994): 28–42 (quotation: 39); Solomon, *Soviet Criminal Justice*,
    125 (discharge); Hagenloh, *Stalin's Police*, 143 (compulsory labor).

26 Quotation and statistics from Matthew Lenoe, "Fear, Loathing, Conspiracy: The Kirov
    Murder as Impetus for Terror," in *The Anatomy of Terror*, ed. Harris, 195–215 [here:
    199].

27 Statistic in Solomon, *Soviet Criminal Justice*, 232.

28 Gabor T. Rittersporn, "Extra-Judicial Repression and the Courts: The Relationship in
    the 1930s," in *Reforming Justice in Russia, 1864–1994: Power, Culture, and the Limits
    of Legal Order*, ed. Peter H. Solomon, Jr. (Armonk, NY, and London: M. E. Sharpe,
    1997), 207–27 [here: 208]; Solomon, *Soviet Criminal Justice*, 82, 127.

29 See Hagenloh, *Stalin's Police*, 189.

30 Statistic in Solomon, *Soviet Criminal Justice*, 186.

31 Statistic in Solomon, *Soviet Criminal Justice*, 217.

32 David R. Shearer and Vladimir Khaustov, eds., *Stalin and the Lubianka: A
    Documentary History of the Political Police and Security Organs in the Soviet Union,
    1922–1953* (New Haven, CT, and London: Yale University Press, 2009), 195.

33 Statistics cited in Oleg V. Khlevniuk, "The Politburo, Penal Policy, and 'Legal Reforms'
    in the 1930s," in *Reforming Justice in Russia, 1864–1994*, ed. Solomon, 190–227 [here:
    201].

34 Statistic in J. Arch Getty, Gábor T. Rittersporn, and Viktor N. Zemskov, "Victims
    of the Soviet Penal System in the Pre-War Years: A First Approach on the Basis
    of Archival Evidence," *The American Historical Review* 98, no. 4 (October 1993):
    1017–49 [here: 1034].

35 For this terrible statistic, see Getty, Rittersporn, and Zemskov, "Victims of the Soviet Penal System," 1022.

36 Wendy Z. Goldman, *Inventing the Enemy: Denunciation and Terror in Stalin's Russia* (Cambridge: Cambridge University Press, 2011), 26.

37 See Goldman, *Inventing the Enemy*, 73.

38 Statistics in Solomon, *Soviet Criminal Justice*, 272.

39 Statistic from Shearer and Vladimir Khaustov, eds., *Stalin and the Lubianka*, 235.

40 Statistic and quotation from Solomon, *Soviet Criminal Justice*, 308, 311.

41 Statistics from Solomon, *Soviet Criminal Justice*, 330–31.

42 Statistics in Getty, Rittersporn, and Zemskov, "Victims of the Soviet Penal System," 1019–20.

43 As noted in V. N. Zemskov, "Spetspolentsy (1930–1959)," in *Naselenie Rossii v 1920–1950-e gody: Chislennost', poteri, migratsii: Sbornik nauchnykh trudov*, ed. Iu. A. Poliakov, et al. (Moscow: Institut rossiiskoi istorii RAN, 1994), 145–94 [here: 151].

44 Statistic from Hagenloh, *Stalin's Police*, 299.

45 Statistic from Shearer and Khaustov, eds., *Stalin and the Lubianka*, 247.

46 Statistic cited in Amir Weiner, *Making Sense of War: The Second World War and the Fate of the Bolshevik Revolution* (Princeton, NJ: Princeton University Press, 2001), 148.

47 See Getty, Rittersporn, and Zemskov, "Victims of the Soviet Penal System," 1041.

48 Statistics from Pavel Polian, *Against Their Will: The History and Geography of Forced Migrations in the USSR* (Budapest: Central European University Press, 2004), 329–32.

49 Statistics from Solomon, *Soviet Criminal Justice*, 343.

50 Statistics from James Heinzen, "Corruption among Officials and Anticorruption Drives in the USSR, 1945–1964," in *Russian Bureaucracy and the State: Officialdom from Alexander III to Vladimir Putin*, ed. Don Karl Rowney and Eugene Huskey (London: Palgrave Macmillan, 2009), 169–88 [here: 173–74].

51 Statistic in Heinzen, "Corruption among Officials," 175.

52 Statistic from Solomon, *Soviet Criminal Justice*, 435n70.

53 Statistic quoted from William Taubman, *Khrushchev: The Man and His Era* (New York: W. W. Norton, 2004), 207.

54 Statistics in Zemskov, "Spetspolentsy," 162, 165 (settlers); Getty, Rittersporn, and Zemskov, "Victims of the Soviet Penal System," 1040 (Gulag).

55 Statistics from Galina Ivanova, "Eine unbekannte Seite des GULag: Lagersondergerichte in der UdSSR (1945–1954)," *Jahrbücher für Geschichte Osteuropas* 53, no. 1 (2005): 25–41 [here: 26].

56 See Stephen G. Wheatcroft, "The Great Terror in Historical Perspective: The Records of the Statistical Department of the Investigative Organs of OGPU/NKVD," in *The Anatomy of Terror*, ed. Harris, 287–305 [here: 305].

57 Statistic from Zemskov, "Spetspolentsy," 152.

Chapter 6

1 See Harold Joseph Berman, *Justice in the U.S.S.R.: An Interpretation of Soviet Law* (Cambridge, MA: Harvard University Press, 1963).

2 Statistic from Jeffrey S. Hardy, *The Gulag after Stalin: Redefining Punishment in Khrushchev's Soviet Union, 1953–1964* (Ithaca, NY, and London: Cornell University Press, 2016), 12.

3   Statistics from Miriam Dobson, *Khrushchev's Cold Summer: Gulag Returnees, Crime, and the Fate of Reform after Stalin* (Ithaca, NY, and London: Cornell University Press, 2009), 39.

4   Quotation from Miriam Dobson, "Show the Bandit-Enemies no Mercy!: Amnesty, Criminality, and Public Response in 1953," in *Dilemmas of De-Stalinization: Negotiating Cultural and Social Change in the Khrushchev Era*, ed. Polly Jones (New York: Routledge, 2006), 21–40 [here: 30].

5   Statistics from Dobson, *Khrushchev's Cold Summer*, 199n47 (rehabilitated), 109n2 (released).

6   Marc Elie and Jeffrey Hardy, "'Letting the Beasts out of the Cage': Parole in the Post-Stalin Gulag, 1953–1973," *Europe-Asia Studies* 67, no. 4 (June 2015): 579–605 [here: 579].

7   I am grateful to Marc Elie for sharing with me his expertise based on Russian archives.

8   Statistic in Marc Elie, "Les politiques à l'égard des libérés du Goulag: Amnistiés et réhabilités dans la région de Novosibirsk, 1953–1960," *Cahiers du Monde russe* 47, nos. 1/2 (January–June 2006): 327–47 [here: 330 (May), 337 (August)].

9   Statistics from Brian LaPierre, *Hooligans in Khrushchev's Russia: Defining, Policing, and Producing Deviance during the Thaw* (Madison: University of Wisconsin Press, 2012), 18, 103–4.

10 Statistic in Marc Elie, "Khrushchev's Gulag: The Soviet Penitentiary System after Stalin's Death, 1953–1964," in *The Thaw: Soviet Society and Culture during the 1950s and 1960s*, ed. Denis Kozlov and Eleonory Gilburd (Toronto, Buffalo, NY, and London: University of Toronto Press, 2013), 109–42 [here: 123].

11 Jeffrey S. Hardy, "De-Stalinizing the Gulag: Physical Violence in Soviet Correctional Facilities, 1953–1973," paper presented at the Workshop on Physical Violence and State Legitimacy in Late Socialism, Budapest, 2013.

12 See Jeffrey S. Hardy, "Gulag Tourism: Khrushchev's 'Show' Prisons in the Cold War Context, 1954–59," *The Russian Review* 71, no. 1 (2012): 49–78.

13 Statistic in Elie, "Khrushchev's Gulag," 126.

14 Quoted in Jeffrey S. Hardy, "'The Camp Is Not a Resort': The Campaign against Privileges in the Soviet Gulag, 1957–61," *Kritika: Explorations in Russian and Eurasian History* 13, no. 1 (Winter 2012): 89–122 [here: 108].

15 Statistics in Hardy, *The Gulag after Stalin*, 122.

16 Statistics in Elie, "Khrushchev's Gulag," 128.

17 Statistic and quotation from Heinzen, "Corruption among Officials," 179.

18 Statistics in Gordon Smith, "Popular Participation in the Administration of Justice in the Soviet Union: Comrades' Courts and the Brezhnev Regime," *Indiana Law Journal* 49 (Winter 1974): 238–52 [here: 246].

19 Statistics from Dobson, *Khrushchev's Cold Summer*, 175.

20 See Marianne Armstrong, "The Campaign against Parasites," in *Soviet Policy-Making*, ed. Peter Juviler and Henry Morton (Santa Barbara, CA: Praeger Publishers, 1967), 163–82 [here: 163–72].

21 Statistics in Sheila Fitzpatrick, "Social Parasites: How Tramps, Idle Youth, and Busy Entrepreneurs Impeded the Soviet March to Communism," *Cahiers du monde russe* 47, nos. 1–2 (2006): 377–408 [here: 396].

22 See Yuri Feofanov and Donald D. Barry, *Politics and Justice in Russia: Major Trials of the Post-Stalin Era* (Armonk, NY: M. E. Sharpe, 1996), 22–30.

23   Statistics from Robert Hornsby, *Protest, Reform and Repression in Khrushchev's Soviet Union* (New York: Cambridge University Press, 2013), 116.

24   Shelley, *Policing Soviet Society*, 181.

25   Statistic from Robert Hornsby, *Protest, Reform and Repression*, 221.

26   Hornsby, *Protest, Reform and Repression*, 239–52.

27   See Fridrikh Neznansky, *The Prosecution of Economic Crimes in the USSR, 1954–1984* (Falls Church, VA: Delphic Associates, Inc., 1985), 12–16.

28   See V. M. Savitski, "Criminal Procedure," in *The Criminal Justice System of the USSR*, ed. M. Cherif Bassiouni and V. M. Savitski (Springfield, IL: Charles C. Thomas, 1979), 45–92 [here: 66].

29   Episode recounted in Louise Shelley, "Party Members and the Courts—Exploitation of Privilege," in *Ruling Communist Parties and Their Status under Law*, ed. D. A. Loeber (Dordrecht: Martinus Nijhoff, 1986): 75–90 [here: 84].

30   Statistics from Huskey, "The Politics of the Soviet Criminal Process," 105.

31   George P. Fletcher, "The Ongoing Soviet Debate about the Presumption of Innocence," *Criminal Justice Ethics* 69, no. 3 (Winter/Spring 1984): 69–75 [here: 72].

32   Statistics in Neznansky, *The Prosecution of Economic Crimes in the USSR*, 43.

33   Statistics from Ilya Zeldes, *The Problems of Crime in the USSR* (Springfield, IL: C.C. Thomas, 1981), 78–80.

34   Statistics from Walter D. Connor, "Juvenile Delinquency in the U.S.S.R.: Some Quantitative and Qualitative Indicators," *American Sociological Review* 35, no. 2 (April 1970): 283–97.

35   Quoted from Rhiannon Dowling, "Soviet Women in Brezhnev's Courts: 'The Case of Two Boys,' Gender, and Justice in Late Soviet Russia," *Russian History* 43 (2016): 245–74 [here: 261].

36   See Savitski, "Criminal Procedure," 72.

37   Statistics from Hornsby, *Protest, Reform and Repression*, 134, 221n93.

38   Quoted in Feofanov and Barry, *Politics and Justice in Russia*, 42.

39   Statistic from Yoram Gorlizki, "Delegalization in Russia: Soviet Comrades' Courts in Retrospect," *American Journal of Comparative Law* 46, no. 3 (Summer 1998): 403–25 [here: 425].

40   Statistics from Sinikukka Saari, *Promoting Democracy and Human Rights in Russia* (London and New York: Routledge, 2010), 153n53 (21,000); Ger P. Van den Berg, "The Soviet Union and the Death Penalty," *Soviet Studies* 35, no. 2 (April 1983): 154–74 (diminished: 160).

41   Statistics quoted from Marc Elie and Jeffrey Hardy, "'Letting the Beasts out of the Cage': Parole in the Post-Stalin Gulag, 1953–1973," *Europe-Asia Studies* 67, no. 4 (June 2015): 579–605 [here: 597, 599].

42   Statistic from Shelley, *Policing Soviet Society*, 167.

43   Statistic in Gordon Smith, *The Soviet Procuracy and the Supervision of Administration* (Alphen aan den Rijn, The Netherlands: Sijthoff & Noordhoff, 1978), 21.

44   Statistic in Robert Rand, *Comrade Lawyer: Inside Soviet Justice in an Era of Reform* (Boulder, CO: Westview Press, 1991), 25–26.

45   See William A. Clark, *Crime and Punishment in Soviet Officialdom: Combating Corruption in the Political Elite, 1965–1990* (Armonk, NY: M. E. Sharpe, 1993), 119–24.

46   See Clark, *Crime and Punishment in Soviet Officialdom*, 152–55.

47   Statistic in Clark, *Crime and Punishment in Soviet Officialdom*, 162.

48   Statistic cited in Shelley, *Policing Soviet Society*, 51.

49   See Clark, *Crime and Punishment in Soviet Officialdom*, 184–85.

50   Statistic cited in Robert Sharlet, *Soviet Constitutional Crisis: From De-Stalinization to Disintegration* (Armonk, NY: M. E. Sharpe, Inc., 1992), 79.

51   Statistic in Clark, "Crime and Punishment in Soviet Officialdom," 261.

52   See Theresa C. Smith and Thomas A. Oleszczuk, *No Asylum: State Psychiatric Repression in the Former USSR* (New York: New York University Press, 1996), 3, 104.

53   Statistic cited in Louise Shelley, "Crime and Criminals in the USSR," in *Understanding Soviet Society*, ed. Michael Stacks and Jerry Pankhurst (Boston: Unwin Hyman, 1988), 193–219 [here: 197].

54   Statistics from Jay Bhattacharya, Christina Gathmann, and Grant Miller, "The Gorbachev Anti-Alcohol Campaign and Russia's Mortality Crisis," *American Economic Journal. Applied Economics* 5, no. 2 (April 2013): 232–60 [here: 237–38].

55   Feofanov and Barry, *Politics and Justice in Russia*, 101–23.

56   As quoted from Peter H. Solomon, Jr., "Reforming Criminal Law under Gorbachev: Crime, Punishment, and the Rights of the Accused," in *Toward the Rule of Law in Russia? Political and Legal Reform in the Transition Period*, ed. Donald D. Barry (Armonk, NY: M. E. Sharpe, 1992), 235–55 [here: 238].

57   Statistic from Solomon, "Reforming Criminal Law under Gorbachev," 241.

58   Statistics in Olga B. Semukhina and John F. Galliher, "Death Penalty Politics and Symbolic Law in Russia," *International Journal of Law, Crime and Justice* 37 (2009): 131–53 [here: 137].

59   See Shelley, *Policing Soviet Society*, 53, 56, 167, 173.

60   See Donald D. Barry, "The Quest for Judicial Independence: Soviet Courts in a *Pravovoe Gosudarstvo*," in *Toward the Rule of Law in Russia?*, ed. Barry, 257–75.

61   Statistic in Rand, *Comrade Lawyer*, 44.

62   See Hornsby, *Protest, Reform and Repression*, 232.

Chapter 7

1   Quotation from Matthew Light and Nikolai Kovalev, "Russia, the Death Penalty, and Europe: The Ambiguities of Influence," *Post-Soviet Affairs* 29, no. 6 (2013): 528–66 [here: 541].

2   Eugene Huskey, "Speedy, Just, and Fair: Remaking Legal Institutions in Putin's Russia," in *Perspectives on the Russian State in Transition*, ed. Wolfgang Danspeckgruber (Washington, DC: Woodrow Wilson Center, 2006), 28–65 [here: 45–46].

3   Statistics in Peter H. Solomon, Jr., "The Criminal Procedure Code of 2001: Will It Make Russian Justice More Fair?," in *Ruling Russia: Law, Crime, and Justice in a Changing Society*, ed. William Alex Pridemore (Lanham, MD: Rowman & Littlefield, 2005), 77–98 [here: 79].

4   Statistics from Gordon B. Smith, *Reforming the Russian Legal System* (Cambridge: Cambridge University Press, 1996), 117 (reported crime); Alexandra Lysova and Nikolay Shchitov, "What Is Russia's Real Homicide Rate? Statistical Reconstruction and the 'Decivilizing Process,'" *Theoretical Criminology* 19, no. 2 (2015): 257–77 [here: 258 (homicide)]; Natalia S. Gavrilova, Leonid A. Gavrilov, Victoria G. Semyonova, Galina N. Evdokushkina, and Alla E. Ivanova, "Patterns of Violent Crime in Russia," in *Ruling Russia*, ed. Pridemore, 117–45 [here: 137 (proportion)]; Daniel G.

Rodeheaver and James L. Williams, "Juvenile Crime and Juvenile Justice in Post-Soviet Russia," in *Ruling Russia*, ed. Pridemore, 225–46 [here: 233 (juvenile)]; Olga Semukhina, "Unreported Crimes, Public Dissatisfaction of Police, and Observed Police Misconduct in the Volgograd Region, Russia: A Research Note," *International Journal of Comparative and Applied Criminal Justice* 38, no. 4 (2014): 305–25 [here: 306 (underreported)].

5   Statistics in Roy King and Laura Piacentini, "The Russian Correctional System during the Transition," in *Ruling Russia*, ed. Pridemore, 261–81 [here: 268–69].

6   Statistic in Smith, *Reforming the Russian Legal System*, 155.

7   See Peter H. Solomon, Jr., "Threats of Judicial Counter-reform in Putin's Russia," *Demokratizatsiya* 13, no. 3 (Summer 2005): 325–45 [here: 335 (higher standard)]; Smith, *Reforming the Russian Legal System*, 147–49 (recruited).

8   See David Remnick, "The Trial of the Old Regime," *The New Yorker* (November 30, 1992): 104–21.

9   Statistics in Light and Kovalev, "Russia, the Death Penalty, and Europe," 542–43.

10 Statistic from Peter H. Solomon, Jr., "Criminalization, Decriminalization and Post-Communist Transition: The Case of the Russian Federation," in *Building Justice in Post-Transition Europe? Processes of Criminalisation within Central and East European Societies*, ed. William Munro and Margaret Murdoch (London and New York: Routledge, 2013), 95–114 [here: 104].

11 Quoted in Mark Galeotti, "'Who's the Boss: Us or the Law?' The Corrupt Art of Governing Russia," in *Bribery and Blat in Russia*, ed. Lovell, et al., 270–87 [here: 270].

12 See Olga Schwartz, "The Creation of an Independent Judiciary and the Changing Nature of Courts and the Courtroom," in *Ruling Russia*, ed. Pridemore, 70.

13 See Kathryn Hendley, *Everyday Law in Russia* (Ithaca, NY, and London: Cornell University Press, 2017).

14 Quotation from Huskey, "Speedy, Just, and Fair," 30.

15 Quotations from Solomon, "The Criminal Procedure Code of 2001," 83.

16 Quoted in William Burnham and Jeffrey Kahn, "Russia's Criminal Procedure Code Five Years Out," *Review of Central and East European Law* 33, no. 1 (2008): 1–94 [here: 3].

17 Statistics in Solomon, "The Criminal Procedure Code of 2001," 96 (drugs); Peter H. Solomon, Jr., "Plea Bargaining Russian Style," *Demokratizatsiya* 20, no. 3 (Summer 2012): 282–99 [here: 282 (option)]; Peter H. Solomon, Jr., "Post-Soviet Criminal Justice: The Persistence of Distorted Neo-inquisitorialism," *Theoretical Criminology* 19, no. 2 (2015): 159–78 [here: 167 (reconciliation)].

18 Statistic in Rodeheaver and Williams, "Juvenile Crime and Juvenile Justice in Post-Soviet Russia," 240.

19 Statistic in Schwartz, "The Creation of an Independent Judiciary," 72.

20 Statistics from Huskey, "Speedy, Just, and Fair," 40 (doubled); Peter B. Maggs, Olga Schwartz, and William Burnham, *Law and Legal System of the Russian Federation*, 6th ed. (Huntington, NY: Juris, 2015), 85 (2013).

21 See Maria Popova, *Politicized Justice in Emerging Democracies: A Study of Courts in Russia and Ukraine* (Cambridge: Cambridge University Press, 2012), 134–35.

22 Statistics from Peter H. Solomon, Jr., "Accusatorial Bias in Russian Criminal Justice," in *Sociology of Justice in Russia*, ed. M. Kurkchiyan and Agnieszka Kubal (Cambridge: Cambridge University Press, 2018) (all trials); Solomon, "The Criminal Procedure Code of 2001," 96 (jury trials); Solomon, "Threats of Judicial Counter-reform in Putin's Russia," 335 (9 percent).

23 As quoted in Solomon, "Threats of Judicial Counter-reform in Putin's Russia," 337.

24 Quotation from Dorothea Schönfeld, "Tilting at Windmills? The European Response to Violations of Media Freedom in Russia," *Review of Central and East European Law* 37, nos. 2–3 (2012): 233–90 [here: 252)].

25 Solomon, "Post-Soviet Criminal Justice," 165 (restrictions); Alexei Trochev, "How Judges Arrest and Acquit: Soviet Legacies in Post-Communist Criminal Justice," in *Historical Legacies of Communism in Russia and Eastern Europe*, ed. Mark Beissinger and Stephen Kotkin (Cambridge: Cambridge University Press, 2014), 152–78 [here: 169–70 (statistics)].

26 See Steven Lee Myers, "Verdict in Russian Courts: Guilty Until Proven Guilty," *The New York Times* (June 20, 2004), WK3 (cell); Kathryn Hendley, "'Telephone Law' and the 'Rule of Law': The Russian Case," *Hague Journal on the Rule of Law*, no. 1 (2009): 241–62 [here: 257–58 (regional)]; Alena Ledeneva, "Telephone Justice in Russia: An Update," *The EU-Russia Center Review*, no. 18 (2011): 4–22 [here: 18–19 (surveys)].

27 See Alena V. Ledeneva, *Can Russia Modernise? Sistema, Power Networks and Informal Governance* (Cambridge: Cambridge University Press, 2013), 182–88.

28 Statistics in Jordan Gans-Morse, "Threats to Property Rights in Russia: From Private Coercion to State Aggression," *Post-Soviet Affairs* 28, no. 3 (2012): 263–95 [here: 268 (plummeted), 274 (levies), 275 (2010)].

29 Statistics in Peter H. Solomon, Jr., "Assessing the Courts in Russia: Parameters of Progress under Putin," *Demokratizatsiya* 16, no. 1 (Winter 2008): 63–74 [here: 71].

30 Statistics in Alena V. Ledeneva, "Telephone Justice in Russia," *Post-Soviet Affairs* 24, no. 4 (October–December 2009): 324–50 [here: 340–41].

31 Statistics in Semukhina, "Unreported crimes," 306 (underreporting), 309 (11 million).

32 Statistics in Lauren A. McCarthy, *Trafficking Justice: How Russian Police Enforce New Laws, from Crime to Courtroom* (Ithaca, NY, and London: Cornell University Press, 2015), 22 (globe), 102 (extorted), 182–83 (jumped), 219 (worst).

33 Quoted in Peter H. Solomon, Jr., "President Medvedev and the Courts: The Start of a New Era?" in *From Putin to Medvedev: Continuity or Change?*, ed. J. L. Black and Michael Johns (Manotick, Ontario: Penumbra Press, 2009), 25–37 [here: 25 (red tape)]; Hendley, *Everyday Law in Russia*, 13 (disregard).

34 Statistics in Solomon, "Criminalization," 107 (huge decline); Olga Semukhina "Public Contacts with Russian Police in Life-Threatening Situations," *Policing: An International Journal of Police Strategies & Management* 37, no. 2 (2014): 420–37 [here 420 (mortal danger)].

35 See Judith Pallot, "The Gulag as the Crucible of Russia's Twenty-First-Century System of Punishment," in *The Soviet Gulag: Evidence, Interpretation, and Comparison*, ed. Michael David-Fox (Pittsburgh: Pittsburgh University Press, 2016), 286–313 [here: 311 (penitentiaries)]; Peter H. Solomon, Jr., "Courts, Law and Policing under Medvedev: Many Reforms, Modest Change, New Voices," in *Russia after 2012: From Putin to Medvedev to Putin - Continuity, Change, or Revolution?* ed. Larry Black and Michael Johns (London and New York: Routledge, 2013), 19–41 [here: 21–22 (violations)].

36 Ledeneva, *Can Russia Modernise?*

37 Statistics in Ledeneva, *Can Russia Modernise?*, 177 (2009); Vladislav Starzhenetskii, "Assessing Human Rights in Russia: Not to Miss the Forest for the Trees: A Response to Preclik, Schönfeld and Hallinan," *Review of Central and East European Law* 37, nos. 2–3 (2012): 349–56 [here: 350 (hundreds), 352 (procedural)]; Courtney

Hillebrecht, *Domestic Politics and International Human Rights Tribunals: The Problem of Compliance* (New York: Cambridge University Press, 2014), 119–21 (partially).

38 See Solomon, "Courts, Law and Policing under Medvedev," 32.

39 Pallot, "The Gulag as the Crucible of Russia's Twenty-First-Century System of Punishment," 312 (scrapped); Teuvo Laitila, "Russia: Atheism, 'Blasphemy,' and Orthodox Christianity," in *The Atheist Bus Campaign: Global Manifestations and Responses*, ed. Steven Tomlins and Spencer Culham Bullivant (Leiden and Boston: Brill, 2017), 262–85 [here: 278 (quotation)].

40 See quotation from Julia Gerlach, *Color Revolutions in Eurasia* (Cham, Switzerland: Springer, 2014), 24.

41 Quotation and numbers quoted from Valerie Sperling, *Sex, Politics, and Putin: Political Legitimacy in Russia* (Oxford and New York: Oxford University Press, 2015), 74.

42 See Solomon, "Post-Soviet Criminal Justice," 165.

43 See Nadezhda Tolokonnikova, "Pussy Riot's Nadezhda Tolokonnikova: Why I have gone on hunger strike," *The Guardian* (September 23, 2013). https://www.theguardian.com/music/2013/sep/23/pussy-riot-hunger-strike-nadezhda-tolokonnikova.

44 See Joshua Yaffa, "Putin's New War On 'Traitors,'" *The New Yorker* (March 28, 2014). http://www.newyorker.com/news/news-desk/putins-new-war-on-traitors (Zubov); Anton Vshivtsev, "Uroki istorii v Verkhovnom sude," *Novoe vremia* (September 2, 2016). https://newtimes.ru/stati/xroniki/uroki-istorii-v-verxovnom-sude.html (Luzhin).

45 Lauri Mälksoo, "Russia's Constitutional Court Defies the European Court of Human Rights: Constitutional Court of the Russian Federation Judgment of 14 July 2015, No 21-П/2015," *European Constitutional Law Review* 12, no. 2 (September 2016): 377–95 [quotation: 381].

46 See http://www.transparency.org/news/feature/corruption_perceptions_index_2016.

47 See Ivan Nechepurenko, "Russia Moves to Soften Domestic Violence Law," *The New York Times* (January 26, 2017), A7 (battery); Neil Macfarquhar and Ivan Nechepurenko, "Putin Rival Is Barred from Presidential Run," *The New York Times* (February 9, 2017), A6 (ineligible); Ivan Nechepurenko, "Kremlin Critic Says Graft Fueled Premier's Empire," *The New York Times* (March 3, 2017), A9 (report).

48 Statistics from Ella Paneyakh, "Faking Performance Together: Systems of Performance Evaluation in Russian Enforcement Agencies and Production of Bias and Privilege," *Post-Soviet Affairs* 30, nos. 2/3 (2014): 115–36 [here: 121 (acquittals)]; Solomon, "Accusatorial Bias in Russian Criminal Justice" (rate).

49 Paneyakh, "Faking Performance Together," 128 (statistic), 131 (quotation).

50 As quoted from Paneyakh, "Faking Performance Together," 126 (chain), 131 (confession).

Conclusion

1 See Richard Wortman, "Russian Monarchy and the Rule of Law: New Considerations of the Court Reform of 1864," *Kritika: Explorations in Russian and Eurasian History* 6, no. 1 (Winter 2005): 145–70 [here: 147].

2 See Raeff, "Codification et droit en Russie impériale," 11.

3 See Muravyeva, "Russian Early Modern Criminal Procedure and Culture of Appeal," 297.

4   See Kollmann, *Crime and Punishment in Early Modern Russia*, 5.

5   See Antonov, *Bankrupts and Usurers of Imperial Russia*, 19.

6   As quoted from Burbank, *Russian Peasants Go to Court*, 74.

7   Quotation from Hendley, *Everyday Law in Russia*, 3.

8   See Cathy A. Frierson, "'I Must Always Answer to the Law …' Rules and Responses in the Reformed Volost' Court," *Slavonic and East European Review* 75, no. 2 (April 1997): 308–34.

9   See Solomon, "Accusatorial Bias in Russian Criminal Justice."

10 See Daly, "On the Significance of Emergency Legislation in Late Imperial Russia," 613.

11 Wayne Dowler, *Russia in 1913* (DeKalb: Northern Illinois University Press, 2010), 214.

12 See Pipes, *Russia under the Old Regime, passim*; Wortman, "Russian Monarchy and the Rule of Law," 145–70 [here especially: 168].

13 Günther Schlee, "Regularity in Chaos: The Politics of Difference in the Recent History of Somalia," in *Imagined Differences: Hatred and the Construction of Identity*, ed. Günther Schlee (Münster: Lit, 2002), 251–80 (here: 266) as quoted in Dittmar Schorkowitz, "Imperial Formations and Ethnic Diversity: Institutions, Practices, and Longue Durée, Illustrated by the Example of Russia," Working Paper no. 165 (Halle/Saale: Max Planck Institute for Social Anthropology, 2015), 4.

14 As quoted from Butler, "Russian Legal History," 22.

GLOSSARY

adversarial: A form of judicial procedure with two equal parties

advocates (*advokaty*): University-trained legal experts who have passed the bar exam and are permitted to represent criminal defendants

anti-parasite law: A statute adopted in 1961 criminalizing the shirking of gainful employment

arbitrariness (*proizvol*): Lack of restraint in the use of authority, absolutist power; characteristic of autocracy

banishment: The removal by administrative procedure of a person deemed harmful to society

birch rods (*rozgi*): The most lenient instrument for corporal punishment in prerevolutionary Russia

branding: A method for marking criminals until the mid-nineteenth century in Russia

carceral: Of, relating to, or suggesting incarceration

Central Committee: The main governing body of the Communist Party

Charters to the Nobility and to the Towns: Grants of civil rights by Catherine II in 1785

Cheka: The Extraordinary Commission, or political police (1917–1922)

civil law: Law relating to personal and interpersonal disputes

clearance rate: Proportion of crimes for which arrests and charges are made

collective responsibility (*krugovaia poruka*): Traditional Russian norm of mutual obligation

College of Justice: One of several central government institutions founded by Peter I in 1717

Commissariat of Justice: Institution for overseeing the Soviet judicial system until 1946

committee on administrative exile (*Osoboe soveshchanie*): Special board that approved requests to exile "troublemakers" both before and after 1917

Complete Collection of Laws of the Russian Empire (1830): First codification of laws since 1649

comrades' courts: Informal Soviet courts for simple criminal and civil cases

conscience courts: First- instance court established in 1775 with more lenient procedure

Council of People's Commissars (SNK): Name of the Soviet government, 1917–1946

court bailiffs: Police officials to protect courts and enforce judgments beginning in late 1990s

criminal law: Law relating to offenses in which the state takes a direct interest; opposed to civil law

customary law: Informal rules and norms governing societies before official laws were adopted

Department of Police: Central police institution (1880–1917)

dekulakization: A campaign against peasants resisting collectivization

deprivation of freedom:
Incarceration, exile, and analogous judicial punishments

deprivation of rights: Punishment involving loss of official honors and status

Digest of Laws (1835): Systematic organization of laws codified in 1832

districts (*uezdy*)**:** Political units into which a province was divided before 1917

domestic passport: Document required for identification and travel in Russia

*druzhiny***:** *See* voluntary brigades

duma: A representative political assembly

enemies of the people: Expression widely used from 1937

exile: A judicial or administrative punishment consisting in removal to a specified location

fiat law: Rules established by an autocrat

*fiskaly***:** Officials appointed, beginning in 1711, to root out government malfeasance and corruption

FSB: Federal Security Service, or political police (1991–present)

gauntlet: *See* running the gauntlet

Gendarmerie: Paramilitary force (1837–1917)

GPU: The Main Political Administration, or political police (1922–1923)

Great Terror: Stalin's witch-hunt for "enemies of the people" in 1937–1938

Gulag (or Gulag archipelago)**:** The network of Soviet forced-labor camps

hard labor (*katorga*)**:** Harsh judicial punishment involving exile and forced labor, abolished in 1917

His Imperial Majesty's Own Chancellery: Parallel bureaucracy under Nicholas I

hostage-taking: Early Bolshevik method of controlling population groups

Imperial Russia: From 1721 to 1917

inquisitorial: Judge-centered judicial procedure without contest of parties

judicial torture: Violence and other pressure applied to suspects to extract confessions

jurist (*iurist*)**:** University-trained legal experts without the right to represent criminal defendants

justice of the peace courts: Lower instance courts handling simple civil and criminal cases

Kadet Party: Liberal party advocating civil rights, the rule of law, and constitutionalism

KGB: Committee for State Security, or political police (1954–1991)

kissing the cross: Judicial oaths in early modern Russia

knout: A brutal form of whip for corporal punishment; abolished in 1845

Komsomol: The Communist Youth League

*krugovaia poruka***:** *See* collective responsibility

kulak operation: Police operation aimed at rooting out enemies; launched the Great Terror in 1937

"kulak": A rich or allegedly rich peasant persecuted for resisting collectivization; in quotation marks because it was almost exclusively a political construct

labor camps: Principal place of incarceration during the Soviet era

labor colonies: Soviet places of incarceration with a moderately strict regime

land captain (*zemskii nachalnik*)**:** Administrative and judicial official in rural Russia (1889–1917)

legal nihilism: Disbelief in or contempt for the law

legality: *See zakonnost'*

Little Deal: Informal policy under Brezhnev to turn a blind eye to unlawful business dealings

MGB: Ministry of State Security, or political police (1946–1953)

Military-Criminal Codex (*Artikul voinsky*) **of 1715:** Penal and procedural code

military field court: Military courts with a streamlined procedure in 1906–1907

military revolutionary tribunal: Early Bolshevik courts with streamlined procedure

militia (*militsiia*): Regular police force (1917–2011); replaced by *politsiia*

Ministry of the Interior: Central police and administrative institution (1802–1917 and 1947–present)

Muscovite: Referring to Russia before the Imperial era (before 1721)

New Economic Policy (NEP): A program temporarily relaxing antimarket policies in 1921–1928

NKVD: The People's Commissariat of Internal Affairs or political police (1934–1946)

nomenklatura: Ruling elite of the Soviet Union

noncustodial punishments: Judicial punishments not including incarceration

OGPU: The Unified Main Political Administration, or political police (1923–1934)

oprichnina: Arbitrary state within a state under Ivan the Terrible

Order No. 00447: Political police operational order of 1937 launching the Great Terror

Party line: Informal but obligatory policies imposed by the Communist Party leadership

Penal Code of 1845: Russia's first Penal Code since 1649

people's commissar: Head of a Bolshevik government agency until 1947

People's Commissariat: Main government department or ministry until 1947

people's courts: First-instance courts (1917–1996)

Politburo: Committee of top Communist Party leaders

political crime: Political actions deemed criminal acts

political reliability (*politicheskaia blagonadezhnost'*): Status of political trustworthiness

politsiia: Police in Russia before 1917 and starting in 2011

power institutions: In post-Soviet times, influential agencies like the FSB, military, and Interior Ministry

Pravda: The flagship newspaper of the Russian Communist Party

pravo: Abstract sense of the law

pravovoe gosudarstvo: "State of law" or state governed by laws; similar to German *Rechtstaat*; a state-centered concept falling short of the rule of law

precinct (*chast'*): District of a city in the Imperial period

prikazy: Government agencies until the establishment of Colleges in 1717

procedure, criminal: Rules governing criminal justice

Procuracy: Supervisory agency with oversight over all legal matters within the state apparatus

procurator: Supervisor of legality and prosecutor

procurator general: Highest supervisory official with oversight over the bureaucracy

proizvol: *See* arbitrariness

qualification collegia: Bodies of judicial self-regulation created at the regional and national levels in 1989 to oversee the appointment, promotion, and dismissal of judges

Red Terror: Early Bolshevik policy of arbitrary violence in 1918–1919

regime cities: Cities with strict residency rules in the Soviet and post-Soviet eras. See also residency permit

rehabilitation: Act of restoring a convicted person's social status and judicial innocence

republican: *See* republic

republic: Large administrative districts of the USSR lacking political autonomy and free elections

residency permit (*propiska*): Required document for residing in major cities in Soviet and post-Soviet eras. See also regime cities

revolutionary consciousness: Bolshevik idea that good behavior and judgment flow from ideological awareness

revolutionary legality: Bolshevik concept of law mediated by revolutionary consciousness

revolutionary tribunal: Higher court for serious and all political crimes (1917–1922)

rule of law: Ideal and practice of predictable and rational legal systems, where government is constrained by and under the law. See also *pravovoe gosudarstvo*

running the gauntlet: A harsh punishment instituted by Peter the Great; abolished in 1863

Russian Federation: Name of Russia since 1991

Russian Socialist Republic (RSFSR): Name of Russia from 1918 to 1991

Russkaia Pravda: Earliest Russian law code; influenced but superseded by *Ulozhenie* of 1649

Sachsenspiegel: Medieval Germanic law code

samosud: Mob justice

Secret Expedition of the Senate: Political police agency under Catherine the Great

security bureaus: Political police institutions functioning from 1866 to 1917

Security Law of 1881: Emergency legislation adopted in 1881 and in force until 1917

Senate: Highest institution of state and highest appeals court (1711–1917)

shel'movanie: Civil death, deprivation of rights and status in Imperial Russia

show trials (*pokazatel'nye protsessy*): Trials put on with didactic purpose in the Soviet era

slovo i delo: Political crime cases in early modern Russia

socialist legality: A concept aimed at restoring respect for the law in the early Khrushchev era

socialist substitutes: Ordinary people brought into various government agencies to supplement existing staff

Soviet power: Soviet government, authority, rule, regime

special sections (*osobye otdely*): Political police in military units during the Russian Civil War

special settlements: Remote settlements of exiled "kulaks" formed during collectivization; later applied to other population groups

speculation: Profiteering or the act of engaging in normal market relations

State Council: Highest consultative body (1810–1906); upper chamber of legislature (1906–1917)

state crime: *See* political crime

State-Legal Administration: Parallel government committee under Yeltsin

superbureaucracy: Parallel government structures, intended to supervise the regular bureaucracy

telephone justice (or law): Soviet and post-Soviet practice of administrative officials interfering in the judicial process

Third Section of His Imperial Majesty's Own Chancellery: Political police (1826–1880)

township (*volost'*): Political units into which a district (*uezd*) was divided in Imperial Russia

township courts: Lowest instance courts created for all peasants in 1861

troika: Unit of three leaders, often representing the Party, Soviet, and political police with broad administrative power

***Ulozhenie* of 1649:** Detailed law code in force until 1835

volost': *See* township

voluntary brigades (*druzhiny*)**:** Groups of police assistants (*druzhinniki*) in the Soviet era

whip (*pleti*): Instrument for corporal punishment replacing the knout in 1845

Workers' and Peasants' Militia: *See* militia

***zakon*:** A law

zakonnost': Legality or lawfulness; implies restraint on the absolutist power of the ruler or the government; opposed to arbitrariness (*proizvol*)

zemstvos: Institutions of local self-government (1864–1917)

WORKS CITED

List A consists of works repeatedly drawn upon in the preparation of this book, though to which few or no references have been made. List B includes all other works cited in the endnotes.

List A

Daly, Jonathan W. "On the Significance of Emergency Legislation in Late Imperial Russia." *Slavic Review* 54 (Fall 1995): 602–29.

Daly, Jonathan W. *Autocracy under Siege: Security Police and Opposition in Russia, 1866–1905*. DeKalb: Northern Illinois University Press, 1998.

Daly, Jonathan W. *The Watchful State: Security Police and Opposition in Russia, 1906–1917*. DeKalb: Northern Illinois University Press, 2004.

Daly, Jonathan. "Russian Punishments in the European Mirror." In *Russia in the European Context, 1789–1914: A Member of the Family*. Edited by Susan McCaffray and Michael Melancon. New York: Palgrave Macmillan, 2005. Pp. 161–88.

Efremova, N. N. *Sudoustroistvo Rossii v XVIII–pervoi polovine XIX vv. Istoriko-pravovoe issledovanie*. Moscow: Nauka, 1993.

Hagenloh, Paul. *Stalin's Police: Public Order and Mass Repression in the USSR, 1926–1941*. Baltimore: The John Hopkins University Press, 2009.

Hardy, Jeffrey S. *The Gulag after Stalin: Redefining Punishment in Khrushchev's Soviet Union, 1953–1964*. Ithaca, NY, and London: Cornell University Press, 2016.

Jacobson, M., and M. B. Smirnov. "Sistema mest zakliucheniia v RSFSR i SSSR, 1917–1930." In *Sistema ispravitel'no-trudovykh lagerei v SSSR, 1923–1960: Spravochnik*. Edited by M. B. Smirnov. Moscow: Zvenie, 1998. Pp. 10–24.

Kollmann, Nancy Shields. *Crime and Punishment in Early Modern Russia*. Cambridge: Cambridge University Press, 2012.

LeDonne, John P. *Absolutism and Ruling Class: The Formation of the Russian Political Order, 1700–1825*. New York and Oxford: Oxford University Press, 1991.

McReynolds, Louise. *Murder Most Russian: True Crime and Punishment in Late Imperial Russia*. Ithaca, NY, and London: Cornell University Press, 2013.

Mironov, Boris. *A Social History of Imperial Russia, 1700–1917*, 2 vols. With Ben Eklof. Boulder, CO: Westview Press, 2000.

Portnov, V. P., and M. M. Slavin. *Stanovlenie pravosudiia Sovetskoi Rossii, 1917–1922 gg*. Moscow: Nauka, 1990.

Shearer, David R. *Policing Stalin's Socialism: Repression and Social Order in the Soviet Union, 1924–1953*. New Haven, CT: Yale University Press, 2009.

Shelley, Louise I. *Policing Soviet Society: The Evolution of State Control*. New York: Routledge, 1996.

Solomon, Peter H., Jr. *Soviet Criminal Justice under Stalin*. Cambridge: Cambridge University Press, 1996.

List B

Adams, Bruce F. *The Politics of Punishment: Prison Reform in Russia, 1863–1917*. DeKalb: Northern Illinois University Press, 1996.

Alexopoulos, Golfo. *Stalin's Outcasts: Aliens, Citizens, and the Soviet State, 1926–1936*. Ithaca, NY, and London: Cornell University Press, 2003.

Alexander, R. S. *Europe's Uncertain Path, 1814–1914: State Formation and Civil Society*. Chichester, UK: Wiley-Blackwell, 2012.

Antonov, Sergei. *Bankrupts and Usurers of Imperial Russia: Debt, Property, and the Law in the Age of Dostoevsky and Tolstoy*. Cambridge, MA, and London: Harvard University Press, 2016.

Antonov, Sergei. "Russian Capitalism on Trial: The Case of the Jacks of Hearts." *Law and History Review* 36, no. 1 (February 1918).

Antonov, Sergei, and Katherine Pickering Antonova. "The Maiden and the Wolf: Law, Gender, and Sexual Violence in Imperial Russia." *Slavic Review* 77, no. 1 (Spring 2018).

Armstrong, Marianne. "The Campaign against Parasites." In *Soviet Policy-Making*. Edited by Peter Juviler and Henry Morton. Santa Barbara, CA: Praeger Publishers, 1967. Pp. 163–82.

Atwell, John W., Jr. "The Russian Jury." *Slavonic and East European Review* 53 (January 1975): 44–61.

Baberowski, Jörg. *Autokratie und Justiz: Zum Verhältnis von Rechsstaatlichkeit und Rückständigkeit im ausgehenden Zarenreich, 1864–1914*. Frankfort am Main: Vittorio Klostermann, 1996.

Baberowski, Jörg. "Stalinismus 'von oben': Kulakendeportationen in der Sowjetunion 1929–1933." *Jahrbücher für Geschichte Osteuropas* 46 (1998): 572–95.

Baiburin, Al'bert. "Vvedenie pasportnoi sistemy v SSSR." In *Status dokumenta: Okonchatel'naia bumazhka ili otchuzhdennoe svidetel'stvo?* Edited by I. M. Kaspe. Moscow: NLO, 2012. Pp. 75–102.

Balashov, E. M. "Novoe obshchestvo—'Novyi chelovek.'" In *Petrograd na perelome epokh: Gorod i ego zhiteli v gody revoliutsii i grazhdanskoi voiny*. Edited by V. A. Shishkin, et al. St. Peterburg: Dmitrii Bulanin, 2000. Pp. 272–73.

Bartlett, Roger. "Serfdom and State Power in Imperial Russia." *European History Quarterly* 33 (2003): 29–64.

Berman, Harold J. *Justice in the U.S.S.R.: An Interpretation of Soviet Law*. Cambridge, MA: Harvard University Press, 1963.

Bhattacharya, Jay, Christina Gathmann, and Grant Miller. "The Gorbachev Anti-Alcohol Campaign and Russia's Mortality Crisis." *American Economic Journal. Applied Economics* 5, no. 2 (April 2013): 232–60.

Blum, Jerome. "The Internal Structure and Polity of the European Village Community from the Fifteenth to the Nineteenth Century." *The Journal of Modern History* 43 (December 1971): 541–76.

Bryner, Cyril. "The Issue of Capital Punishment in the Reign of Elizabeth Petrovna." *The Russian Review* 49, no. 4 (October 1990): 389–416.

Burbank, Jane. *Russian Peasants Go to Court: Legal Culture in the Countryside.* Bloomington: Indiana University Press, 2004.

Bushnell, John. *Mutiny amid Repression: Russian Soldiers in the Revolution of 1905–1906.* Bloomington: Indiana University Press, 1985.

Butler, William E. "On the Formation of a Russian Legal Consciousness: The Zertsalo." In *Russia and the Law of Nations in Historical Perspective.* London: Wildy, Simmonds & Hill Pub., 2009. Pp. 91–101.

Butler, William E. "Russia, Legal Traditions of the World, and Legal Change." In *Russia and the Law of Nations in Historical Perspective.* London: Wildy, Simmonds & Hill Pub., 2009. Pp. 170–76.

Butler, William E. "Russian Legal History: The Pre-revolutionary Heritage." In *Russia and the Law of Nations in Historical Perspective.* London: Wildy, Simmonds & Hill Pub., 2009. Pp. 3–23.

Chistiakov, O. I., ed. *Zakonodatel'stvo pervoi poloviny XIX veka*, vol. 6 of *Rossiiskoe zakonodatel'stvo X–XX vekov.* Moscow: Iuridicheskaia literatura, 1988.

Clark, William A. "Crime and Punishment in Soviet Officialdom, 1965–90." *Europe-Asia Studies* 4, no. 2 (1993): 259–79.

Clark, William A. *Crime and Punishment in Soviet Officialdom: Combating Corruption in the Political Elite, 1965 -1990.* Armonk, NY: M. E. Sharpe, 1993.

Connor, Walter D. "Juvenile Delinquency in the U.S.S.R.: Some Quantitative and Qualitative Indicators." *American Sociological Review* 35, no. 2 (April 1970): 283–97.

Conquest, Robert. *The Harvest of Sorrow: Soviet Collectivization and the Terror-Famine.* New York: Oxford University Press, 1986.

Corruption Perceptions Index. http://www.transparency.org/news/feature/corruption_perceptions_index_2016.

Daly, Jonathan. *Hammer, Sickle, and Soil: The Soviet Drive to Collectivize Agriculture.* Stanford, CA: Hoover Institution Press, 2017.

Dahlke, Sandra. "Old Russia in the Dock: The Trial against Mother Superior Mitrofaniia before the Moscow District Court, 1874." *Cahiers du monde russe* 53, no. 1 (2012): 95–120.

de Madariaga, Isabel. "Catherine II and the Serfs: A Reconsideration of Some Problems." *The Slavonic and East European Review* 52, no. 126 (January 1974): 34–62.

de Madariaga, Isabel. *Russia in the Age of Catherine the Great.* New Haven, CT: Yale University Press, 1981.

de Madariaga, Isabel. "Penal Policy in the Age of Catherine II." In *Politics and Culture in the Eighteenth Century: Collected Essays by Isabel de Madariaga.* London and New York: Longman, 1998. Pp. 97–123.

Dixon, Simon. *Catherine the Great.* London: Profile Books, 2001.

Dobozy, Maria, trans. and ed. *The Saxon Mirror: A Sachsenspiegel of the Fourteenth Century.* Philadelphia: University of Pennsylvania Press, 1999.

Dobson, Miriam. "Show the Bandit-Enemies no Mercy!: Amnesty, Criminality and Public Response in 1953." In *Dilemmas of De-Stalinization: Negotiating Cultural and Social Change in the Khrushchev Era.* Edited by Polly Jones. New York: Routledge, 2006. Pp. 21–40.

Dobson, Miriam. *Khrushchev's Cold Summer: Gulag Returnees, Crime, and the Fate of Reform after Stalin*. Ithaca, NY, and London: Cornell University Press, 2009.

Dowling, Rhiannon. "Soviet Women in Brezhnev's Courts: 'The Case of Two Boys,' Gender, and Justice in Late Soviet Russia." *Russian History* 43 (2016): 245–74.

Eisner, Manuel. "Long-Term Historical Trends in Violent Crime." *Crime and Justice* 30 (2003): 83–142.

Elie, Marc. "Les politiques à l'égard des libérés du Goulag: Amnistiés et réhabilités dans la région de Novosibirsk, 1953–1960." *Cahiers du Monde russe* 47, nos. 1–2 (January–June 2006): 327–47.

Elie, Marc. "Khrushchev's Gulag: The Soviet Penitentiary System after Stalin's Death, 1953–1964." In *The Thaw: Soviet Society and Culture during the 1950s and 1960s*. Edited by Denis Kozlov and Eleonory Gilburd. Toronto, Buffalo, NY, and London: University of Toronto Press, 2013. Pp. 109–42.

Elie, Marc, and Jeffrey Hardy. "'Letting the Beasts out of the Cage': Parole in the Post-Stalin Gulag, 1953–1973." *Europe-Asia Studies* 67, no. 4 (June 2015): 579–605.

Esper, Thomas. "Hired Labor and the Metallurgical Industry of the Urals during the Late Serf Period." *Jahrbücher für Geschichte Osteuropas* 29 (1980): 62–70.

Ezhenedel'nik chrezvychainykh komissii po bor'be s kontr-revolutsiei i spekulatsiei, no. 1 (September 22, 1918).

Feofanov, Yuri, and Donald D. Barry. *Politics and Justice in Russia: Major Trials of the Post-Stalin Era*. Armonk, NY: M. E. Sharpe, 1996.

Finkel, Stuart. *On the Ideological Front: The Russian Intelligentsia and the Making of the Public Sphere*. New Haven, CT: Yale University Press, 2007.

Fitzpatrick, Sheila. "Social Parasites: How Tramps, Idle Youth, and Busy Entrepreneurs Impeded the Soviet March to Communism." *Cahiers du monde russe* 47, nos. 1–2 (2006): 377–408.

Fitzpatrick, Sheila. "The Great Departure: Rural–Urban Migration in the Soviet Union, 1929–1933." In *Social Dimensions of Soviet Industrialization*. Edited by William G. Rosenberg and Lewis H. Siegelbaum. Bloomington and Indianapolis: Indiana University Press, 1993. Pp. 15–40.

"Food Scarcity in Russia," The *Times* (December 6, 1932): 13.

Frame, Murray. "State Expansion and the Criminal Investigation Militia during the Russian Civil War." *History* 98 (July 2013): 406–27.

Frederick Starr, S. *Decentralization and Self-Government in Russia, 1830–1870*. Princeton, NJ: Princeton University Press, 1972.

Frierson, Cathy. "Crime and Punishment in the Russian Village: Rural Concepts of Criminality at the End of the Nineteenth Century." *Slavic Review* 46, no. 1 (1987): 55–69.

Frierson, Cathy A. "'I Must Always Answer to the Law … 'Rules and Responses in the Reformed Volost' Court." *Slavonic and East European Review* 75, no. 2 (April 1997): 308–34.

Fuller, William C., Jr. "Civilians in Russian Military Courts, 1881–1904." *The Russian Review* 41, no. 3 (July 1982): 288–305.

Gans-Morse, Jordan. "Threats to Property Rights in Russia: From Private Coercion to State Aggression." *Post-Soviet Affairs* 28, no. 3 (2012): 263–95.

Gatrell, V. A. C. *The Hanging Tree: Execution and the English People, 1770–1868*. New York: Oxford University Press, 1994.

Gavrilov, G. A. "Rol' chekistov v stanovlenii Sovetskoi vlasti na territorii Viatskoigubernii v 1918 godu." In *Iz istorii Viatskikh spetssluzhb (pervaia polovina XIX–vtoraia polovina XX v.v.).* Edited by V. E. Musikhin. Kirov: Triada-S, 1997. Pp. 53–62.

Gavrilova, Natalia S., Leonid A. Gavrilov, Victoria G. Semyonova, Galina N. Evdokushkina, and Alla E. Ivanova. "Patterns of Violent Crime in Russia." In *Ruling Russia: Law, Crime, and Justice in a Changing Society.* Edited by William Alex Pridemore. Lanham, MD: Rowman and Littlefield, 2005. Pp. 117–45.

Gentes, Andrew A. "The Institution of Russia's Sakhalin Policy, from 1868 to 1875." *Journal of Asian History* 36, no. 1 (2002): 1–31.

Gentes, Andrew A. *Exile to Siberia, 1590–1822.* Basingstoke, UK: Palgrave Macmillan, 2008.

Gentes, Andrew A. *Exile, Murder, and Madness in Siberia, 1823–61.* Basingstoke, UK: Palgrave Macmillan, 2010.

Gentes, Andrew A. "'Completely Useless': Exiling the Disabled to Tsarist Siberia." *Sibirica* 10, no. 2 (2011): 26–49.

Gerlach, Julia. *Color Revolutions in Eurasia.* Cham, Switzerland: Springer, 2014.

Gernet, M. N. *Istoriia tsarskoi tiur'my,* 5 vols., 3rd ed. Moscow: Gos. izd. iuridicheskoi literatury, 1961–1963.

Getty, J. Arch, Gábor T. Rittersporn, and Viktor N. Zemskov. "Victims of the Soviet Penal System in the Pre-War Years: A First Approach on the Basis of Archival Evidence." *The American Historical Review* 98, no. 4 (October 1993): 1017–49.

Gilbert, George. *The Radical Right in Late Imperial Russia: Dreams of a True Fatherland?* London and New York: Routledge, 2016.

Goldman, Wendy Z. *Inventing the Enemy: Denunciation and Terror in Stalin's Russia.* Cambridge: Cambridge University Press, 2011.

Gooding, John. "The Liberalism of Michael Speransky." *The Slavonic and East European Review* 64, no. 3 (July 1986): 401–24.

Gorlizki, Yoram. "Delegalization in Russia: Soviet Comrades' Courts in Retrospect." *American Journal of Comparative Law* 46, no. 3 (Summer 1998): 403–25.

Harding, Neil. *Lenin's Political Thought: Theory and Practice in the Democratic and Socialist Revolutions.* Chicago: Haymarket Books, 2009.

Hardy, Jeffrey S. "'The Camp Is Not a Resort:' The Campaign against Privileges in the Soviet Gulag, 1957–61." *Kritika: Explorations in Russian and Eurasian History* 13, no. 1 (Winter 2012): 89–122.

Hardy, Jeffrey S. "Gulag Tourism: Khrushchev's 'Show' Prisons in the Cold War Context, 1954–59." *The Russian Review* 71, no. 1 (2012): 49–78.

Hardy, Jeffrey S. "De-Stalinizing the Gulag: Physical Violence in Soviet Correctional Facilities, 1953 -1973." Paper presented at the Workshop on Physical Violence and State Legitimacy in Late Socialism, Budapest, 2013.

Hartley, Janet. "Bribery and Justice in the Provinces in the Reign of Catherine II." In *Bribery and Blat in Russia: Negotiating Reciprocity from the Middle Ages to the 1990s.* Edited by Stephen Lovell, Alena Ledeneva, and Andrei Rogachevskii. New York: St. Martin's Press, 2000. Pp. 48–64.

Hartley, Janet M. "Catherine's Conscience Court: An English Equity Court?"
    In *Russia and the West in the Eighteenth Century*. Edited by A. G. Cross.
    Newtonville, MA: Oriental Research Partners, 1983. Pp. 306–18.
Hartley, Janet M. *Alexander I*. London and New York: Longman, 1994.
Hasegawa, Tsuyoshi. "Crime and Police in Revolutionary Petrograd, March 1917–
    March 1918: Social History of the Russian Revolution Revisited." *Acta Slavica
    Iaponica* 13 (1995): 1–41.
Heinzen, James. "Corruption among Officials and Anticorruption Drives in the
    USSR, 1945–1964." In *Russian Bureaucracy and the State: Officialdom from
    Alexander III to Vladimir Putin*. Edited by Don Karl Rowney and Eugene
    Huskey. London: Palgrave Macmillan, 2009. Pp. 169–88.
Hellie, Richard, ed. *The Muscovite Law Code (Ulozhenie) of 1649*, Part 1: Text
    and Translation. Irvine, CA: Charles Schlaks, 1998.
Hellie, Richard. "Early Modern Russian Law: The Ulozhenie of 1649." *Russian
    History* 15, nos. 2–4 (1988): 155–79.
Hellie, Richard. "Migration in Early Modern Russia, 1480s–1780s." In *Coerced
    and Free Migration: Global Perspectives*. Edited by David Eltis. Stanford:
    Stanford University Press, 2002. 292–323.
Hendley, Kathryn. "'Telephone Law' and the 'Rule of Law': The Russian Case."
    Hague Journal on the Rule of Law, no. 1 (2009): 241–62.
Hendley, Kathryn. *Everyday Law in Russia*. Ithaca, NY, and London: Cornell
    University Press, 2017.
Hillebrecht, Courtney. *Domestic Politics and International Human Rights
    Tribunals: The Problem of Compliance*. New York: Cambridge University Press,
    2014.
Hollingsworth, Barry. "John Venning and Prison Reform in Russia, 1819–1830."
    The Slavonic and East European Review 48, no. 113 (October 1970): 537–56.
Hood, Roger, and Carolyn Hoyle. *The Death Penalty: A Worldwide Perspective*,
    5th ed. Oxford: Oxford University Press, 2015. Pp. 11–13.
Hornsby, Robert. *Protest, Reform and Repression in Khrushchev's Soviet Union*.
    New York: Cambridge University Press, 2013.
Hughes, Lindsey. *Russia in the Age of Peter the Great*. New Haven, CT, and
    London: Yale University Press, 1998.
Huskey, Eugene. "The Politics of the Soviet Criminal Process: Expanding the Right
    to Counsel in Pretrial Proceedings." *American Journal of Comparative Law* 34,
    no. 1 (Winter 1986): 93–112.
Huskey, Eugene. "Speedy, Just, and Fair: Remaking Legal Institutions in Putin's
    Russia." In *Perspectives on the Russian State in Transition*. Edited by Wolfgang
    Danspeckgruber. Washington, DC: Woodrow Wilson Center, 2006. Pp. 28–65.
Iarov, S. V. *Krest'ianin kak politik: Krest'ianstvo severo-zapada Rossii v 1918–1919
    gg.: Politicheskoe myshlenie i massovyi protest*. St. Petersburg: Dmitrii Bulanin,
    1999.
Ivanova, Galina. "Eine unbekannte Seite des GULag: Lagersondergerichte in der
    UdSSR, 1945–1954." *Jahrbücher für Geschichte Osteuropas* 53, no. 1 (2005):
    25–41.
Ivnitskii, N. A. *Repressivnaia politika sovetskoi vlasti v derevne, 1928–1933*.
    Moscow: Institut rossiiskoi istorii RAN, 2000.

Ivnitskii, N. A. *Golod 1932–1933 godov v SSSR: Ukraina, Kazakhstan, Povolzh'e, Tsentral'no-Chernozemnaia oblast', Zapadnaia Sibir', Ural.* Moscow: Sobranie, 2009.

Jansen, Mark. "The Bar during the First Years of the Soviet Regime: N. K. Murav'ev." *Revolutionary Russia,* no. 2 (1990): 211–23.

Jones, Robert E. *Provincial Development in Russia: Catherine II and Jacob Sievers.* New Brunswick, NJ: Rutgers University Press, 1984.

Kahn, Jeffrey. "Russia's Criminal Procedure Code Five Years Out." *Review of Central and East European Law* 33, no. 1 (2008): 1–94.

Kazantsev, Sergei M. "Judicial Reform of 1864 and the Procuracy." In *Reforming Justice in Russia, 1864–1996: Power, Culture, and the Limits of Legal Order.* Edited by Peter H. Solomon, Jr. Armonk, NY, and London: M.E. Sharpe, 1997. Pp. 44–60.

Keep, John. "No Gauntlet for Gentlemen: Officers' Privileges in Russian Military Law, 1716–1855." *Cahiers du monde russe et soviétique* 34, nos. 1–2 (January–June 1993): 171–92.

Khaustov, V. N., V. P. Naumov, and N. S. Plotnikov, eds. *Lubianka: Stalin i VChK-GPU-OGPU-NKVD, ianvar' 1922–dekabr' 1936.* Moscow: Materik, 2003.

Khlevniuk, Oleg V. "The Politburo, Penal Policy, and 'Legal Reforms' in the 1930s." In *Reforming Justice in Russia, 1864–1996: Power, Culture, and the Limits of Legal Order.* Edited by Peter H. Solomon, Jr. Armonk, NY, and London: M.E. Sharpe, 1997. Pp. 190–227.

King, Roy, and Laura Piacentini. "The Russian Correctional System during the Transition." In *Ruling Russia: Law, Crime, and Justice in a Changing Society.* Edited by William Alex Pridemore. Lanham, MD: Rowman and Littlefield, 2005. Pp. 261–81.

Kolodizh, B. N. "Iul'skoe 1918 goda antibol'shevistskoe vosstanie v Iaroslavle: Politiko-istoricheskoe osmyslenie." In *Iaroslavskoe vosstanie, iiul' 1918.* Edited by V. Zh. Tsvetkov, et al. Moscow: Posev, 1998. Pp. 19–27.

Kosakovskii, A. A. "Bol'sheviki utverzhdaiut gosudarstvennuiu vlast'." In *Drama rossiiskoi istorii: Bol'sheviki i revoliutsiia.* Edited by O. V. Volobuev, et al. Moscow: Novyi khronograf, 2002. Pp. 345–426.

Kucherov, Samuel. *Courts, Lawyers, and Trials under the Last Three Tsars.* New York: Praeger, 1953.

Kucherov, Samuel. *The Organs of Soviet Administration of Justice: Their History and Operation.* Leiden: E. J. Brill, 1970.

Kvashonkin, A. V., et al., eds. *Bol'shevistskoe rukovodstvo: Perepiska, 1912–1927: Sbornik dokumentov.* Moscow: Rosspen, 1996.

Laitila, Teuvo. "Russia: Atheism, 'Blasphemy,' and Orthodox Christianity." In *The Atheist Bus Campaign: Global Manifestations and Responses.* Edited by Steven Tomlins and Spencer Culham Bullivant. Leiden and Boston: Brill, 2017. Pp. 262–85.

LaPierre, Brian. *Hooligans in Khrushchev's Russia: Defining, Policing, and Producing Deviance during the Thaw.* Madison: University of Wisconsin Press, 2012.

Ledeneva, Alena. "Telephone Justice in Russia: An Update." *The EU-Russia Center Review,* no. 18 (2011): 4–22.

Ledeneva, Alena V. *Can Russia Modernise? Sistema, Power Networks and Informal Governance.* Cambridge: Cambridge University Press, 2013.

LeDonne, John P. "The Judicial Reform of 1775 in Central Russia." *Jahrbücher für Geschichte Osteuropas* 21, no. 1 (1973): 29–45.

LeDonne, John P. "The Evolution of the Governor's Office, 1727–1764." *Canadian-American Slavic Studies* 12, no. 1 (Spring 1978): 86–115.

LeDonne, John P. *Ruling Russia: Politics and Administration in the Age of Absolutism, 1762–1796.* Princeton, NJ: Princeton University Press, 1984.

LeDonne, John P. "The *Guberniia* Procuracy during the Reign of Catherine II, 1764–1796." *Cahiers du monde russe* 36, no. 3 (July–September 1995): 221–48.

Leggett, George. *The Cheka: Lenin's Political Police.* Oxford: Clarendon Press, 1981.

Lentin, A. "Beccaria, Shcherbatov, and the Question of Capital Punishment." *Canadian Slavonic Papers* 24, no. 2 (June 1982): 128–37.

Lenoe, Matthew "Fear, Loathing, Conspiracy: The Kirov Murder as Impetus for Terror." In *The Anatomy of Terror.* Edited by James Harris. Oxford and New York: Oxford University Press, 2013. Pp. 195–215.

Leonov, S. V. *Rozhdenie sovetskoi imperii: Gosudarstvo i ideologiia, 1917–1922 gg.* Moscow: Dialog-MGU, 1997.

Light, Matthew, and Nikolai Kovalev. "Russia, the Death Penalty, and Europe: The Ambiguities of Influence." *Post-Soviet Affairs* 29, no. 6 (2013): 528–66.

Lincoln, W. Bruce. *In the Vanguard of Reform: Russia's Enlightened Bureaucrats, 1825–1861.* DeKalb: Northern Illinois University Press, 1982. Pp. 72–74.

Lindenmeyr, Adele. "The First Soviet Political Trial: Countess Sofia Panina before the Petrograd Revolutionary Tribunal." *The Russian Review* 60, no. 4 (October 2001): 505–25.

Litvin, A. L. *Krasnyi i belyi terror v Rossii, 1918–1922 gg.* Kazan: Tatarskoe gazetno-zhurnal'noe izd., 1995.

Lohr, Eric. *Nationalizing the Russian Empire: The Campaign against Enemy Aliens during World War I.* Cambridge, MA: Harvard University Press, 2003.

Lohr, Eric. *Russian Citizenship, From Empire to Soviet Union.* Cambridge, MA, and London: Harvard University Press, 2012.

Lysova, Alexandra, and Nikolay Shchitov. "What Is Russia's Real Homicide Rate? Statistical Reconstruction and the 'Decivilizing Process.'" *Theoretical Criminology* 19, no. 2 (2015): 257–77.

Macfarquhar, Neil, and Ivan Nechepurenko. "Putin Rival Is Barred from Presidential Run." *The New York Times* (February 9, 2017): A6.

Maggs, Peter B., Olga Schwartz, and William Burnham. *Law and Legal System of the Russian Federation*, 6th ed. Huntington, NY: Juris, 2015.

Mälksoo, Lauri. "Russia's Constitutional Court Defies the European Court of Human Rights: Constitutional Court of the Russian Federation Judgment of 14 July 2015, No 21-П/2015." *European Constitutional Law Review* 12, no. 2 (September 2016): 377–95.

Manning, Roberta T. "The Rise and Fall of the Extraordinary Measures, January–June, 1928: Towards a Reassessment of the Onset of the Stalin Revolution." *The Carl Beck Papers in Russian and East European Studies*, no. 1504 (January 2001): 1, 33.

McCarthy, Lauren A. *Trafficking Justice: How Russian Police Enforce New Laws, from Crime to Courtroom.* Ithaca, NY, and London: Cornell University Press, 2015.

McLaren, Angus. *The Trials of Masculinity: Policing Sexual Boundaries, 1870–1930*. Chicago and London: The University of Chicago Press, 1997.

Melancon, Michael. "Revolutionary Culture in the Early Soviet Republic: Communist Executive Committees versus the Cheka, Fall 1918." *Jahrbücher für Geschichte Osteuropas* 57, no. 1 (2009): 1–22.

Monas, Sidney. *The Third Section: Police and Society under Nicholas I*. Cambridge, MA: Harvard University Press, 1961.

Morris, Norval, and David J. Rothman, eds. *The Oxford History of the Prison: The Practice of Punishment in Western Society*. New York and Oxford: Oxford University Press, 1998.

Morrissey, Susan K. *Suicide and the Body Politic in Imperial Russia*. New York: Cambridge University Press, 2006.

Moutchnik, Alexander. "Soziale und wirtschaftliche Grundzüge der Kartoffelaufstände von 1834 und von 1841–1843 in Russland." In *Volksaufstände in Rußland: Von der Zeit der Wirren bis zur "Grünen Revolution" gegen die Sowjetherrschaft*. Edited by Heinz-Dietrich Löwe. Wiesbaden: Harrassowitz Verlag, 2006. Pp. 427–51.

Mozokhin, O. B. "Vnesudebnye polnomochiia VChK" In *Istoricheskie chteniia na Liubianke, 1998 god: Rossiiskie spetssluzhby na perelome epokh: Konets XIX veka-1922 god*. Edited by A. A. Zdanovich, M. N. Petrov, and V. N. Khaustov. Moscow: Velikii Novgorod, 1999. Pp. 75–81.

Muravyeva, Marianna. "Russian Early Modern Criminal Procedure and Culture of Appeal." *Review of Central and East European Law* 38 (2013): 295–316.

Muravyeva, Marianna. "'Till Death Us Do Part': Spousal Homicide in Early Modern Russia." *The History of the Family* 18, no. 3 (2013): 306–30.

Musaev, V. I. *Prestupnost' v Petrograde v 1917–1921 gg. i bor'ba s nei*. St. Petersburg: Dmitrii Bulanin, 2001.

Myers, Steven Lee. "Verdict in Russian Courts: Guilty Until Proven Guilty." *The New York Times* (June 20, 2004): WK3.

Naumov, V. P., and A. A. Kosakovskii, eds. "Kronshtadtskaia tragediia 1921 goda." *Voprosy istorii*, no. 4 (1994): 3–21.

Nechepurenko, Ivan. "Russia Moves to Soften Domestic Violence Law." *The New York Times* (January 26, 2017): A7.

Neznansky, Fridrikh. *The Prosecution of Economic Crimes in the USSR, 1954–1984*. Falls Church, VA: Delphic Associates, Inc., 1985.

Ostroumov, S. S. "Repressii tsarskogo pravitel'stva protiv revoliutsionnogo dvizhenia v Rossii v period imperializma: Ugolovno-statistichekoe issladovanie." *Vestnik moskovskogo universiteta*, Series 8: Pravo, no. 3 (1976): 40.

Pallot, Judith. "The Gulag as the Crucible of Russia's Twenty-First-Century System of Punishment." In *The Soviet Gulag: Evidence, Interpretation, and Comparison*. Edited by Michael David-Fox. Pittsburgh: Pittsburgh University Press, 2016. Pp. 286–313.

Paneyakh, Ella. "Faking Performance Together: Systems of Performance Evaluation in Russian Enforcement Agencies and Production of Bias and Privilege." *Post-Soviet Affairs* 30, nos. 2/3 (2014): 115–36.

Park, Nancy. "Imperial Chinese Justice and the Law of Torture." *Late Imperial China* 29, no. 2 (December 2008): 37–67.

Pavlov, D. B. "Tribunal'nyi etap sovetskoi sudebnoi sistemy, 1917–1922 gg." *Voprosy istorii*, no. 6 (2007): 3–16.

Peregudova, Z. I. *Politicheskii sysk Rossii, 1880–1917*. Moscow: Rosspen, 2000.

Perrie, Maureen. "The Russian Peasant Movement of 1905–1907: Its Social Composition and Revolutionary Significance." *Past & Present* 57 (November 1972): 123–55.

Peterson, Claes. *Peter the Great's Administrative and Judicial Reforms: Swedish Antecedents and the Process of Reception*. Stockholm: Juridska Fakulteten, 1979.

Piontkovskii, A. A. "Kontr-revoliutsionnye prestupleniia v Ugolovnom Kodekse R.S.F.S.R." Sovetskoe pravo, no. 1(7) (1924): 7-40.

Pipes, Richard. *Russia under the Old Regime*. New York: Charles Scribner's Sons, 1974.

Pipes, Richard. "Lenin's Gulag." *International Journal of Political Science and Development* 2, no. 6 (June 2014): 140–46.

Polian, Pavel. *Against Their Will: The History and Geography of Forced Migrations in the USSR*. Budapest: Central European University Press, 2004.

Portnov, V. P. *VchK, 1917–1922*. Moscow: Iuridicheskaia literatura, 1987.

Pravilova, E. A. "Organizatsiia sistemy administrativnoi iustitsii v Rossii: Pravovye reformy Vremennogo pravitel'stva." In *Rossiia v XIX–XX: Sbornik statei k 70-letiiu so dnia rozhdeniia Rafaila Sholomovich Ganelina*. Edited by A. A. Fursenko. St. Petersburg: Dmitrii Bulanin, 1998.

Raeff, Marc. *Siberia and the Reforms of 1822*. Seattle: University of Washington Press, 1956.

Raeff, Marc. "Codification et droit en Russie impériale: Quelques remarques comparatives." *Cahiers du monde russe et soviétique* 20, no. 1 (1979): 5–13.

Raeff, Marc. *The Well-Ordered Police State: Social and Institutional Change Through Law in the Germanies and Russia, 1600–1800*. New Haven, CT: Yale University Press, 1983.

Raeff, Marc. "Russia's Autocracy and Paradoxes of Modernization." In *Political Ideas and Institutions in Imperial Russia*. Boulder, CO: Westview Press, 1994. Pp. 116–40.

Raleigh, Donald J. *Experiencing Russia's Civil War: Politics, Society, and Revolutionary Culture in Saratov, 1917–1922*. Princeton, NJ: Princeton University Press, 2002.

Rand, Robert. *Comrade Lawyer: Inside Soviet Justice in an Era of Reform*. Boulder, CO: Westview Press, 1991.

Rendle, Matthew. "Revolutionary Tribunals and the Origins of Terror in Early Soviet Russia." *Historical Research* 84, no. 226 (November 2011): 693–721.

Rendle, Matthew. "Mercy amid Terror? The Role of Amnesties during Russia's Civil War." *The Slavonic and East European Review* 92, no. 3 (July 2014): 449–78.

Retish, Aaron B. "Controlling Revolution: Understandings of Violence through the Rural Soviet Courts, 1917–1923." *Europe-Asia Studies* 65 (November 2013): 1789–1806.

Retish, Aaron B. "Breaking Free from the Prison Walls: Penal Reforms and Prison Life in Revolutionary Russia." *Historical Research* 90, no. 247 (February 2017): 134–50.

Rodeheaver, Daniel G., and James L. Williams. "Juvenile Crime and Juvenile Justice in Post-Soviet Russia." In *Ruling Russia: Law, Crime, and Justice in a Changing Society*. Edited by William Alex Pridemore. Lanham, MD: Rowman and Littlefield, 2005. Pp. 225–46.

Saari, Sinikukka. *Promoting Democracy and Human Rights in Russia*. London and New York: Routledge, 2010.

Savitski, V. M. "Criminal Procedure." In *The Criminal Justice System of the USSR*. Edited by M. Cherif Bassiouni and V. M. Savitsk. Springfield, IL: Charles C. Thomas, 1979. Pp. 45–92.

Schönfeld, Dorothea. "Tilting at Windmills? The European Response to Violations of Media Freedom in Russia." *Review of Central and East European Law* 37, nos. 2–3 (2012): 233–90.

Schorkowitz, Dittmar. "Imperial Formations and Ethnic Diversity: Institutions, Practices, and Longue Durée Illustrated by the Example of Russia." Working Paper no. 165. Halle/Saale: Max Planck Institute for Social Anthropology, 2015.

Schrader, Abby M. *Languages of the Lash: Corporal Punishment and Identity in Imperial Russia*. DeKalb: Northern Illinois University Press, 2002.

Schwartz, Olga. "The Creation of an Independent Judiciary and the Changing Nature of Courts and the Courtroom." In *Ruling Russia: Law, Crime, and Justice in a Changing Society*. Edited by William Alex Pridemore. Lanham, MD: Rowman & Littlefield, 2005. Pp. 59–76.

Semukhina, Olga. "Public Contacts with Russian Police in Life-Threatening Situations." *Policing: An International Journal of Police Strategies & Management* 37, no. 2 (2014): 420–37.

Semukhina, Olga. "Unreported Crimes, Public Dissatisfaction of Police, and Observed Police Misconduct in the Volgograd Region, Russia: A Research Note." *International Journal of Comparative and Applied Criminal Justice* 38, no. 4 (2014): 305–25.

Severov, "Golodovka levykh sots.-rev. v Butyrskoi tiur'me." In *Kreml' za reshchetkoi: Podpol'naia Rossiia*. Edited by M. A. Spiridonova and A. A. Izmailovich. Berlin: Izd. "Skify," 1922. Pp. 70–82.

Sharlet, Robert. *Soviet Constitutional Crisis: From De-Stalinization to Disintegration*. Armonk, NY: M. E. Sharpe, Inc., 1992.

Shearer, David R., and Vladimir Khaustov, eds. *Stalin and the Lubianka: A Documentary History of the Political Police and Security Organs in the Soviet Union, 1922–1953*. New Haven, CT, and London: Yale University Press, 2009.

Shelley, Louise. "Female Criminality in the 1920s: A Consequence of Inadvertent and Deliberate Change." *Russian History* 9, nos. 2/3 (1982): 265–84.

Shelley, Louise. "Party Members and the Courts—Exploitation of Privilege." In *Ruling Communist Parties and Their Status under Law*. Edited by D. A. Loeber. Dordrecht: Martinus Nijhoff, 1986. Pp. 75–90.

Shelley, Louise. "Crime and Criminals in the USSR." In *Understanding Soviet Society*. Edited by Michael Stacks and Jerry Pankhurst. Boston: Unwin Hyman, 1988. Pp. 193–219.

Shishkin, V. I., ed. *Sibirskaia Vandeia*, 2 vols. Moscow: Mezhdunarodnyi fond "Demokratiia," 2001.

Siljak, Ana. *Angel of Vengeance: The "Girl Assassin," the Governor of St. Petersburg, and Russia's Revolutionary World*. New York: St. Martin's Press, 2008.

Smith, Gordon. "Popular Participation in the Administration of Justice in the Soviet Union: Comrades' Courts and the Brezhnev Regime." *Indiana Law Journal* 49 (Winter 1974): 238–52.

Smith, Gordon. *The Soviet Procuracy and the Supervision of Administration.* Alphen aan den Rijn, The Netherlands: Sijthoff & Noordhoff, 1978.

Smith, Gordon B. *Reforming the Russian Legal System.* Cambridge: Cambridge University Press, 1996.

Smith, Theresa C., and Thomas A. Oleszczuk. *No Asylum: State Psychiatric Repression in the Former USSR.* New York: New York University Press, 1996.

Solomon, Peter H., Jr. "Soviet Penal Policy, 1917–1934: A Reinterpretation." *Slavic Review* 39, no. 2 (June 1980): 195–217.

Solomon, Peter H., Jr. "Reforming Criminal Law under Gorbachev: Crime, Punishment, and the Rights of the Accused." In *Toward the Rule of Law in Russia? Political and Legal Reform in the Transition Period.* Edited by Donald D. Barry. Armonk, NY: M. E. Sharpe, 1992. Pp. 235 -55.

Solomon, Peter H., Jr. "Criminal Justice and the Industrial Front." In *Social Dimensions of Soviet Industrialization.* Edited by William G. Rosenberg and. Lewis H. Siegelbaum. Bloomington and Indianapolis: Indiana University Press, 1993.

Solomon, Peter H., Jr. "The Criminal Procedure Code of 2001: Will It Make Russian Justice More Fair?" In *Ruling Russia: Law, Crime, and Justice in a Changing Society.* Edited by William Alex Pridemore. Lanham, MD: Rowman & Littlefield, 2005. Pp. 77–98.

Solomon, Peter H., Jr. "Threats of Judicial Counter-reform in Putin's Russia." *Demokratizatsiya* 13, no. 3 (Summer 2005): 325–45.

Solomon, Peter H., Jr. "Assessing the Courts in Russia: Parameters of Progress under Putin." *Demokratizatsiya* 16, no. 1 (Winter 2008): 63–74.

Solomon, Peter H., Jr. "President Medvedev and the Courts: The Start of a New Era?" In *From Putin to Medvedev: Continuity or Change?* Edited by J. L. Black and Michael Johns. Manotick, Ontario: Penumbra Press, 2009. Pp. 25–37.

Solomon, Peter H., Jr. "Plea Bargaining Russian Style." *Demokratizatsiya* 20, no. 3 (Summer 2012): 282–99.

Solomon, Peter H., Jr. "Criminalization, Decriminalization and Post-Communist Transition: The Case of the Russian Federation." In *Building Justice in Post-Transition Europe? Processes of Criminalisation within Central and East European Societies.* Edited by William Munro and Margaret Murdoch. London and New York: Routledge, 2013. Pp. 95–114.

Solomon, Peter H., Jr. "Courts, Law and Policing under Medvedev: Many Reforms, Modest Change, New Voices." In *Russia after 2012: From Putin to Medvedev to Putin - Continuity, Change, or Revolution?* Edited by Larry Black and Michael Johns. London and New York: Routledge, 2013. Pp. 19–41.

Solomon, Peter H., Jr. "Post-Soviet Criminal Justice: The Persistence of Distorted Neo-inquisitorialism." *Theoretical Criminology* 19, no. 2 (2015): 159–78.

Solomon, Peter H., Jr. "Accusatorial Bias in Russian Criminal Justice." In *Sociology of Justice in Russia.* Edited by M. Kurkchiyan and Agnieszka Kubal. Cambridge: Cambridge University Press, 2018.

Sperling, Valerie. *Sex, Politics, and Putin: Political Legitimacy in Russia.* Oxford and New York: Oxford University Press, 2015.

Starzhenetskii, Vladislav. "Assessing Human Rights in Russia: Not to Miss the Forest for the Trees: A Response to Preclik, Schönfeld and Hallinan." *Review of Central and East European Law* 37, nos. 2–3 (2012): 349–56.

Stites, Richard. *The Four Horsemen: Riding to Liberty in Post-Napoleonic Europe* (Oxford and New York: Oxford University Press, 2014.

Tagantsev, N. S. *Russkoe ugolovnoe pravo: Letktsii: Chast' obshchaia*, 2 vols. Moscow: Nauka, 1994.

Taranovski, Theodore. "The Aborted Counter-Reform: Muravév Commission and the Judicial Statutes of 1864." *Jahrbücher für Geschichte Osteuropas* 29, no. 2 (1981): 161–84.

Taubman, William. *Khrushchev: The Man and His Era*. New York: W. W. Norton, 2004.

Tolokonnikova, Nadezhda. "Pussy Riot's Nadezhda Tolokonnikova: Why I Have Gone on Hunger Strike." *The Guardian* (September 23, 2013). https://www.theguardian.com/music/2013/sep/23/pussy-riot-hunger-strike-nadezhda-tolokonnikova.

Torke, Hans J. "Crime and Punishment in the Pre-Petrine Civil Service: The Problem of Control." *In Imperial Russia, 1700–1917: State, Society, Opposition: Essays in Honor of Marc Raeff*. Edited by Ezra Mendelsohn and Marshall S. Shatz. DeKalb: Northern Illinois University Press, 1988. Pp. 7–21.

Trochev, Alexei. "How Judges Arrest and Acquit: Soviet Legacies in Post-Communist Criminal Justice." In *Historical Legacies of Communism in Russia and Eastern Europe*. Edited by Mark Beissinger and Stephen Kotkin. Cambridge: Cambridge University Press, 2014. Pp. 152–78.

Tsarevskaia, T. V. "Prestuplenie i nakazanie: Paradoksy 20-x godov." In *Revoliutsiia i chelovek: Byt, nravy, povedenie, moral'*. Edited by P. V. Volobuev, et al. Moscow: Institut rossiiskoi istorii RAN, 1997. Pp. 214.

Tsvigun S. K., et al., eds. *V. I. Lenin i VChK: Sbornik dokumentov, 1917–1922 gg.* Moscow: Izd. Politicheskoi literatury, 1975.

Van den Berg, Ger P. "The Soviet Union and the Death Penalty." *Soviet Studies* 35, no. 2 (April 1983): 154–74.

Velychenko, Stephen. *State Building in Revolutionary Ukraine: A Comparative Study of Governments and Bureaucrats, 1917–1922*. Toronto, Buffalo, NY, and London: University of Toronto Press, 2011.

Vshivtsev, Anton. "Uroki istorii v Verkhovnom sude." *Novoe vremia* (September 2, 2016). https://newtimes.ru/stati/xroniki/uroki-istorii-v-verxovnom-sude.html.

Weickhardt, George B. "The Modernization of Law in 17th-Century Muscovy." In *Modernizing Muscovy: Reform and Social Change in Seventeenth-Century Russia*. Edited by Jarmo Kotilaine and Marshall Poe. London: RoutledgeCurzon, 2004. Pp. 76–92.

Weiner, Amir. *Making Sense of War: The Second World War and the Fate of the Bolshevik Revolution*. Princeton, NJ: Princeton University Press, 2001.

Weissman, Neil. "Rural Crime in Tsarist Russia: The Question of Hooliganism, 1905–1914." *Slavic Review* 37 (June 1978): 228–40.

Werth, Nicholas. "A State against Its People: Violence, Repression, and Terror in the Soviet Union." In *The Black Book of Communism: Crimes, Terror, Repression*. Edited by Stéphane Courtois, et al.; trans. Mark Kramer and Jonathan Murphy. Cambridge, MA: Harvard University Press, 1999.

Wheatcroft, Stephen G. "The Crisis of the Late Tsarist Penal System." In *Challenging Traditional Views of Russian History*. Edited by Stephen G. Wheatcroft. Basingstoke, UK: Palgrave Macmillan, 2002. Pp. 27–54.

Wheatcroft, Stephen G. "The Great Terror in Historical Perspective: The Records of the Statistical Department of the Investigative Organs of OGPU/NKVD." In *The Anatomy of Terror: Political Violence under Stalin*. Edited by James Harris. Oxford and New York: Oxford University Press, 2013. Pp. 287–305.

Wood, Alan. "Sex and Violence in Siberia: Aspects of the Tsarist Exile System." In *Siberia: Two Historical Perspectives*. Edited by John Massey Stewart and Alan Wood. London: The Great Britain-USSR Association and The School of Slavonic and East European Studies, 1984. Pp. 23–42.

Wood, Alan. "Administrative Exile and the Criminals' Commune in Siberia." In *Land Commune and Peasant Community in Russia: Communal Forms in Imperial and Early Soviet Society*. Edited by Roger Bartlett. New York: St. Martin's Press, 1990. Pp. 395–414.

Worobec, Christine D. "Horse Thieves and Peasant Justice in Post-Emancipation Russia." *Journal of Social History* 21 (Winter 1987): 281–93.

Wortman, Richard S. *The Development of a Russian Legal Consciousness*. Chicago and London: University of Chicago Press, 1976.

Wortman, Richard. "Russian Monarchy and the Rule of Law: New Considerations of the Court Reform of 1864." *Kritika: Explorations in Russian and Eurasian History* 6, no. 1 (Winter 2005): 145–70.

Yaffa, Joshua. "Putin's New War On 'Traitors.'" *The New Yorker* (March 28, 2014). http://www.newyorker.com/news/news-desk/putins-new-war-on-traitors.

Zavrazhin, S. A. "Juvenile Courts in the Russian Empire." *Russian Education and Society* 38, no. 2 (1996): 67–74.

Zeldes, Ilya. *The Problems of Crime in the USSR*. Springfield, IL: C.C. Thomas, 1981.

Zelenin, I. E. "'Revoliutsiia sverkhu': Zavershenie i tragicheskie posledstviia." *Voprosy istorii*, no. 10 (1994): 28–42.

Zemskov, V. N. "Spetsposelentsy: Po dokumentam NKVD—MVD SSSR." *Sotsiologicheskie issledovaniia*, no. 11 (1990): 3–17.

Zemskov, V. N. "Spetspolentsy, 1930–1959." In *Naselenie Rossii v 1920–1950-e gody: Chislennost', poteri, migratsii: Sbornik nauchnykh trudov*. Edited by Iu. A. Poliakov, et al. Moscow: Institut rossiiskoi istorii RAN, 1994. Pp. 145–94.

Zhiromskaia, V. B. "Golod 1932–1933 gg.: Liudskie poteri." In *Golod v SSSR, 1929–1934: Dokumenty*, 3 vols. Edited by V. V. Kondrashin, et al. Moscow: Mezhdunarodnyi fond "Demokratiia," 2011–2013, vol. 3. Pp. 649–718.

INDEX